THE ORIGINS OF ARGENTINA'S REVOLUTION OF THE RIGHT

RECENT TITLES FROM THE HELEN KELLOGG INSTITUTE
FOR INTERNATIONAL STUDIES

Scott Mainwaring, *general editor*

Michael Fleet and Brian H. Smith, eds.
The Catholic Church and Democracy in Chile and Peru (1997)

A. James McAdams, ed.
Transitional Justice and the Rule of Law in New Democracies (1997)

Carol Ann Drogus
Women, Religion, and Social Change in Brazil's Popular Church (1997)

Víctor E. Tokman and Guillermo O'Donnell, eds.
Poverty and Inequality in Latin America: Issues and New Challenges (1998)

Brian H. Smith
Religious Politics in Latin America, Pentecostal vs. Catholic (1998)

Tristan Anne Borer
Challenging the State: Churches as Political Actors in South Africa, 1980–1994
(1998)

Juan E. Méndez, Guillermo O'Donnell, and Paulo Sérgio Pinheiro, eds.
The (Un)Rule of Law and the Underprivileged in Latin America (1999)

Guillermo O'Donnell
Counterpoints: Selected Essays on Authoritarianism and Democratization (1999)

Howard Handelman and Mark Tessler, eds.
*Democracy and Its Limits: Lessons from Asia, Latin America, and the Middle
East* (1999)

Larissa Adler Lomnitz and Ana Melnick
Chile's Political Culture and Parties: An Anthropological Explanation (2000)

Kevin Healy
*Llamas, Weavings, and Organic Chocolate: Multicultural Grassroots
Development in the Andes and Amazon of Bolivia* (2000)

Ernest J. Bartell, C.S.C., and Alejandro O'Donnell
The Child in Latin America: Health, Development, and Rights (2000)

Vikram K. Chand
Mexico's Political Awakening (2001)

Sylvia Borzutzky
Vital Connections (2002)

Ruth Berins Collier and David Collier
Shaping the Political Arena (2002)

Glen Biglaiser
Guardians of the Nation? (2002)

For a complete list of titles from the Helen Kellogg Institute for International
Studies, see http://www.undpress.nd.edu

THE ORIGINS OF ARGENTINA'S REVOLUTION OF THE RIGHT

Alberto Spektorowski

University of Notre Dame Press
Notre Dame, Indiana

Published in the United States of America

Library of Congress Cataloging-in-Publication Data
Spektorowski, Alberto, 1952–
The origins of Argentina's revolution of the right / Alberto
Spektorowski.
p.   cm.
"From the Helen Kellogg Institute for International Studies."
Includes bibliographical references and index.
ISBN 0-268-02010-8 (cloth : alk. paper)
ISBN 0-268-02011-6 (pbk. : alk. paper)
1. Conservatism—Argentina—History—20th century.
2. Nationalism—Argentina—History—20th century.
3. Argentina—Politics and government—20th century.   1. Title.
JC573.2.A7 S64   2002
982.06—dc21
2001006427

To the memory of my father Lazaro

To my mother Susana

Contents

Acknowledgments

The ideas of this book first took shape during several seminars and conferences on fascism and modernization directed by Professor Zeev Sternhell at the Hebrew University of Jerusalem. Sternhell introduced me and other students of comparative politics and political theory to the understanding of fascism as a complex ideology deeply grounded in the history of European political thought. It is logical that my first debt should be to him, for inspiring me and advising me throughout the process of analyzing the development of fascist ideology in a non-European setting.

This is also my opportunity to thank the group of people working with Professor Sternhell who helped me shape these ideas. I am grateful to David Ohana, Reuven Shoshani, Amos Iovel, Maia Asheri, and especially Professor Mario Sznajder of the Hebrew University of Jerusalem, who in the course of endless talks became one of my closest advisors in the writing of this book.

My thanks also go to a large number of scholars, experts in fascism and Latin American politics, who have read different versions of this book: Professors Juan Linz, David Rock, Fernando Lopez Alves, Sandra McGee Deutsch, Carlos Waisman, Roger Eatwell, Roger Griffin, Zvi Medin, and Cristián Buchrucker and Enrique Zuleta Alvarez, the most enlightened experts on Argentinean right-wing nationalism.

Other scholars in comparative politics have also read this text and provided useful comments at different stages of writing. My thanks to my colleagues at Tel Aviv University, Professors Yoav Peled, Yosi Shain, and Gad Barzilai, and to Professor Luis Roniger of the Hebrew University.

Special thanks are due to Professors Stanley Payne and Guillermo O'Donnell, the readers and referees of this text for the University of

Notre Dame Press. Their comments caused me to review several ideas, which led to an improvement in the final text.

This book could not have been written without the financial aid bestowed by Professor Shlomo Ben Ami and the Sourassky Chair in Iberian and Latin American Studies at the University of Tel Aviv, and by the Truman Institute for Peace at the Hebrew University of Jerusalem. My thanks to them for trusting that I could accomplish this project.

I am deeply indebted to the Kellogg Institute at the University of Notre Dame, and especially to Professors Scott Mainwaring, Michael Coppedge, and Frances Hagopian, for permitting me spend a semester at the institute, where this book was completed. My stay at the Kellogg allowed me to taste the spirit of belonging to an outstanding intellectual family and to meet colleagues from different fields of comparative politics and political thought, including Venelin Ganev, Larissa Lomnitz, Walker Frank, Vibha Pinglé, and others. To the administrative staff of the Kellogg as well as to most of its senior researchers, including Ernest Bartell, Samuel Valenzuela, and Maria Rosa Olivera Williams, my sincere thanks.

I thank the director of the University of Notre Dame Press, Barbara Hanrahan, and the assistant director, Jeffrey Gainey, for opening the doors of the press to my book. I am grateful to Rebecca DeBoer for her editorial work. She and Phillip Berryman contributed during endless revisions of the text to making me clarify central ideas. My last thanks go to my research assistant, Liza Ireni, for her constant support.

All those whom I thank have contributed to the development of this book. Its shortcomings are entirely my own responsibility.

Alberto Spektorowski
Tel Aviv University

Introduction

The Right and the Idea
of Reactionary Modernism

This book deals with political ideas. More specifically, it traces the intellectual threads of Argentina's antiliberal nationalism emerging in the early decades of the twentieth century and their influence and impact on politics. In this book I define this process as a revolution of the right. However, I am aware that the term itself may raise questions regarding its theoretical consistency as well as the validity of its application in Argentina's political framework.

The right is usually associated with antimodernist reaction and the left is associated with revolutionary change. While liberal and socialist thinkers are generally thought to be connected with democracy and progressive politics, the radical right has been regarded as opposed to democracy and even modernity. In Latin America, analysts have associated the national populism of the 1940s with modern anti-imperialist politics and the national left in the 1960s with social justice and economic development.

In contrast, the political tradition of the conservative or the radical right has been linked to policies that exclude the working class. Furthermore, the right has been accused of serving foreign political and economic imperialism, and in Argentina in particular, observers have blamed it for the culture of fear and violence prevailing in the 1970s. Hence, the idea of associating the political tradition of Argentina's nationalist right not only with authoritarianism, but also with anti-imperialism, nationalistic modernization, and social justice, would seem somewhat strange.

This book will nevertheless challenge the common view just outlined by examining one of the most sophisticated, intellectually and ideologically antiliberal, right-wing movements in Latin America between the two world wars.

With the publication in the 1980s of Zeev Sternhell's books on the origins of fascism in France, *La droite révolutionnaire* and *Neither Right nor Left*, the idea of the *"droite révolutionnaire"* appears as a concept describing an ideological development that preceded and accompanied fascism in Europe.[1] Its chief characteristic was that it rejected old-style conservatism in the name of a new type of plebeian "national populism," which was both hierarchical and popular. In most cases, this revolutionary right found a common ground with a non-Marxist revolutionary left, followers of Georges Sorel. Together they delegitimized liberal democracy and Marxist socialism and created the framework for fascism, which combined the ideas of an organic nation, organized as a syndicalist state.

The question is to what extent this ideological phenomenon, which laid the groundwork for the fascist and national-socialist "revolution of the right," could be called a revolution. Indeed, the revolution of the right was a conservative revolution and differed from a social class revolution. It was a revolution that aimed to preserve the integrity and morality of the nation from liberal disintegration and Marxist revolution. At the same time it cannot be reduced simply to a military coup d'état and labeled as a counterrevolution against the revolutionary left. It was an alternative right-wing revolution against the liberal democratic order. Although it endorsed some of the motives of the left, it was a revolution not in the name of the proletariat and universal values but in the name of the nation. The fascist political regime did not change the socioeconomic order in Italy, for example. However, it still could be defined as a national revolution, for it involved a new type of popular mobilization and political style, a new type of socioeconomic organization, and new social and political values.

Several books and essays written in the last decades have proven thoroughly that the revolutionary right, fascism, and national socialism were first and foremost political ideologies. Most of these new studies (by Ernst Nolte, Zeev Sternhell, Roger Eatwell, Roger Griffin, and others) have stressed the role of intellectuals in these political phenomena. This does not mean that fascist or national populist leaders adopted in a complete form the ideological constructions of antidemocratic intellectuals. However, as noted by Gordon Craig in reference to the Weimar Conservative Revolutionaries, the latter were the avant-garde of the rightist revolution that was to be effected in 1933. Although contemptuous of national socialism and Hitler, they did much to pave his road to power.[2] Following this line of analysis, the present book traces how antidemocratic intellectuals in Argentina adapted to Argentine reality the more important concepts coming from the European conservative revolution and shaped the political repertoire of most antiliberal political elites following the military upheaval of 1930.

This book thus analyzes the ideological process leading from conservative authoritarianism in 1930 to the revolution of the right in 1943. Although this analysis is bounded by the early Peronist years, it hints that the ideological legacy of the revolutionary right went beyond this period. The "nationalist" repertoire survived these regimes, just as fascist ideology survived the vanishing of the fascist political regimes. In other words, the political impact of the right-wing nationalist intellectuals was not limited to the writing of essays. Despite their lack of success in forming a mass political party, they had direct connections to military and political elites, and the issues they raised became an integral part of Argentina's political culture. Not only were several military regimes imprinted by the values of the revolutionary right. Radical movements of the Peronist right and left, and rebellious military men like Muhamed Sinheldin and Aldo Rico in the 1980s, displayed the same repertoire of ideas. The question is how these ideas originated and flourished.

This intellectual revolt was essentially a reaction to domestic developments, namely, economic dependency on Great Britain, cultural decadence, and fraudulent politics. However, I also argue, as noted below, that the Argentine nationalist upheaval in the 1930s and the shift in political development to which it contributed were representative of a new wave of right-wing ideological uprisings around the world during an era of mass politics, expanding capitalism, and radical technological progress. These uprisings constituted a rebellion against liberal society and cosmopolitan values, and indeed against liberal modernity itself. Like Enrico Corradini and Gabriele D'Annunzio in Italy, Charles Maurras and Maurice Barrès in France, and Arthur Moeller van den Bruck, Ernst Jünger, and Carl Schmitt in Germany, the representative figures of this rebellious generation in Argentina included the brothers Rodolfo and Julio Irazusta, Leopoldo Lugones, the brothers Carlos (Jr.) and Federico Ibarguren, Enrique Osés, Julio Meinvielle, and others. Working in most cases independently of one another, these intellectuals helped popularize a new framework of values, pseudoscientific truths, and emotionally laden expressions whose implications for political practice were decisive in the 1930s and 1940s.

The ideologues and intellectuals of this generation—even those born in France, the motherland of democratic liberalism—conceived of modern liberalism and bourgeois society as at odds with the spirit of the nation. All of them, even those who were citizens of powerful modern nations, felt that their countries were on the "losing side" of international competition. They portrayed their countries as "peripheral" modernizers, held back by the power of foreign and domestic capitalists. To them, "peripheral" meant that a nation's development was economically and culturally dependent on other nations, and this was incompatible with national pride and the concept of national sovereignty.

Italian and French antiliberal intellectuals blamed liberal politicians and liberal bourgeois culture for defeat at Adowa and for the loss of Alsace-Lorraine. German right-wing nationalist intellectuals believed that the liberal order imposed on Germany after the First World War was alien to the German spirit. One characteristic that most of them shared was their belief that the concept of political modernity inherent in liberal and socialist theories undermined the communitarian bonds of the nation. Nonetheless, in contrast to old-style reactionary Catholicism or conservative and romantic rejections of the "modern world," they endorsed modern technology, industrialization, and the new techniques and discourse of mass mobilization. In other words, while they rejected the synthesis between industrial society and the idea of enlightened civilization, they advocated a new blend of antimodernist romantic values, technological virtues, and mass mobilization, which was to provide the basis for a reactionary road to modernity.[3]

The common ground shared by European and Latin American radical right-wing nationalists was that they all pressed for the renewal of the national soul in a modern setting, and all of them believed that national renewal would require political authoritarianism and an integrated self-sufficient society. Where radical right-wing nationalists in Latin American countries differed was in their greater emphasis on cultural and economic anti-imperialism and on social justice, issues hardly considered by their European counterparts.

Based on that ideological framework, I argue that in Argentina between the 1930s and 1940s a new political discourse arose that blended a reactionary politics with popular mobilization, anti-imperialism, and themes of social justice.

Argentina's new nationalists believed that liberalism had made Argentina politically and economically dependent on Great Britain and that it was antithetical to Argentina's collective identity. This new political discourse, produced in intellectual laboratories of right-wing and left-wing antiliberal nationalists and combining integralist and populist ideas, antedated and helped shape the military revolution of 1943 and Peronism.[4] In other words, although in Europe these new brands of nationalists shared a common program with revolutionary syndicalism, setting the stage for fascism, in Argentina a common ground formed between political views that were at first sight opposed—right-wing integral nationalism and left-wing populist nationalism—thus creating the ideological framework for Peronism.

I argue that most of the new repertoire of political and social ideas applied by these regimes—the combination of elements which at first glance appear to be at odds, that is, "anti-Marxist" social justice, anti-imperialism, and national industrialism in combination with reactionary Catholicism and state corporativism—had been introduced in Argentina by these new brand of right-wing and populist nationalist intellectuals who were prominent in influential circles in Buenos Aires in the 1920s and 1930s. They constituted neither an organized political party nor a unified or coherent ideological movement, but through newspapers, cultural associations, paramilitary parades, and the like, they influenced key figures in the military, the church, and political life. They provided these political elites with an alternative concept of modernization, which laid the foundation for one of the most dramatic political shifts in Argentine political history.

The impact of this intellectual tradition on Argentina's political development, especially for the military revolution of 1943 and subsequent Peronism, is undeniable. In the 1940s Argentina was a rich country with good prospects for becoming an industrial democracy. Yet the military revolution of 1943 adopted the nationalist discourse of peripheral modernity and shifted the direction of political and economic development from liberalism to nationalist-authoritarian autarkic development.

More than once in Argentina, liberals have called for military intervention in order to "save" the constitutional order from populist, left-wing pressures. As some scholars have noted, the propensity toward authoritarian politics has also been a part of the liberal political tradition.[5] However, the category of integral nationalism promoted by the left and right components of Argentina's revolution of the right, goes beyond the idea of an authoritarian "solution" to crises of liberalism. The new nationalism did not want to save liberalism, but to surpass it. In other words, Argentina's liberal-conservatives had been authoritarian, although they paid tribute to a liberal constitution; the new integral nationalists, by contrast, strove to change the very definition of democracy, and they replaced the liberal and socialist path to modernity with a new rhetoric of cultural and political anti-imperialism. Therefore, this study focuses on a more destructive and long-term form of authoritarianism, namely, nationalist authoritarianism, which, in contrast to political authoritarianism, attempts to redefine the parameters of the country's collective identity and of legitimate political participation. I argue that this new political culture has been the most critical obstacle to the development of a liberal democratic political culture in Argentina.

I suggest that this work complements, builds upon, and in some cases substantially contrasts with recent works on Argentina's antiliberal nationalism. It differs from David Rock's *Authoritarian Argentina*,[6] and likewise with most of the contributors to *The Argentine Right: Its History and Intellectual Origins, 1910 to the Present*, edited by Sandra McGee Deutsch and R. H. Dolkart. Most of these authors draw a clear dividing line between the fascist-oriented "authoritarian right" and the populist left, who claimed to be the "authentic" nationalists. The former has usually been regarded as the reactionary and counterrevolutionary face of Argentine nationalism and as that which inspired military authoritarianism; the latter has been identified with populist anti-imperialism and social reform. In her comparative study *Las Derechas: The Extreme Right in Argentina, Brazil, and Chile, 1890–1939*, Deutsch seeks to correct old views of the right by stressing the anti-imperialist and pro-labor characteristics of the Latin American extreme right between World Wars I and II.[7]

The present book challenges all those views, but not by downplaying the distinction between counterrevolutionary and national populist currents, or between foreign and "authentic" sources. It differs from those other works inasmuch as it traces the conceptual synthesis of these opposing trends by interpreting them within a new framework of reactionary modernization. I suggest that the revolution of the right, which paradoxically resulted from a blend of right-wing corporativism and left-wing populism, rejected the liberal and reformist socialist concepts of progress and modern society. It held that liberalism and socialism were rooted in similar principles, and both led to economic dependency and cultural decadence. The retrieval of "Hispanic" and "*caudillista*" cultural values served as the basis for pursuing a different path to political and socioeconomic modernity. In sharp contrast to David Rock, who holds that the ultimate loyalties of Argentina's right lay with conservative clericalism,[8] this work stresses the fact that in the 1930s the Argentine right shifted toward national populism and the elaboration of a new discourse of peripheral modernization. Contrary to most of the literature, I bring the traditions of the nationalist right and left together into a common struggle against the advocates—whether conservatives, liberals, reformist socialists, or communists—of the liberal type of political modernization.

Obviously, the idea of a rapprochement between the ideology of counterrevolution and that of national populism is controversial, not only because of the gap in their intellectual roots. The democratic populist regime of Hipólito Yrigoyen was toppled by a military revolution, whose leaders' intellectual mentors were integral nationalists like the Irazusta brothers, Juan Carulla, Ernesto Palacio, and others who were associated with the newspaper *La Nueva República*. Most works on Argentine nationalism have emphasized the fact that this breakdown of democracy was paradigmatic of the persistent attempts of Argentine liberalism to block the advance of popular democracy. The argument here does not contradict that position, but the emphasis is on tracing the evolution of those young intellectuals from a conservative antidemocratic posture toward support for a national-populist authoritarian order and a fascist style of mobilization.

As mentioned earlier, I claim that the broad intellectual and ideological framework of rebellion against liberal modernity offered these Argentine nationalists the inspiration for a new model of nationalist mobilization under state corporativist control. However, the new climate of ideas also coincided with a period in Argentina's political and economic history that enabled such ideas to be accepted. Argentina was basically a limited political democracy with a dynamic and modern civil society characterized by expanding economic growth. Fraudulent elections and political and economic dependence on England, along with a long-standing reluctance on the part of the upper classes to integrate the lower classes into the nation, paved the way for a redefinition of right- and left-wing political discourse. That domestic background allowed proud right-wing nationalist sectors to denounce imperialism, demand a reorientation of the economy toward industrialization, and strive for mass support. The new right likewise disavowed the conservative elites' techniques of electoral fraud in order to adopt the more modern fascist techniques of political mobilization and pro-labor language under a corporativist-authoritarian state. Thus, while the pre-1930 right in Argentina combated liberal populism and its redistributive politics, from the 1930s onwards its main enemy appeared to be the liberal conservative oligarchy with its socialist democratic "partners."

In contrast to the Liga Patriótica movement analyzed by Sandra McGee Deutsch,[9] which represented the old type of authoritarian conservative reaction against working-class demands and communism, the new groups of the 1930s, like the Legión Cívica, Liga Republicana, and Alianza Nacionalista, although anticommunist, were first and foremost antiliberal and displayed a fascist style. They were more than a response to a communist threat, as some analysts have emphasized. These movements were represented by Catholic priests, such as Julio Meinvielle and Gustavo Franceschi; integral nationalists, such as the brothers Rodolfo and Julio Irazusta, the brothers Carlos and Federico Ibarguren, and Ernesto Palacio; and fascists, such as the poet Leopoldo Lugones. They rejected the liberal path to modernity because it contributed to social disintegration.[10] They were authoritarian, although most of them evolved to the point of accepting a new type of controlled populist mobilization.

The 1930s were also the time when the discourse of the national left, based on political and economic anti-imperialism and the abandonment of liberal populism, took firm hold. After the fall of Yrigoyen, a young group of hard-line Radicals who rejected the conservative tendencies in the Radical party came together in a group named FORJA (Fuerza de Orientación Radical de la Juventud Argentina). They focused on reestablishing "popular sovereignty" through popular mobilization and economic and cultural anti-imperialism. The most prominent figures within FORJA—Arturo Jauretche, Dario Alessandro, Manuel Ortiz Pereyra, Luis Dellepiane, and even Raúl Scalabrini Ortiz (who never was a direct member of the group)—were far from being fascist counterrevolutionaries, even though they were antiliberal nationalists. They supported a new type of "anti–political party" populist democracy, and they conceived of the nation as an organic unit mobilized by authentic leaders. Therefore, although their critique was focused on Argentine liberalism and the sources of economic imperialism, they developed a concept of republican populism and a direct approach to democratic justice that generally disdained formal democratic procedures. They saw themselves as nationalists of the future and came to emphasize the gap between their modernizing approach and the nostalgic one of the integralists. As noted by Jauretche, right-wing intellectuals like Meinvielle, Rodolfo and Julio Irazusta, and others, were nostalgic nationalists who reminded him of the "love of a son for his father's grave."[11]

I argue that despite their different sources, which are clearly emphasized in this book, both strains of nationalism, starting in the 1930s, evolved toward a common "nationalist authoritarian order." They were different but complementary faces of a common reaction against the liberal elite approach to modernization, and of a common third way blending nostalgic and modernizing motifs.

Both versions of nationalism put forward cultural and economic anti-imperialist ideas and revived the pre-liberal myth of the struggle of the *caudillos* against liberal modernization. For both, the army would play a central modernizing role. FORJA idealized the army as a popular institution, and the integral nationalists admired its hierarchical organization. For both, it was the organic representation of the nation, an example of an ordered, heroic, and multiclass "democracy." Both had been supporters of neutrality during World War I. Unlike the integralists, FORJA and several other anti-imperialist nationalist movements worldwide did not support fascism, but like many nationalists worldwide, they understood fascism to be a national and cultural revolution against the "plutocratic" democratic nations and an alternative to socialist and liberal ideologies.

In short, both varieties of nationalism attacked liberalism, democratic political institutions, the liberal approach to modernization promoted by the nineteenth-century elite, and basically the synthesis between nationalism and liberalism. Instead, they advanced a new set of political values and looked for alternative political ideologies as inspiring models through which the links between popular participation and state institutionalization could be redefined. The values behind modern cosmopolitan society were delegitimized, and old social and cultural values, such as "*caudillismo*" and "*hispanismo*," were retrieved as symbols of a true cultural identity. Values of heroism, national vitality, and political intolerance were prized over values of bourgeois materialism and tolerance. At the political level, institutions of liberal society like the parliament and political parties were labeled as the instruments of national decadence and economic dependency. In contrast, institutions such as the church and the army were celebrated as the institutions of a new type of "organic democracy" through which an "emancipated," self-sufficient path to modernization would be mapped out.

As the Italian embassy in Buenos Aires correctly recognized, only a combination of antiliberal versions of nationalism would be able to produce what might be defined as a local fascist ideology.[12] Although Argentina's alternative nationalism did not directly mimic fascism, the question of fascism in Argentina cannot simply be reduced to a complex relationship with German or Italian immigrants in Argentina.[13] Most of Argentina's nationalist intellectuals had been critical of fascism. Yet like other antiliberal and antisocialist nationalists between the two world wars, they conceived of an organic "third way" to modernization stressing national integration and technical modernization, while totally rejecting modern values such as egalitarianism and individual freedom. Fascism was the most successful political expression of this ideological trend.

Although it is a matter of debate whether the influence of this national-fascist model extends to the present-day process of democratic consolidation, it is clear that the nationalist ideological revolt analyzed in this book helped shape a political repertoire that became an integral part of military regimes as well as of important sectors of society. Indeed, for a long period

of Argentina's political history, concepts such as socioeconomic modernization, social justice, and national pride were difficult to reconcile with
liberal democracy. The new discourse was that of national mobilization
and mythic heroic rebellion, invoked by generations of young nationalists
from the right and the left in opposition to capitalism and its local liberal
associates. It was paradoxically also the language of the same right-wing
and left-wing nationalists who killed one another before the dirty war of
the 1970s, but who effusively applauded—despite political repression and
human rights violations—the military junta adventure in the Malvinas/
Falklands in 1982, in the name of national pride and anti-imperialism.
Their bitter struggle among themselves notwithstanding, they had a common enemy, and they developed a common vision of an Argentina emancipated from liberalism. In essence, most Argentine nationalists envisioned
the new Argentina as an authoritarian, communitarian, and mobilized
coun try with scant regard for democratic procedures and individual rights,
which they associated with economic and political imperialism.

Those seeking political and ideological explanations for Argentina's
lack of a liberal civic culture during a long period of its political history
could blame the liberals themselves for failing to articulate liberal and
democratic rights. I suggest, however, that this is not enough. We should
pay especial attention not only to the shortcomings of liberal ideologues
and corrupt politicians in Argentina but also to the construction of alternative ideological paradigms which legitimized antiliberal politics. The
nationalist right and left made a substantive and radical contribution to
Argentina's antiliberal political culture by creating this new paradigm.
They were firm in prying the ideas of social justice, cultural authenticity,
and industrial development away from liberal and socialist ideologies and
inextricably associating these ideas with a new concept of populist and
authoritarian nationalism.

Chapter 1 of this book deals with the theoretical background of fascist
conservative revolutionaries and national populist ideologies. It introduces
the debate on the question of fascist ideology, its concept of modernity,
and its links to nationalism and the conservative revolution, while testing
its political and ideological importance for societies of modern but dependent development. The distinctions and connecting points between
the development of cultural nationalism, national populism, and national
socialism in Argentina and Europe are analyzed in this chapter.

Chapter 2 focuses on the sociopolitical and cultural setting that permitted the political hegemony of the liberal oligarchic elites. It analyzes
the roots of their project of national modernization and emphasizes the
gap between their vision of economic liberalism and political liberalism.

I attempt to demonstrate that the liberal oligarchic elites and socialist reformist parties, despite their differences, were enclosed within similar cultural parameters; that is, their proposals were "civilized," in contrast to the "authentic" forces of nationalism that erupted with the populist Radical party and with the first seeds of cultural nationalism originating in the works of Ricardo Rojas and Manuel Gálvez. This chapter also discusses the cultural and social background behind the first modern national populist movement in Argentina, which was embodied in the personality of Hipólito Yrigoyen. It explains the links between Yrigoyen's idea of the nation and democratic populism, stressing the fact that this new type of national populism expanded the concept of democratic participation. At the same time, it limited and weakened the ideas of liberal democratic procedures, by enhancing the virtues of plebiscitary presidentialism in contrast to parliamentary limitations, by interfering in the provinces and in the army, and basically by behaving with an "oppositionist" or contentious attitude, even when in power.

Chapter 3 deals with the incipient ideological roots of integral nationalism, stressing the influences of the poet Leopoldo Lugones (an Argentine D'Annunzio) and the intellectuals gathered around *La Nueva República*. It analyzes the formative years of a conservative-authoritarian ideology whose fundamental goal was to prevent the expansion of democracy. It traces the personal and ideological links of *La Nueva República* intellectuals, like the Irazusta brothers, Ernesto Palacio, and Juan Carulla, to important sectors of the army, especially to Felix de Uriburu, the leader of the military upheaval of 1930. I also deal with the legacy of Uriburu's ideas, expressed fundamentally in the appearance of fascist-style leagues (Liga Republicana, Legión Cívica, and the like), which emphasized anti-liberalism and antisocialism, while at the same time advocating a new type of nationalist social justice.

Chapter 4 focuses on the embryonic stages of the integralist populist synthesis and critically analyzes the links between fascism, national populism, and Catholic integralism. It examines these developments during a special period of Argentina's social and political history, the "Década Infame" (Decade of Shame), so called because it was the time when Argentina became most dependent on Great Britain.

Chapter 5 considers how Argentine nationalists of the right and left dealt with the country's crisis of liberalism. It analyzes the idea of right-wing anti-imperialism and the concepts of "productionism" and social justice advocated by Leopoldo Lugones and Alejandro Bunge. It attempts first to distinguish between their proposals for industrial production and the idea of import-substitution promoted by Socialist leaders. It then addresses the differences and similarities between right-wing anti-imperialism and the anti-imperialist ideology propagated by the leftist FORJA.

Chapter 6 traces the ideological synthesis of right-wing integralism and left-wing populism and stresses the fact that only when the integralist right embraced Yrigoyenist nationalism did it abandon old-style conservatism and become a conservative revolutionary right resembling fascism. In this chapter, I highlight the debate over Argentine neutrality during World War II and stress its correlation with the country's internal politics. The debate on neutrality and the rapprochement to the Axis powers was emblematic of a broader ideological discussion of Argentine political identity. Several works have emphasized that the traditional neutralist position was promoted by the liberals and continued by Yrigoyen. These works have also stressed the fact that during World War II there were rational economic interests, even those of Britain, driving Argentine neutrality. Without disregarding these interests, I analyze the debate on neutrality as part of a discussion on Argentina's cultural identity, which could not be severed from the ideological models in dispute in a worldwide ideological conflict.[14] World War II catalyzed and radicalized differences on cultural and ideological matters. The issue became national identity rather than foreign policy. Antiliberal right-wing and national populist intellectuals defended a "pro-Axis" neutrality with a different intonation: they believed that the emerging "new world order" served their nationalist revolutionary aspirations. Liberals, conservatives, communists, and reformist socialist modernizers differed with and opposed each other, but their view of the nation and their idea of sociopolitical development shared similar cultural parameters. During World War II they supported the Western powers, while domestically, their view of national modernity challenged the integralist populist formula devised by the "revolution of the right" and later by Peronism.

Chapter 7 deals with the 1943 military revolt and the emergence of Peronism as a combination of integralist and populist ideology. It indicates the differences between this military upheaval and Uriburu's earlier attempt to establish a corporativist state, and emphasizes the connecting and divergent lines between the GOU (Grupo de Oficiales Unidos) and subsequent Peronism. Finally, it attempts to define Peronism as a unique movement, an expression of a collective sentiment of the social pride of a great part of Argentina's population. At the same time, I explain why Perón's populism cannot be disentangled from the ideological framework of the revolution of the right.

Juan Perón himself was quite aware of the theoretical importance and continuing appeal of fascist national-socialist ideology for dependent societies in the Third World, and of the role that Argentina's nationalist legacy played in setting the stage for a political and cultural revolution such as Peronism.[15] This does not mean that Perón adopted all the political and cultural strategies of the nationalists, especially those elaborated by the integralist right. Perón employed them several times, but in the end he rejected them.

I am not suggesting that Argentina's rightists approved of Perón's regime. Obviously, none of the integralists at *La Nueva República* could have imagined the social and aesthetic revolution that would be unleashed by Perón. Despite the fact that some of the "pro-labor" and plebeian characteristics of Peronism had already appeared with the Alianza Nacionalista in the mid-1930s, the impact of Perón's "*descamisados*" probably went beyond the image of controlled mobilization and the new type of antiliberal communitarian state sought by nationalist intellectuals. Furthermore, the nationalist intellectuals placed a great deal of importance on historical revisionism, quite unlike Perón himself. Some, such as the Irazusta brothers, were far from convinced by Perón's populist and anti-imperialist rhetoric. Like those Europeans whose ideas paved the way for fascism and Nazism but who later became contemptuous of how these regimes developed, most of the intellectuals of Argentina's revolution of the right were unlikely to sympathize with the plebeian characteristics of Peronism.

These differences notwithstanding, the ideological background studied in this book can scarcely be distinguished from Peronism. Perón's populism and direct approach to the working class do not prove the existence of a gap between him and fascist and integralist ideologies. Peronism was not anti-hierarchical or anti-authoritarian, and Argentina's nationalists were not pure reactionary supporters of the oligarchic conservative order. They shared a primary conviction that in the modern era of mass mobilization, only controlled authoritarian means could lead to social integration. Moreover, the only way to survive in an imperialist world was through an integrated industrialized society, a goal which, according to the new nationalists, was scarcely reconcilable with political liberalism. They rejected the dichotomy between progressive social policies and popular mobilization on the one side, and reactionary politics on the other; the Peronist "third way" provided a synthesis of both. Hence, this line of thought that characterized a third path to modernity was incorporated into Argentine political culture. In most countries this ideological formula was abandoned after the defeat of the Axis powers in World War II. The political tragedy of Argentina was that, as a result of Peronism, it continued to be a formula for national liberation, national pride, and social justice in Argentina.

CHAPTER 1

Reactionary Modernism, Fascism, and the Language of Cultural Emancipation

The Fascist Right and the Question of Anti-Imperialism

Argentina's "revolution of the right" took place during the interwar period when fascism arose in Europe. Not coincidentally, its foremost proponents were nationalist intellectuals influenced by the fascist revolution. Most of them admitted that the fascist spiritual and political revolution against European liberalism contributed to their own rebellion against Argentine liberalism and against the oligarchic elite model of political modernization, which they saw as the contextual framework that condemned Argentina to cultural and economic dependency. In this book, I define this type of reactionary stance against liberal modernity and against any type of Marxist socialist modernity as a reactionary type of modernism. This was a "third way" toward political modernity, one that combined conservative values, such as high regard for the traditional organic community, with industrial modernization under authoritarian rule.

Scholars have been reluctant to label this third path of modernization as political modernity. They have little trouble in identifying a left-wing modernizing tradition and contrasting it with democratic liberalism, but they have been ambivalent about the existence of a fascist or a national-socialist modernist tradition.[1] In other words, while liberalism and Marxist-Leninist ideologies and movements have been seen as promoting alternative paths to political modernization, fascism has usually been associated with imperialist policies and an authoritarian reaction of the bourgeoisie against working-class mobilization. This reasoning has been transported to the analysis of non-European societies. Consequently, analysts of Latin American politics have generally agreed that Marxist-Leninism provided a concept of anti-imperialist revolution and democratic mobilization that inspired revolutionaries around the world. However, the notion that there might be fascist or radical right-wing concepts of anti-imperialism and popular mobilization has been met with skepticism. The Marxist view was promoted in Latin America during the 1960s, when a number of intellectuals in the "dependency" school used the term "dependent fascism." Drawing on a Marxist perspective, their theories related the nature of hegemonic crises of capitalism and different authoritarian forms of response to a basic theory of imperialism and the dependence it produces. They concluded that fascism was introduced into Latin America not from "Berlin, but from Washington."[2]

Few perceived, however, that radical right and fascist ideologues in Europe, even though they rejected a Leninist type of revolution, were far from being agents of world capitalism or political reactionaries. Likewise, few recognized that "right-wing" fascist movements in Europe and Latin America during the interwar period were not necessarily supportive of bourgeois rights against popular demands. Such movements presented a radical, sometimes leftist, view of society that was quite different from revolutionary Leninism. Moreover, few were aware that fascist, national socialist, and radical right-wing movements and intellectuals, by advancing a total critique of both liberal and Marxist-socialist ideologies of modernization, established the conceptual framework for an alternative road to modernity that was especially suited to underdeveloped or economically and culturally dependent societies.

In this chapter, I try to cast these issues in a different light by examining an idea of modernity and national revolution embedded not in the Marxist revolutionary left but in a new type of conservative revolution encompassing fascist, radical right, and national socialist movements and ideologies. I argue that this ideological framework, which was the outcome of an intellectual rebellion against liberal democracy and Marxist socialism during the interwar period, set the stage for a theory of cultural and political emancipation for "dependent" societies in the non-European world.

Charles Maurras and Maurice Barrès in France, Arthur Moeller van den Bruck, Carl Schmitt, and Oswald Spengler in Germany, Enrico Corradini and Gabriele D'Annunzio in Italy, and Juan Carulla, Ernesto Palacio, and the Irazusta brothers in Argentina exemplify those intellectuals who were vehemently antiliberal but conservative in harking back to the "organic community" and its historical myths.[3] Most of them were modernizers inasmuch as they lauded technological modernization and mass mobilization and in most cases displayed a leftist progressive view on integrating society. Yet they were reactionary inasmuch as they dismissed the moral values of Enlightenment modernity, liberal rights, democratic procedures, and bourgeois society, while praising traditionalist hierarchical values. In short, most of these intellectuals were reactionary in their stance on individual rights and social and political progress, while at the same time they supported social rights for the workers of the nation within the framework of a corporativist state.[4] Several of these intellectuals called themselves fascists, while others refused to be labeled as such. The question is how to characterize this ideological phenomenon, namely, whether these intellectuals were part of the specific ideological realm of fascism, or whether they belonged to a wider intellectual realm that could be defined as the conservative revolution. In this chapter, I claim that fascism was the most radical and modernizing expression of a conservative revolution that encompasses other types of antiliberal and antidemocratic ideologies. I examine the conceptual differences and similarities among movements and intellectuals comprising the conservative revolution. I then draw a conceptual distinction between the ideology of the conservative revolution and what commonsense wisdom perceives as political authoritarianism. I stress that, while the former ideological construction was made up of nationalists who aspired to shift the direction of the country's route toward development from liberalism to self-sufficient corporativism, the latter used authoritarian means to save the bourgeois order and protect a Western "liberal" cultural identity. Finally, I explain the emergence of an alternative political and cultural identity in Argentina within the context of the sociopolitical debate on fascism and populism in Latin America in general and in Argentina in particular.

As a point of departure, I will attempt to clarify the concept of fascism and fascist modernity within the parameters of the conservative revolution. Despite the impact of fascism, scholars have not reached a consensus on defining the phenomenon itself. Simple empirical observation shows us that Italian fascism and German national socialism, for instance, differed from each other in some of their principal characteristics. Moreover, these two central models differed from the French, British, and other variants of fascism that flourished in industrialized Europe, to say nothing of the authoritarian-conservative regimes of Eastern Europe and the Iberian peninsula. It is debatable whether movements like Action Française or the Croix de Fois should be seen as fascist. Some of the movements widely associated with fascism, like the Romanian Iron Guard, rarely used the term to describe themselves, while others, like the Spanish Falange or the

English nationalist movement, repudiated it. Most of Argentina's national-ist leagues, like the Legión Cívica, Liga Republicana, Guardia Argentina, and so forth, also rejected the term "fascism."

The matter is no easier for intellectuals. How can we classify together integralist Catholics like Leon Degrelle, leader of the Belgian Rex move-ment, social monarchists like Charles Maurras of L'Action Française, national communists like George Valois of the French *fasciaux*, ethnic regionalists like Drieu la Rochelle, socialist leaders like Hendrik de Man in Belgium, nationalists like Leopoldo Lugones in Argentina, and national socialists like Jorge González von Marées in Chile? All of them were linked to fascism in many ways, even though at first glance they had few things in common. All of them shared a common disdain for bourgeois culture, decadent materialism, alienated individualism, and liberal demo-cratic values. They differed, however, in their visions of a future society and the type of revolution they advocated. All of them were nationalists who would accept José Antonio Primo de Rivera's assertion that fascism "was a universal attitude of return to one's [national essence]."[5] In other words, a great number of intellectuals who could not be properly labeled fascists considered fascism to be the new universal spirit of national resur-rection, in opposition to liberal or socialist universalist ideologies.

Most scholars have regarded fascism as a "latecomer" movement, an outgrowth of mass politics and industrialization.[6] Some analysts, like Stanley Payne, have emphasized fascist negations: antiliberalism, anticon-servatism, and anti-Marxism.[7] Other analysts emphasize characteristics such as fascism's dynamic quality, cult of action, and political violence.

Recent theories stress the antidoctrinaire character of the fascist ideo-logical core. Roger Griffin, for instance, defines fascism's mythical core as a palingenetic form of "populist ultranationalism."[8] Roger Eatwell states that fascism was an ideology seeking a rebirth of society based on a holis-tic, national, radical third way.[9] Social scientists like Zeev Sternhell have focused on the ideological elaboration of the fascist formula and stressed that the revolutionary characteristics of fascism are the result of a particu-lar combination of ideas from nationalist followers of Maurras and from Sorelian leftist revolutionary syndicalism. The argument is that both lines of thought provided the basis for a revolutionary third way, a "national-socialist" formula, an alternative to Marxist socialism and liberal democ-racy.[10] Georges Sorel's syndicate became a revolutionary school against bourgeois society, liberalism, and socialist-reformist parties.[11] The new nationalism expressed by Maurras and Barrès appropriated the syndicalist mythology, based on authentic hierarchical leadership and organized mobilization in the nation. The Sorel-Maurras synthesis produced a third way to political modernization and set the basis of the national-syndicalist state. However, more than a path to political modernization, fascism represented a new type of community which, as defined by Ernst Jünger, was "a community of sacrifice" or "blood socialism," whose underlying values stood in stark contrast to the materialist, utilitarian, and rationalist values sustaining liberal, Marxist-socialist, or social-democratic ideologies.

Some analysts emphasize other features of fascism that could be identified as rational. As technocratic fascists like Hendrik de Man and Oswald Mosley showed, fascism through *"plannisme"* (state planning) produced rational solutions to economic and social crises. In Italy the national-corporativist state, based on the organic unity of the nation, was a response to the divisiveness of parliamentary politics, social strife, and the underdevelopment besetting the Italian economy. In such a state, as Edmondo Rossoni, the head of fascist syndicates between 1922 and 1925, concluded, "free competition can be no more than a sham. . . . a state like ours . . . needs to know not only what is being produced, but also the conditions under which it is produced."[12] His views were complemented by Enrico Corradini's production-oriented vision of a proletarian nation. On economic grounds, Corradini argued rationally for the welfare of a society of producers. He recommended that a proletarian nation such as Italy should improve workers' lives by matching high wages to large-scale production. The Dopolavoro, for instance, was "a consequence of the fascist concept that does not consider the worker as a human subspecies, but as the class that produces national wealth."[13] The consequence seemed to be a concept of social justice different from that promoted by socialists.

> There are two principles which are used to support high salaries, one of them socialist, the other nationalist. The first of these supports them as a sort of divine right of the proletariat, leaving aside any question of productivity; the second supports their steady increase in accordance with the gradual increase of the national product.[14]

In other words, improvement of the workers' condition was contingent upon the greatness of the nation, which was defined as a community of producers. Moreover, the worker was perceived as the hero of the productive process, a frontline soldier of the homeland.

Domestically, the nation of producers was contrasted to the "disintegrative" forces of the nation: the nonproductive financial bourgeoisie, foreigners, Jews, liberals, and international socialists. Internationally, this conflict was translated into placing "national socialist" nations in confrontation with bourgeois-plutocratic ones. Corradini's idea of a totally mobilized "proletarian nation" was so conceived in order to save the nation from political decadence and transform it from a nondeveloped into an aggressive developed one, ready to compete for empire. This would be an imperialism of the "poor nations" against the imperialism of the "plutocratic nations." Corradini's formula was in agreement with the Italian revolutionary-syndicalist assessment that proletarian nations would be able to take the path to modernity only by first undergoing a national revolution. Indeed, according to Antonio Labriola and Enrico Leone, both representatives of Italian revolutionary syndicalism, Italy was an underdeveloped country that had to pass through a "national revolution" before a socialist one. In his theory of the proletarian nation, Labriola held that Italians were exploited as a nation, not as a social class.[15]

Did this production-oriented conception represent a welfare utopia? Not at all. While the fascist program of national modernization permitted industrialization and national mobilization under authoritarian control and, at first glance, a new path to political modernity, ultimately, fascism's dynamic character contained the seeds of its own self-destruction. Fascism does not share the liberal and socialist aims of change and improvement as the basis for the democratization of public life. Yet it cannot be identified merely as political authoritarianism. One of the most important things to be borne in mind is that fascism's characteristic dynamism and mobilization are not only a means but an end in themselves. Fascism was thus represented by a new antibourgeois spirit of heroism, a new vitality that demanded constant mobilization. It disavowed old elites and was plebeian, or mass-oriented, and secular; although, as noted by Alfredo Roco, its corporativist system might make the fascist revolution turn conservative, its dynamic of permanent confrontation made it the most radical and modernist of the conservative revolutions. As seen by some of its followers, fascism was

> not a political doctrine, nor was it an economic doctrine. . . . Fascism was a spirit: it was first of all an anticonformist, antibourgeois spirit, in which disrespect played its part. It was a spirit opposed to prejudices, to class prejudices and all other prejudices as well.[16]

In the words of Giovanni Gentile, the Italian fascist philosopher, fascism was "above all a total conception of life,"[17] a synthesis of voluntarism and heroism. Therefore, in promulgating an ideology that would be closely linked to action, Mussolini clearly enunciated and embraced a principle that other ideologies might decry but that they were nonetheless obliged to put into practice.[18] In other words, socialists or communists, as stern guardians of an unalterable doctrine, or liberals, as guardians of universal values, are compelled to endlessly rationalize and give countless explanations to justify the process of development, while fascists are free from any such obligation. The reality, the action itself, is thus the fundamental idea. These features of paradigmatic fascism underscore its differences from conservative authoritarian and other radical-right movements.

Authoritarian conservatives and fascists often stood at nearly opposite cultural and ideological poles, while radical right-wing movements tended to span the entire spectrum between fascism and conservative authoritarianism. Limited authoritarian regimes, like Hungary under Miklós Horthy or the original Pilsudski regime in Poland, and that of Agustín Justo in Argentina or the Gabriel Terra regime in Uruguay, preserved certain liberal and parliamentary forms and basically refrained from fully abandoning legal formality. They were more concerned with bureaucratic solutions to economic and political crises, and their ultimate aim was to return to the legal constitutional system.

Still, radical-right and fascist movements had several things in common. Both were militantly opposed to liberal and Marxist socialist visions of modernity, but both promoted social rights and national mobilization under tight political control. Both garnered popular support for reactionary and conservative policies. Thus the fascists and the radical-right movements and intellectuals, their differences notwithstanding, fit within a single category of the conservative revolution. Most of them believed that the nation is an entity that can decay and can thus be regenerated by eliminating liberal politics.

Radical-right movements usually harked back to a reorganized monarchism or an eclectic "neo-Catholic" corporativism and were more doctrinaire than fascist movements. They had a religious component that fascists did not have, and they repudiated the Sorelian and Nietzschian flavor of most fascist movements in favor of a more practical, rational, and schematic approach. In contrast to the fascist exaltation of violence and permanent political mobilization, conservative revolutionaries had a predilection for state power and accountability.

The German Stahlhelm, Italian Nationalist Association (ANI), Portuguese Integralists, French Action Française, Spanish Carlists, and most of Argentina's nationalist leagues in the 1930s rejected liberal society and the liberal order in both theoretical and political terms, yet they relied on elite elements, especially those representing the "authentic nation," who believed that the nation should be regenerated and society should be mobilized and controlled not by a fascist mass-based party but by the army and the Catholic Church. As a political culture, however, fascism was completely different from the conservative authoritarian right, which wanted to freeze the status quo. It differed also from radical right-wing nationalists who were tied to the existing elites, and who were unwilling to accept fully the mass mobilization across class lines, social radicalism, and cultural change demanded by fascism.

Despite differences among conservative revolutionaries themselves, the important analytical distinction that must be borne in mind is that fascist and right-wing radicals were all part of a revolution which implied much more than merely establishing an authoritarian order. In this sense, we are dealing with a new category which makes it possible to distinguish not only between authoritarianism and liberalism, but between authoritarians and conservative revolutionaries. Conservative revolutionaries, whether fascist or right-wing radicals, wanted to surpass economic and political liberalism, by redefining the political realm and the road toward socioeconomic modernization. They were nationalists of a different kind, namely, organic nationalists, and hence their concept of nation was not compatible with democratic organization and liberal rights.

Having thus distinguished between conservative and authoritarian revolutionaries, I shall examine the concept of the conservative revolution by analyzing its theoretical components: a counterrevolutionary theory of state power and a new type of organic nationalism, quite foreign to the republican democratic tradition growing out of the French Revolution. I shall explain why this type of nationalism laid the groundwork for a theory of cultural and political emancipation for "third world" dependent societies.

The Conservative Revolution and Organic Nationalism

Scholars of fascism find connections between the conservative revolution and a wide variety of Weimar intellectuals in the interwar period, such as Arthur Moeller van den Bruck, Oswald Spengler, Martin Heidegger, Carl Schmitt, Ernst Jünger, Ernst Niekisch, Edgar Jung, and others. The shared themes of German conservative revolutionaries were nationalism and the celebration of the superiority of the German *Volk*, in opposition to the destructive influences of the West. Most of them attempted to convert technology from a component of alien Western *Zivilisation* to an organic part of German *Kultur*.[19] This tradition regarded German *Kultur* as the authentic mentality for technological advancement, one not shared by all peoples. According to Gordon Craig, conservative revolutionaries in Germany, for instance, helped legitimize Nazism intellectually.[20]

In this study, however, I endorse Stefan Breuer's position that this entire group of German intellectuals was not the product of a German *Sonderweg*, of the unique condition of the German way.[21] Rather they typified, with different variants, a broad intellectual environment of rebellious intellectuals of a new kind, who aspired to "save" their national community from liberal and socialist cosmopolitan civilization, whose forces they blamed for their own country's cultural and political decadence.

The intellectual forerunners of a counterrevolutionary theory of power were Juan Donoso Cortés, Marcelino Menéndez y Pelayo, and Ramiro de Maeztu in Spain; Louis Gabriel Ambroise de Bonald and Charles Maurras in France; the French (although British-educated) philosopher Hilaire Belloc (1870–1953) in England; the Russian Nikolai Berdyaev (1874–1948); and Carl Schmitt and Oswald Spengler. All presented a total critique of liberal civilization. For them the purpose of politics was clear: to reverse this state of chaos and decadence, of pointless elections, superfluous and self-interested parties, paralyzed parliaments, and so forth.[22]

These thinkers maintained that the character of modern liberal society was alien to the spirit and tradition of their peoples. Although liberal ideology was attuned to the distinct national traditions of each country, it was essentially alike in every country.[23] "National culture" was counterposed to "liberal civilization," or in the case of Argentine nationalists, "Hispanic" values were placed in opposition to liberal ones. These conservatives were advocates of *Gemeinschaft* as something inherently good and unified, as opposed to a divided and fragmented *Gesellschaft*. A central idea was that the French Revolution, Rousseau's social contract, and the concept of popular sovereignty were at the root of the concept of liberal secular modernization, which presaged the destruction of the natural order. In contrast to democratic egalitarianism, most conservative revolutionaries praised the "natural" hierarchies of the Middle Ages and advocated a central role for Christianity, seeing both as repositories of traditional "popular consent."

As noted by Edgar Jung, conservative revolutionaries attempted to rescue those elementary values and laws, without which man loses all links with nature and God:

> Genuine worth is established rather than equality; just integration into a hierarchized society, rather than the drift of society; organic emergence of leaders rather than mechanical elections; the internal responsibility of true inner prompting rather than bureaucratic coercion; the right of the community of the people rather than mass contentment.[24]

The underlying framework of this political thought derived from Joseph de Maistre's anti-Enlightenment stance. Maistre contended that Enlightenment skepticism toward the biblical God led to a violent hatred of political authority. He identified the central sin of modern thought as the deification of the self or the belief that the world can become wholly transparent to the sovereign human mind. The popular conclusion that human beings by nature live in society is not wholly empirical. According to Maistre, one of the capital errors of modern democratic thought was to represent the state as the consequence of a choice based on the consent of men. Only institutions that are sacralized can survive, as he saw very clearly in "Essai sur le principle generateur des constitutions politiques" (1814). Every form of sovereignty comes from God. The logical conclusion was that human nature required an absolute monarchy, supported by the church.

Maistre's basic political conceptions were followed and developed by Bonald and Berdyaev. Bonald attacked the theory of popular sovereignty, claiming that political power was independent of men since it resides in natural law, and Berdyaev stressed the concept of the "organic will of the people," as opposed to the idea of the rational social contract represented by parliamentary politics. For Berdyaev, the organic will of the people is embodied in strong governments, which are sustained by "professional corporate associations."

One of the most important theoretical claims of Maistre and his followers was expressed by Bonald's well-known assertion that the great danger of liberal representative government lay in the opportunity it offered for foreigners to intervene (in national affairs) with their gold.[25] They believed that in the long process of secularization and democratization of the modern world, the "vital" natural economic and cultural resources of the homeland were repressed. A return to God and tradition, therefore, became the first step of a cultural revolution, a revolution of tradition, as opposed to a socialist revolution that would only continue the imperialism and decadence of the Enlightenment.

This spirit was clearly present in Carl Schmitt's belief that "The concept of humanity is an especially useful ideological instrument of imperialist expansion, and in its ethical humanitarian form it is a specific vehicle of economic imperialism."[26] In other words, the concept of universal humanism was seen as the basis for cultural and economic imperialism. The real revolution against liberalism would not be a universal socialist revolution. What was needed was a national and cultural revolution that would rescue the authentic natural order of each society. In this sense, the idea of cultural resurrection and authenticity was set over against liberal modernity.

Some of the most important and influential Spanish philosophers of the generation of 1898—José Ortega y Gasset, Miguel de Unamuno, and later Ramiro de Maeztu, with whom the Argentine nationalists felt a keen affinity—pointed to the dichotomy between cultural authenticity and liberal cosmopolitanism. Ortega's teachings were at first glance ambivalent. He urged that Spain become more European, and at the same time he insisted on the urgency with which Spain and Latin America should seek their own cultural and political identity. In other words, although Ortega was a Europeanist who felt that Spain was the disease and Europe the remedy, that remedy was not rooted in the liberal Europe, whose decadence was announced by Spengler. Ortega's theoretical ambivalence was complemented by Unamuno's own critique of Spanish Westernization. Unamuno addressed the youth of Spain, confident that the collective spirit of the Spanish people would overcome the paralyzing atomization that still plagued it. In a clearly Heideggerian mood, he confessed an inner repugnance for the scientific orthodoxy of the day, as well as for Western utilitarian philosophy and economics. He called for a return to "popular wisdom," by refusing to imitate foreign models. This idea of cultural regeneration was taken up by two of the most prominent figures of Spanish counterrevolutionary thought, Marcelino Menéndez y Pelayo and Ramiro de Maeztu. In his book *Defensa de la Hispanidad*, Maeztu, one of the most important exponents of Acción Española, provided the clearest image of a new type of "permanent community," based not on territory or race, but on language and religion. This proposal was shared by Menéndez y Pelayo, one of the ideological mentors of the Spanish Falange, who in the nineteenth century led the quest to restore what he called Spain's true Catholic self. In the Middle Ages, he argued, Spaniards always saw themselves as one people.

All these thinkers saw an intrinsic link between a theory of cultural revitalization and a counterrevolutionary theory of the state: for all of them, retrieving their culture would entail dismantling the liberal state. At first glance, there is a critical theoretical gap between this type of antimodernist ideology and modern nationalism. However, we should bear in mind that by the end of the nineteenth century two different forms of modern nationalism existed and were in competition with one another: "democratic" Jacobinic nationalism and antidemocratic integral nationalism. While the former adjusted to the path of liberal modernity and the idea of progress embodied in the Enlightenment tradition, the integralist current was tied to the counter-Enlightenment and to a counterrevolutionary theory of state power.

I now turn to examine the characteristics of these two concepts, democratic nationalism and integral nationalism. I will argue that the two faces of integral nationalism, the corporativist and the populist, established a new model of political modernization combining reactionary and modernizing features. This definition raises new theoretical questions about the prevailing analysis of nationalism as a hallmark of modernity.

Democratic Nationalism vs. Integral Nationalism

Current theories of nationalism have explained the emergence of "national collective identities" as a result of capitalist development and egalitarian culture.[27] Ernst Gellner, Eric Hobsbawm, Benedict Anderson, and others have held that nations are an invention of modernity. Gellner locates the emergence of nations in the transition from agrarian-mercantile societies regulated by structure to industrial societies whose mode of integration is cultural. Hobsbawm relates the formation of nations to the requirements of capitalism, a system which calls for large-scale, centralized territorial and political units that provide the necessary legal framework and market outlets. He describes the birth of the nation very much in the spirit of John Breuilly,[28] locating the state as the "social engineer" of the nation: "Nations do not make the state and nationalism but the other way around."[29] Pursuing the theory of modernity from a different perspective, Anderson says that modern nations are an artifact of print capitalism whose genres—the newspaper and the novel—make the nation imaginable.[30]

One of the latest attempts to connect nationalism with modernity has been made by Liah Greenfeld. Greenfeld claims that nationalism is the fundamental vector for modernity. The nation "is the bearer of sovereignty, the basis of solidarity, and the supreme object of loyalty."[31] Not only is the nation a form of republicanism, it is also potentially democratic: "Nationalism, indeed, was the form in which democracy appeared in the world."[32]

Most of these theories express the spirit of the romantic age of nationalism, dominated by faith in democratic progress. Indeed, advocates of nationalism during the mid-nineteenth century were romantic republicans who expressed a strong spirit of optimism in the universal scope and regenerative role of their particular culture. From Giuseppe Mazzini's liberal nationalism, which invoked a utopia of democratic peace and progress, to the historicism and antiliberal approach of Ernst Renan and Johann Gottlieb Fichte, the central belief was that there should be no contradiction between nationalism, democratic rule, and a high human (universal) culture.[33] Although Fichte and Renan could be understood as a turning point toward antiliberalism, this romantic spirit did not necessarily run counter to the concept of democratic progress.

In some societies, however, this spirit stirred up very antidemocratic attitudes. Particularly important within this process is what Greenfeld calls the "resentment" directed at a foreign culture. In Germany, for instance, nationalism was a creed formulated by intellectuals drawn from the middle ranks of society who rejected the culture of the German courts, dominated as it was by French language and literature. The universal values of the Enlightenment were replaced by an appeal to history and the particular values of the nation. In Russia during the 1840s, romantic nationalism emerged among the Slavophiles who defended the Orthodox Church and idealized the medieval past in criticism of Western individualism. Russian nationalism was not based simply on romantic patriotism. While it endorsed the romantic critique of enlightened modernity, in contrast to romantic French republicanism, it rejected the idea of egalitarianism and the concept of popular sovereignty resulting from a "rational" social contract. In Germany and Russia, therefore, we can perceive the seeds of an organic concept of nationalism that was reactionary and hardly democratic, evolving at different stages of political and social development in Europe. This type of romantic upheaval could be explained by the fact that these countries did not pass through complete bourgeois revolutions. What must be stressed, however, is that this nationalist spirit of reaction against liberal modernity was first conceived ideologically in France, the very country in which the bourgeois revolution originated.

Post-Revolution France was more representative of the modern democratic world than any other country. It had rebounded from military defeat to spectacular success in the new imperialism, and its economy was prospering. Nonetheless, from the beginning of the twentieth century, a wide range of integralist monarchists and different types of revolutionary movements rose up against the decadent Third Republic, which had permitted the loss of territories to the Germans. Bourgeois society, the Jews, and political democracy were all part of the decadent democratic republic. The new nationalism as defined by these intellectuals was to be authentic, purely French, and socialist. It was a new political doctrine, designed specifically to save France, but its scope was actually universal. Two of the clearest exponents of this form of nationalism are Charles Maurras and Maurice Barrès. Despite their differences, they are representative of the synthesis between two apparently contradictory but in reality complementary strains of integral nationalism, the corporativist and the populist.

Maurras had a particularly significant influence on Argentine nationalists. As noted by Julio Irazusta, the monarchist formula of Maurras was valid only for France, where for historical reasons "the monarchy was good and the republic was evil."[34] In other societies the unifying role played by the monarchy in France should be taken by other political organizations representing the "real" country. What Maurras had in mind was a theory of nationalism and of political power in opposition to liberal society and its political institutions. Maurras argued that it was necessary to create a theory of the French as Fichte had done for the Germans. This theory was not simply one of patriotism, love of one's country, but one of nationalism. For Maurras, nationalism was more than something subjectively desirable; it was an absolute necessity, the great fact of the modern world. Nationalism symbolized the exercise of a rational obligation: true humanity began with what was near to us, claimed Maurras. Not only was the nation natural, it was rationally and morally the most coherent manifestation of humanity.

Maurras objected to the idea of rationality and political progress espoused by democrats and republicans. Indeed, he criticized both for claiming "progressiveness" as their hallmark. He argued that democrats had prided themselves on having a critical and scientific spirit and had dedicated it to the battle against obscurantism and superstition. But their principle of equality, which was a purely abstract one, was in direct opposition to scientific laws.[35] With regard to the political realm, Maurras claimed that the parliamentary regime, which is considered by liberals as modern in contrast to reactionary monarchies, in reality is too slow and too cumbersome to respond to the conditions of the new order. What was needed, according to Maurras, was a new mechanism of government based on science and on progress, but one severed from republican "scientism," which he defined as a scientific fanaticism that spells the doom of science and of society.[36] An ideology based on science and democracy leads to anarchy, while a science of politics leads to an ordered society. The political conclusions of Maurras became the battle cry of L'Action Française, which boasted that it was a modern movement composed of a proud youth recruited from all classes in the land. Action Française claimed the future and relegated the democrats and republicans to the side of the moribund and the rigid.[37] Maurras therefore supported all the antidemocratic and antirepublican tendencies of his time: the attack on the revolutionary system in the name of true liberty; the attack on economic liberty in the name of the liberty of the syndicate, requiring the revival of professional groups; the attack on political liberty in the name of preservation of the nation.

The monarchy was the pole around which Maurras spun his theories. It was the past and the future; it represented a reaction against destructive liberal modernity as a precondition for taking a new path to modernity. The monarchy provided unity and continuity and defended the rational order, in which it reserved for itself the domain of pure politics, diplomacy, war, and the important police and judicial posts. The most important point, however, was that the monarchy should cooperate with Catholicism to serve their mutual interests. Rather than advocating a civic religion, Maurras deployed Catholicism as the creed of the state. For Catholics, however, that was problematic, because it reversed the Thomistic conception of man's temporal well-being in political society as subordinate to his personal salvation, safeguarded by his voluntary obedience to the spiritual sphere. In the theory of Maurras, by contrast, although political society outwardly conformed to the purpose postulated by the church, it did so only insofar as the church appeared to serve the "a priori" ends of the temporal sphere. The religious and political doctrine espoused by Maurras, which might be termed "clerical positivism," anticipated that of Mussolini in more ways than one.[38]

Barrès agreed with Maurras in much of his analysis of nationalism. He agreed that there were differences between French, English, and German types of nationalism. Less rationalistic than Maurras, Barrès's nationalism was valuable not only for rational and religious reasons, but also as a means of exaltation, as a way of feeling and thinking. Barrès advocated the creation of a "mystique" that would reunite all Frenchmen, and he envisioned it as the voice of the ancestors, the celebration of the dead, and the acceptance of determinism. Although Barrès and Maurras rejected an emphasis on race, both defined the idea of a stronger nation as an ethnically pure nation. The means for national revival was resistance to "humanist ideology" and to cosmopolitan France. Like Maurras, Barrès attacked the republican synthesis between nationalism and the French rationalist heritage. At the same time he differed from Maurras in his attitude toward the republican tradition.

For Barrès the republic was more rooted in the French people than was the monarchy.[39] However, he drew a clear distinction between this republican organicism and liberal democracy. The liberal system, he argued, cannot integrate the workers into the nation and cannot propagate the communitarian spirit of the nation. Yet Barrès's concept of republican populism also should be distinguished from Rousseau's democratic "social contract," since the former is rooted in ethnicity rather than in a rational "general will."

Barrès denied the existence of absolute morality. "There is no absolute truth, but only relative truths." During the Dreyfus affair, he distinguished between the "objective truth" and the "French truth," and complained of those "wretches who teach our children the absolute truth . . . [rather] than the French truth, . . . that which is good for the nation." He emphasized the contrast between the Enlightenment intellectuals, who contaminated the nation with rationalist and individualist poison, and the primitive force, the vitality of the people, "the dark will of the masses."[40] Their differences notwithstanding, Barrès and Maurras represented the period when French nationalism relinquished its always tentative associations with liberalism and became firmly attached to the antiliberal right. This was a new type of right-wing antiliberalism, which abandoned old conservative politics in the name of a national populism with the goal of integrating workers into the nation. Both the Maurrasian corporativists and the Barrèsian populists adopted the national-syndicalist model of social organization, and both influenced the model of fascist nationalism. This was a nationalism of resistance to liberal domination that leaned toward self-sufficiency and "national social justice." There was a direct link between this type of nationalism and a syndicalist organization that promoted both popular mobilization and authoritarian control of the masses.[41]

This new type of right-wing nationalism was expressed by the Italian Nationalist Association, which claimed that

> nationalism, which is an integral doctrine of social life, takes full account of the inevitable and irrepressible conflicts between classes and does not ignore the problem of the internal distribution of wealth. . . . it recognizes the need of the working class to be organized, just as it recognizes the need for employers to be organized. Going beyond the economic conceptions of a now superseded liberalism, nationalism has hoisted its colors firmly on the mast of syndicalism.[42]

Hence, this nationalism could never be liberal or democratic. Our question here is whether it was suited for peripheral societies.

Fascism, Conservative Revolution,
and the Structural Question of Peripheral Modernity

It is not surprising that during the 1930s the conservative revolutionary formula competed with Leninism for the attention of modern nationalists worldwide. Although a number of nationalists endorsed revolutionary Leninism in their struggle against imperialism, others considered the "logic" of the fascist type of national revolution and organic modernization to be a higher stage of revolution.[43]

From a sociological standpoint, however, theories of social modernization have been ambivalent regarding the role played by fascism as a political movement and national socialism as an ideological formula beyond the

European cultural and social framework. Scholars have argued that fascism in Europe was a product of the "second stage of political mobilization." In Latin America, by contrast, the 1930s and 1940s were similar to the stage of mobilization of European liberal populism as it was in the 1840s.[44] While fascism has been seen as a movement reflected in the processes of middle-class destabilization and the eruption of the irrational masses into political life, Latin American populism has been seen as the stage at which the masses became "social" citizens. Populist movements, it has been argued, marked the turning point between a society organized as a factory for the export of primary goods and dominated by the liberal laissez-faire model of modernization, and a society of national integration and reform.[45] In this sense, such movements constituted the political expression of popular sectors that lacked organizational autonomy and did not achieve class-consciousness.[46] Other theories of social modernization, however, have blurred the emphasis placed on structural limitation to fascist development in Latin America. Abramo F. K. Organski and Barrington Moore have recognized the potential for fascist regimes to develop in countries outside Europe and especially in Latin America.[47] They focus on the specific regime produced during industrial acceleration, characterized as the take-off phase of development. According to Organski, Peronism fits the definition of fascism better than it does that of Nazism, whereas Moore, who focuses on the Japanese example, admits that fascism could well fit Vargas's "*estado novo*" and Perón's "*justicialismo*." James Gregor has taken this thought further by arguing that "the problems facing Latin America are those that fascism attempted to resolve"[48] through a development-oriented dictatorship.

Some sociologists have regarded the idea of developmentalist dictatorship as fitting the colonial underdevelopment model, characterized by a traditional and structurally heterogeneous society and by economic stagnation. However, Argentina, the case we are studying here, resembled rather the colonial "new country" model, with open spaces and a high potential for capitalist development.[49] It did not pass through excessive mobilization and did not suffer from a deficient institutionalization of participation in accordance with Samuel Huntington's model for forecasting political praetorianism. Argentina's type of economic growth stemmed from complementary relationships with other nations. Its upper and middle classes resembled collaborators, and its culture was imitative rather than innovative. In other words, as noted by Juan Corradi, Argentina was a "peripheral" country characterized by economic and political dependency, where the modernization process was based not on an internal transformation, but rather on a change induced by the development of a worldwide capitalist division of labor that pushed certain countries into the role of agrarian exporters.[50] However, the condition of peripheral development did not mean economic stagnation and underdevelopment. In the late 1920s, Argentina had the potential to become an industrial democracy, in which neither an agrarian nor an industrial class would need a total reversal of political development. In contrast to the developmentalist dictatorship hypothesis, in the conservative modernizing hypothesis, fascism, the radical right, and national populism are regarded as ways of coping with what are defined as the disintegrative consequences of a higher stage of liberal modernity. We are therefore dealing with societies that enjoyed some competitive type of democracy, a Western cultural background, a liberal constitution, and a growing middle class, and which had been politically independent for at least a certain period of time.

The agenda of conservative revolutionaries, whether national populists or national fascists, in modern societies like Argentina, Germany, or Italy, was not determined by the necessity of a take-off from the stage of underdevelopment typical of colonized backward societies in Central America and Africa. As I have already noted, this type of conservative or reactionary modernizing approach was proposed by nationalist ideologues who reacted against liberal bourgeois society and against "imposed" liberalism, and who opposed what they considered a non-authentic path to modernity, one producing social disintegration and a second-class and/or dependent role in world politics.[51]

A problem is that the conservative revolutionary formula produced different political developments resulting from the different socioeconomic settings in which it was applied. As noted by Albert Hirschman, while Europe's "late" industrial countries emphasized the necessity of manufacturing producer goods, "late-late" industrialized nations focused on consumer goods, the basis of "import-substitution." The former developed an ideology of stimulating national production and class integration in order to compete in an imperialist world; the latter were centered on the need for distributive justice and the development of a consumer market.

In both cases, however, the "third way" elaborated by conservative revolutionaries, by those favoring fascist productionism in central countries, and by populists tending more toward distributive politics in peripheral countries, had common features. The political tradition under discussion was not limited to a struggle for the development of a consumer market or for social rights, but aimed at a full-scale cultural and national change. Furthermore, this political tradition, whether in its fascist, radical right, or national populist face, was not limited to struggle against the communist left. While it is true, as noted by Eugen Weber, that in countries like Romania such right-wing nationalists were able to act freely as national revolutionary movements, a level of political action never reached in the (developed) West,[52] it is also true that in Italy and Germany they represented much more than a simple resistance to the left.

In central as well as in peripheral countries, the new conservative revolutionary nationalists presented a similar national-socialist formula. They combined a new type of left- and right-wing authoritarianism, and they elaborated a new approach toward integrating the national working class. What must be borne in mind is that the social policies carried out under this ideological framework were not determined by welfare motives sustained by a universal concept of citizenship and a constitutional protection of civil rights. On the contrary, the idea of social justice built into this new doctrine was based on quite opposite values. The integration of the working class into the nation was a process that had to be totally disconnected from the idea of political democracy based on autonomous working-class institutions and political parties. In other words, only a national authoritarian movement could resolve the social question. This type of movement-oriented nationalist revolution was certainly modernizing and reactionary, authoritarian and anti-Marxist, but at the same time it advocated social reform. There are several examples of political movements that addressed the social question with these characteristics.

In 1919 the National Christian Socialist movement of Romania declared that its goal was not just to defeat communism, but to fight for the rights of the workers. In Hungary, Ferenc Szálasi's national socialist Arrow Cross Party preached a "unified socialist community of workers." In Latin America, the Movimiento Nacional Socialista (MNS) in Chile, Acão Integralista Brasileira (AIB) in Brazil, the Sinarquista movement in Mexico, and the Alianza de la Juventud Nacionalista (AJN) in Argentina were completely anti-Marxist and antisocialist authoritarian groups that advocated social justice and anti-imperialism.[53]

A similar trend, although from the perspective of developed countries, was manifested by labor party leaders such as Oswald Mosley, Leon Degrelle of the Belgian Catholic Rex movement, Marcel Déat of the French Socialists, and Jacques Doriot of the French Communist party. They abandoned their parties in order to seek a new nationalist revolutionary synthesis, albeit far from the Marxist-Leninist formula.

The modern socialism advocated by Marcel Déat and his Rassemblement National Populaire was an authoritarian, populist, anticapitalist system. Many syndicalists and left-wing cadres were members of Déat's group, thus inviting comparisons with the earlier Boulangiste movement, which attracted radical populist cadres from the left as well as from the right. The National Socialism of Déat arose out of left-wing radicalism. Totally opposed to the tradition of liberal democratic values, it had all the mobilizing and reformist elements of the populist movements that were springing up in Latin America.

There was no great difference between the proletarian slant of Perón's *justicialismo* and the fundamental motives of Degrelle's Belgian Rex movement in 1936, which originated as a protest against "inhuman hyper-capitalism, and against profiteering politicians,"[54] in the name of workers of all classes or, in other words, the productive workers. Despite the cultural and economic gap between Belgium and Argentina, both Peronism and Rexism developed a common national populist ideology, which, despite varying definitions, was characterized by a belief in the importance of returning to or adapting simpler, more traditional values emanating from the people, "taken to be the repository of virtue."[55] This was the national ideal as a regenerative myth that would mobilize collective energies in a program of national rebirth and development. As understood by most of these intellectuals and proponents, this trend was characterized by populist mobilization under authoritarian control, regarded as the only political model that would allow for survival in a Darwinian world led by the imperialism of the competing plutocratic nations.

In Argentina, as in most other places, this nationalist idea displayed both a Barrèsian populist and a Maurrasian corporativist face. Although the Barrèsian, national populist strand (FORJA) that emerged from the left of the Radical Party was thoroughly rooted in the "authentic" Argentine traditions, and Maurrasian corporativism drew on European counter-revolutionary sources, they merged in the 1930s. Both rejected the national project promoted by the liberal modernizing elites, claiming that it paved the way for economic and cultural imperialism. Both rejected reformist socialism and revolutionary Leninism, arguing that these political models were rooted in the same antinational principles that characterized liberal ideology. They rejected any socialist democratic theory of universal social rights, but at the same time they promoted workers' rights as conferred by the "organic" nation. They were conservative inasmuch as they wanted to preserve social hierarchies and place the nation and Catholic values over the individual, but they were also revolutionary, inasmuch as they aspired to revolutionize the liberal order. In the words of Lugones, "the conservatives in Argentina are the ones who want to support the demo-liberal ideology of the nineteenth century. In contrast, a revolutionary wants to modify the existent state organization, whatever its fundamental conception."[56] The conservative revolutionaries were nationalists from the right and the left, while those who adhered to the model of dependent modernity were liberals, conservatives, socialists, and even communists. In this sense Argentina's conservative revolutionaries, like most right-wing nationalists worldwide, saw Marxism and liberalism as two complementary ideas that attempt to destroy the spirit of nationalism. Whereas reformist socialists like Alfredo Palacios and Juan B. Justo sought to improve political and social democracy and the Partido Demócrata Nacional (PDN), which represented the old right,[57] yearned to save the liberal regime even by authoritarian means, the new right proposed another type of nationalist revolution. Its underlying aim was a total rejection of the basis for ideological and cultural subjugation of the nation. In contrast to reformist socialism, this new conservative revolutionary right was authoritarian and nationalist in its struggles for social reform. Culturally and economically, it was anti-imperialist in the sense that it attacked the foundations of the concept of liberal or socialist modernity in the name of the organic nation. It was therefore not Marxist socialism but rather fascism that provided the ideological framework for a "peripheral" rebellion against the liberal terms of cultural and economic dependency and for combining production-oriented policies (usually connected with national sacrifices) with policies of social justice and economic redistribution. This revolutionary right aspired to create a new political and cultural order out of the destruction of liberalism rather than from political reformism. In the following chapters I shall examine the political and ideological ground that permitted this national right to find a common ground with Yrigoyen's followers and to adopt the discourse of Yrigoyenist populism, a concept that opposed the idea of constitutional democracy.[58] The merging of right-wing and left-wing discourse produced the model of a new Argentina that was to be based upon a mobilized society under an authoritarian state. In this type of state the national interest would not depend upon individual or social interests or liberal constitutional constraints, which were defined as the tools of economic imperialism.

In summary, both groups of nationalists sought to express a new nationalist spirit politically, not in order to save liberalism through "technocratic-authoritarian" means, but in order to replace liberalism. They rejected the idea of popular sovereignty but promoted popular mobilization under authoritarian control. They rejected laissez-faire economics, but they also rejected all cultural aspects of bourgeois society. For them, nationalist mobilization constituted a means by which the mythological past is used for social and political revolution, a revolution against civic rights, individualism, and the idea of liberal democracy in general.

CHAPTER 2

Nationalism and the Rebellion against Positivism

The Ideology of Positivism and Elitist Liberalism

Since the beginnings of the Argentine Republic, as described by Nicolas Shumway, two broad currents of thought have dominated the country's leading factions. "The first is a liberal, elitist position centered in Buenos Aires and the upper classes that advocated success through imitation of Europe and the United States while denigrating the Spanish heritage.... The other current of thought is an ideologically messy, ill-defined, often contradictory tendency, which could be populist, reactionary, nativist, or genuinely federalist," which Shumway calls "nationalist."[1] Argentina's model of political modernization was determined by the first of these traditions. According to the modernizing elites, a new Argentina, which had emerged from a half-century of civil strife, needed to break away from present conditions and reject the "autochthonous." That rejection was focused on an intellectual attack against the legacy of Juan Manuel de Rosas, the foremost representative of the caudillo image, symbolizing the anarchic, violent, and tyrannical past. The erasing of that legacy became the basis for the creation of a modern political identity. Domingo Sarmiento's novel, *Facundo: Civilización y barbarie* (1845), brought together the guiding ideas of those liberal elites of the independence days and of their ideological heirs: the modernizing generation of 1880. Josefina Ludmer has defined that book as the "first cathedral of Argentina's culture."[2] Probably no other book has been so influential in defining Argentina's cultural identity. "Facundo offers us a dilemma—civilization or barbarism—which can be applied to [Argentina's] entire political process."[3]

Indeed, the story of Facundo has been completed in a number of ways, which have to be seen within context-specific relations of power, institutional constraint, and other circumstances affecting the "uses" to which a book is put.[4] The generation of 1880 promoted a national discourse marked by a forward-looking tension between past and future, portraying the present as the culmination of political legitimacy. It used Facundo to portray the "gaucho's" unwillingness to work and his inability to survive under a rational political order.

Such prominent figures as Bartolomé Mitre and Vicente Fidel Lopez, like Sarmiento and Juan Bautista Alberdi, regarded Argentina as a "barbarous" and ignorant country, as a result of Spanish colonialism.[5] To them "civilization" meant importing Western liberal values to be implanted through education, foreign immigration, economic development, and the erasure of the Hispanic and caudillo tradition. However, the elites' understanding of liberal values was far from political liberalism as we conceive of it today. As noted by one political analyst, the liberal elite, led by Alberdi, failed to understand that the liberal state was in reality an obstacle to democratization.[6] Indeed, despite the process of socioeconomic modernization, the nation's political system remained closed until 1912 because of the liberal elite's fear of democratization. As late as 1910 it was estimated that only about 20 percent of the native male population voted. Political power was concentrated in the hands of the PAN (Partido Autonomista Nacional), which represented the oligarchic interests of liberal economic modernization without promoting democracy. Its hold on power was rooted in a fraudulent and paternalistic political system. As a political analyst of these years observed, the government "accepted all the great ideas of political liberty . . . and universal suffrage . . . but [the government] has a theory which it rarely confesses, but which is its guiding idea, and that is the theory of the tutelary functions of government."[7]

This tutelary type of democracy and the new doctrine of modernization matched the easy prosperity of the time, resulting from the country's integration into the world economic market. By the mid-1850s Argentina began a process of rapid economic growth and was opened completely to foreign investment. The post-1890 period was unquestionably a golden age for Argentina. Its economic growth was similar to that of Canada and Australia until 1920. Argentina was the leading world exporter of frozen beef and corn, and the third in wheat. Per capita income was comparable to that of the most developed countries of Western Europe, and its annual growth rate after 1869 was 6.5 percent.

Faith in progress and order was the basis on which many in the 1890s, led by President Julio A. Roca, received the modernizing legacy of the preceding generation. During Roca's presidency an entire framework of positivist thinking was implemented under the slogan "peace and administration." The government promoted economic development and embodied the basic elitist understanding of liberal modernization in a country that only recently had become an international economic center. The British established new banks, a railroad network, and gas companies, and large numbers of immigrants from Spain, Italy, Ireland, and elsewhere transformed the sociological characteristics of the country. Buenos Aires, the capital, was federalized, the provincial guards who constituted the local base of provincial powers were abolished, currency was unified, and massive improvements were made in education. Political unification, however, also implied the extermination of the Indians and the engineering of society through European immigration. These policies were supported by an intellectual framework that praised social progress and individual success.

In contrast to the 1830s generation, the new modernizers emphasized personal success. At first glance they seemed to be heirs to the liberal elites, ones who were further expanding the elites' basic principles.[8] The problem was that "the second generation, the ones born after the battle of Caseros, . . . had no more worries than the management of day-to-day life in a rather tedious way." For them, the positivist orientation became nothing but pragmatic belief.[9] Carlos Pellegrini, Miguel Cané, Vicente Fidel Lopez, and Bonifacio Lastra were all members of a generation that had to contend with the intellectual consequences of the modernizing utopia of Sarmiento, Alberdi, and Mitre. During the second decade of this century, in the Escuela Normal of Paraná, inspired by José Maria Torres and Jorge Stearns, the first Spencerian principles of political philosophy began to spread in Argentina. The political elites, who believed that power should be held by the fittest, used Auguste Comte's theories in order to promote their own ideological agenda. Carlos Bunge and José Ingenieros, the most representative intellectual figures of the time, based their theories on the assumption that the Latin American continent was ailing because of its racial composition. Clearly influenced by the French psychologist Gustave Le Bon's theory that "each race has a psychological constitution as well as an anatomical constitution," Bunge concluded that all the vices of the continent were related to the Spanish heritage. Even Argentina, the most European country of Latin America, suffered from the dictatorship of Juan Manuel de Rosas, who was a product of the legacy of the past.[10] For those who believed in the positivist solution to social and cultural problems, a liberal democratic society in Latin America would have to be imposed from above. For all these elites, the idea of modern Argentina was conceived in terms of Western constitutional models and was directly connected to European immigration, viewed as essential for achieving stability and progress.[11]

Argentina became an immigrant country because it offered immigrants the illusion of prosperity. The foreign-born constituted about 30 percent of the population in 1914, a percentage that surpassed that of immigrant countries like the United States. Foreign-born white-collar workers, businessmen, craftsmen, and industrialists made up 66 percent of the middle class of Buenos Aires, and foreign-born manual laborers constituted about 86 percent of its lower class.[12] Indeed, immigrants became the bulk of the population of Buenos Aires in the early years of the century. They represented the face of economic growth, but economic growth would produce political stability only if there were a new educated mass available for economic enterprises and for civic participation.

Mass education was therefore initially regarded as the means for creating the republic and consolidating capitalism. The evidence shows that in the minds of the elites, Argentine identity was not a high priority—if by that we mean the internalization of a subjective attachment to something unique. Mass education had a genuine impact when attending school became a mechanism for social mobilization. Schools were instrumental in the "Argentinization" of those children, but such results were most successful when education also became a tool for integrating them into a dynamic capitalism, a development that was particularly effective in coastal areas. For young immigrants or the children of newcomers, school provided not only the bare language but especially the "idiom" of the "high culture" necessary for upward mobility.

However, immigration, which was an integral part of the liberal program of engineering a modern society, became the Achilles heel of the liberal model of national modernization. For structural reasons as well as particular characteristics of immigration, the expectations of the liberal elites were thwarted. From an economic and social perspective, those liberal advocates of immigration who assumed that foreigners would settle in the countryside and become small farmers and laborers were disappointed. In actuality, the upper-class monopoly of land, combined with urban opportunities, steered many immigrants to the cities. From a political perspective, immigration caused the elites to raise new questions on national ideas and the value of citizenship. Because political rights were relatively meaningless before the Reform of 1912, few immigrants felt either the need or the motivation to become citizens. They remained as permanent residents, while refusing to participate in the political life of the country. Political participation in formal democratic parties seemed a frustrating activity to many Argentineans, however, not only immigrants.

Despite limited democracy, the public sphere of Buenos Aires expanded enormously. Newspapers and cultural associations of immigrants prospered. However, as noted by Hilda Sabato, while participation in the public sphere has generally been associated with increased participation in the electoral system, in Buenos Aires this was not the case.[13] This paradoxical situation allowed the elites to reconcile the ideal norms of democracy with their own control over the state and over economic development in the most modern and economically advanced nation in Latin America, as well as one of the richest nations in the world.

At first glance, Argentina seemed made to fit the arguments of Adam Smith and Karl Marx that agrarian countries with a high land-labor ratio and a labor shortage would develop dynamic capitalist economies and democratic policies.[14] These predictions were not realized in the case of Argentina. In spite of the country's economic growth, the political model projected by the liberal elites, which was based on prosperity and a tutelary democracy, was soon delegitimized. By the end of the nineteenth century two different types of rebellions had shaken the liberal utopia. The voices of rebellion against the liberal establishment emerged when the new native-born middle classes (those born in Argentina, including the children of first-generation immigrants), who had risen socially along with economic modernization, sought political participation, and when the representatives of a class-conscious working class raised the flag of social unrest. These two complementary lines of protest were based on different ideological conceptions. The new middle classes were to be the basis of a new nationalist populist ideology, which became the modern representative of a reformist nationalist and rebellious tradition. The other rebellion that seriously threatened the political system was led by the revolutionary anarchists, who were highly influential in a large segment of the working class.

Reformist Socialism, International Anarchism, and National Syndicalism

Since the early years of the twentieth century, anarchists and socialists had competed for the loyalty of the incipient working class (and competed to organize it). The anarchist movement embodied the ideas of social revolution and internationalism; the Socialist Party, founded in 1894 by Juan B. Justo, represented the reformist socialist facet of the process of liberal modernization. The anarchists appealed primarily to the immigrant workers, who were class-conscious as a result of their participation in European revolutionary movements, most notably the First International in Spain and Italy.[15] The anarchists did not aspire to naturalize immigrants or enfranchise them. They did not foster reform of the political system but rather struggled against it through combative syndicalist organizations. The Socialist Party, in contrast, played a leading role in national politics during the first thirty years of labor union activity. Relying on its status as the only working-class organization that strove to enfranchise immigrants, it became the champion of both social reform and political democracy.

Famous anarchist leaders like Enrico Malatesta, who arrived in Buenos Aires in 1885, played an important role in the internal discussions that led to the rise of the mostly immigrant-based syndicalist movement in Argentina. Malatesta, as well as Pietro Gori, formulated a working-class ideology through education in the syndicate. The debate in Europe reached Argentina, and was closely followed by the new anarchist journals. Hector Mattei, an Italian-born anarchist, founded the Anarchist Communist Circle, which followed the ideological line of the Florentine paper *La question sociale*. Mattei's own newspaper, *Il Socialista*, as well as *La Protesta Humana*, reflected the Argentine anarchists' belief in the educational role of the syndicate as the first stage in a total social revolution. The process of trade union formation and the debates on the general strike, both of which took place in the 1890s, formed the basis for a leap forward in organization from 1901. A significant mass action against unemployment, which tactically united socialists and anarchists, preceded the creation in 1901, of the Federación Obrera Argentina (FOA) (Federación Obrera Argentina).

The first FOA congress, with many anarchists in attendance, focused on the issue of strikes, the type of union organization needed, the attitude to be taken toward labor legislation, and so forth. At this first congress some unity of purpose could be found between the anarchists and socialists, but by the second congress the inevitable split had already taken place. The scope and content of the general strike was one of the central debates within the labor movement. The anarchists, or at least the most prominent among them, envisioned the general strike as insurrectionary in nature and as an instrument in the struggle to abolish the state and set up a new society. Most socialists saw the general strike as a tool useful for winning economic benefits in specific pragmatic circumstances. However, a special faction within the socialists, the "revolutionary syndicalists" inspired by Sorel and Labriola, adopted the idea of the general strike as a revolutionary myth which contributes to the unity of the working class, rather than as a pragmatic tool.[16]

From this starting point, a group of anarchists advocated merging with the breakaway syndicalist current of the Socialist Party, thus forming a link between anarcho-syndicalists and revolutionary syndicalists.[17] At first glance it seemed that both anarchist and revolutionary syndicalists would adopt a common attitude toward the general strike and toward violent action against the bourgeois state. In 1910, however, a failed an-archist attempt to overwhelm the centenary celebrations of national in-dependence through a general strike sparked a harsh repression by the regime. The anarchist attempt of 1910 was in fact the culminating point of a series of working-class revolts and repressions by the government, a cycle which had begun in the early days of the century and which threw into question the idea of the revolutionary strike.

The government reacted to the labor agitation, in which immigrants played a central role, primarily by declaring a state of siege, a power granted to the executive branch that allowed for the suspension of con-stitutional guarantees under unusual circumstances. In reality, this legis-lation merely continued earlier legislation tending to outlaw radical politi-cal activities, especially those of foreign anarchists.

Since 1902 the conservative government had introduced legislative measures designed to strengthen and support the state of siege and to dis-courage radical action. The Law of Residence, introduced by the conserva-tive senator Miguel Cané, gave the executive branch the authority to order the expulsion of any foreigner whose conduct threatened national security or disturbed public order. In 1910, after the failed anarchist attempt, a Social Defense Law was approved in order to strengthen security mea-sures. The initial article of the Social Defense Law prohibited the entry of "anarchists and other persons who profess or preconceive an attack by whatever means of force or violence against public officials or governments in general" into the republic.[18] Other articles prohibited the promotion of anarchist doctrines and reflected the deep split in Argentine society, namely, that between the "authentic" nation and the "foreign" nation rep-resented by the disruptive presence of immigrants identified with anarchist and other foreign ideologies. No doubt this repression led the syndicalist to rethink the value of the revolutionary strike. Moreover, it led to the ori-gins of a new syndicalism that would join forces with nationalism.

At FORA's ninth congress (FORA IX) in 1915, the commitment to revolutionary goals was dropped, pushing staunch anarchists, supported by the newspaper *La Protesta Humana*, to reject the decisions of the con-gress and to split away from it. For the next six years, two FORA unions competed with one another: one (FORA V) remained ideologically pure, as defined by FORA's fifth congress, while the other (FORA IX) endorsed a pure syndicalist (or "bread and butter" rather than revolutionary) tendency. The main point for our purposes is that FORA IX reflected two important social and ideological processes that would later have direct implications for the development of Argentina's antiliberal nationalism.

In social terms, FORA IX represented the national and skilled working-class factions, while FORA V, despite some exceptions—such as the syndicalist railway workers—represented unskilled foreign workers.[19] The process of the "nationalization" of the working class, as the native-born workers came to predominate over the foreign-born sectors, strengthened the pure syndicalist bread and butter trend.

In Argentina, FORA IX found common ground with Yrigoyen's Radical Party, which represented a new type of "supra-party" politics, a new framework with which to deal with workers' problems but without the mediation of workers' parties. Indeed, FORA IX syndicalists rejected Socialist Party mediation in workers' affairs. This anti-party syndicalist tendency constituted the "ouvreriste" or pro-labor face of national populism. In ideological terms, this formula blending populism and social reformism would be pitted against the formula of the socialists, which combined social reform with democratic procedures. The Socialist Party became the reformist face of the liberal project of modernization.[20] The prominent leaders of Argentine socialism, such as Juan B. Justo and Alfredo Palacios, did not differ in their basic philosophical and political positions from the elites. They could not free themselves from positivism, and like the liberal elites, they were adverse to the *caudillista* tradition represented by Rosas. Hence it is not surprising that the liberal elites and socialists— their differences notwithstanding—believed in the same philosophical values rooted in the basic concepts of Enlightenment modernity.

The national project of the Socialist Party reflected in part the social background of its principal leaders. As representatives of middle-class consumer interests, the Socialist Party leaders, most of whom were educated middle-class professionals, advocated reformist policies and an honest democratic government. Since their political philosophy was rooted in the revisionist views of European socialists such as Jean Jaurès and Eduard Bernstein, the Argentine socialists were not chauvinistic nor were they primarily concerned with resisting imperialism. Juan B. Justo aspired to create a European-style system of parliamentary democracy, an ambition that aligned him with the philosophical school of the liberal oligarchy. He believed that "creole politics" ought to give way to organized parties based on rational principles and political programs. Justo distinguished between progressive and nonprogressive capitalism, assuming that Argentina must follow the patterns of Western modern development. This goal could be achieved by attracting foreign capital, which he did not distinguish from national capital. Justo accepted the international division of labor and so opposed industrial protectionism. Furthermore, contrary to the laissez-faire "productionist" theories of the Italian syndicalists, Justo's socialism was rooted in the consumer concerns of the urban sectors rather than in an industrialist and production-oriented conception. Justo called Marx's theory of surplus-value a brilliant allegory by which Marx made capitalist exploitation evident.[21] Justo thought that the transformation of capitalism would lead to the desired social system, but until that happened, he thought, very much like Bernstein, that a modern economic system would produce the necessary national wealth to be enjoyed by the national proletariat and the bourgeoisie. He thereby reflected the alignment of the Socialist Party with the liberal democratic principles of national modernization. The emphasis of Justo and his party on avoiding rebellion and on the virtues of programmatic consistency and rational organization suggests immediate parallels with the aims of the reformers of 1912, translated into the aim to create an urban middle class that was organized in democratic political parties capable of integrating social demands under democratic procedures. It is not strange that in 1912 the Socialists gained 30,000 votes in the Buenos Aires elections, a figure that tripled by the 1930s. With the population growing, the Socialist Party's new strength was due to its constant struggle for social reforms, which included a compulsory day of rest and regulation of female and child labor, equality of income between both sexes, separation between church and state, and in the economic realm, support for the abolition of tax restrictions on imports.[22]

The Socialists were committed to a "minimum" program whose approach was liberal rather than collectivist or nationalistically anti-imperialist. Enrico Ferri, an Italian critic visiting Argentina in 1910, declared that the Argentine Socialist Party was in fact a "radical" party (in the French and Italian sense).[23] According to the Argentine leftist critic Rodolfo Puiggrós, socialist intellectuals who did not reject liberalism but sought to perfect it embraced the worldwide dominant bourgeois ideology.[24] Alfredo Palacios and Manuel Ugarte were the only two socialist figures who challenged the reformist approach, thereby attempting to draw the party to the new conception of economic nationalism. Their anti-imperialism and their support for government protection for national industry were among the reasons for their final expulsion from the party in 1913 and 1915. Although Palacios and Ugarte understood that the primary goal of "dependent" countries had to be economic emancipation, the Socialist Party establishment did not change the ideological tendency that made it representative of the urban middle class and the "labor aristocracy."[25]

For socialists like Ugarte, the Socialist Party was incapable of developing ideas of economic nationalism. For syndicalists, whether of the revolutionary Sorelian type or of the reformist type seeking improvement for working-class conditions, the Socialist Party had betrayed the role of the working class. The Sorelians claimed that the Socialist Party was part of the bourgeois parliamentary system, whereas the role of the working class should be to destroy the institutions of bourgeois society.[26] For the non-revolutionary syndicalists, the syndicate rather than the political party should be the basis of a new system of social organization and civilization[27] totally opposed to the morality of party democracy, which is a "morality of imposition and servility."[28] Both thus rejected the Socialist Party's view of democratic practices. The interesting development, however, is that the concern of the Socialist party for political democracy rather than for economic nationalism, and its bourgeois rather than working-class approach, left open an avenue for a new type of synthesis between national populism and syndicalism.

The early roots of this blend came during the rule of President Hipólito Yrigoyen, beginning in 1916. With Yrigoyen a new concept of national populism appeared on the political scene. The national populism of his Radical Party was to present a clear theoretical and practical alternative to the liberal oligarchic approach to the working class. At the same time it presented an alternative to socialist reformism and to the ideological sectarianism of revolutionary anarchism. More importantly, it represented a political party that was not part of the system. The new political style of Yrigoyenism contrasted with the political style of the ruling elites and ultimately reflected an intellectual and cultural uprising against the values that grounded the liberal model of national modernization.

Cultural Nationalism and the Intellectual Origins of National Populism

The Argentine intellectual climate that accompanied the country's economic growth and sociopolitical modernization was one of a profound faith in the ideology of positivism, even as new questions about the real cultural identity of the country were being raised. As Ricaurte Soler correctly pointed out, "the accelerated rhythm of Argentine development made it possible for liberal democracy to meet up with socialism and even communism under the cover of the same positivistic philosophy."[29] Thus the concept of progress was first associated with liberal democratic principles and then with scientific socialism. As noted by Alejandro Korn, Sarmiento's principle of civilization was purely utilitarian and positivist.

Civilization was not merely an abstract concept; it entailed the establishment of a judicial system and an educational system, as well as the opening of ports and rivers to international commerce.[30] This was a cultural, economic, and social project that became the object of severe criticism from a new generation of intellectuals, whose primary aim was to destroy the philosophical positivism of the liberal elites. New spiritual currents that echoed intellectual developments in Europe, as well as new authentic cultural currents, were reflected in magazines and literary groups, most notably in the cosmopolitan capital of the country, Buenos Aires. In fact, the literary supplements of the main newspapers in the capital, *La Nación* and *La Prensa*, published articles written by local intellectuals as well as comments on Ortega y Gasset, Maurice Barrès, Ramiro de Maeztu, and others.

José Ortega y Gasset's first visit to the Americas in 1916 marked an intellectual turning point in the development of genuine anti-positivism in Argentina. The criticism Ortega leveled at his native country's underdevelopment in *España invertebrada* (1922) provided inspiration for local critics of liberal modernization in Latin America. However, his "Letter to an Argentine Student of Philosophy" in particular was a stimulus for Argentine intellectuals. Ortega pointed out the necessity of rescuing the special vitality of the Argentine people. His basic message, which denounced Argentine narcissism and lack of authenticity, supported the belief that Latin America was the vigorous new world that would replace the decadent old world of the West. Ortega's critique was paralleled by José Enrique Rodó's critique of the utilitarian aspects of materialist culture. However, the views of Rodó and Ortega were hardly intended to exalt the "Indian race." Their quest for authenticity was made in the name of a humanistic Latin tradition. For Rodó, one of the greatest problems of modernization was that of the specialization of modern man. Rodó's concept of "*meritocracia*" envisioned not a traditional aristocracy but an intellectual elite that could lead society toward a nonalienated modernity through spiritual values.[31] Rodó commented on the antinomy between the figure of Ariel, who represents the aristocratic, humanistic, and spiritual traits of the Latin American mind, and the materialist Caliban, embodied in the North American neighbor. The dangers posed by Caliban, and the conviction that materialist North American values should not corrupt the Latin American mind, had a powerful effect on the new generation of cultural nationalists who now began to criticize the bourgeois characteristics of liberal democratic society.

Publications such as *Martin Fierro* and *La Revista Nacional* offer a clear impression of aesthetic rupture, thereby reflecting a repudiation of the materialist spirit produced by social and political modernization. They represented a cultural avant-garde that brought together a new generation of nationalists such as Leopoldo Marechal, liberal idealists such as Eduardo Mallea, and ideologically undefined intellectuals such as Jorge Luis Borges. This common sentiment of rupture and contempt for the materialism of liberal bourgeois society was also shared by publications that were at odds ideologically, such as the center-left *Vida Literaria* and the right-wing *Inicial*. In fact, the new cultural rebellion was announcing that the old political formulas were not suited to a country undergoing modernization. A new spirit of antirational dynamism and ideological rupture was evident. In late 1917 and early 1918, the student revolts at the University of Córdoba (discussed below), which were clearly connected to the cultural ideology of the Radical Party, were portents of a deep movement of intellectual change. The manifesto of the "Colegio Novecentista"—a cultural organization founded in Buenos Aires that was based on the ideas of Ortega y Gasset and dedicated to organizing conferences and publishing *cuadernos* (short essays), including those of its leading figures Coroliano Alberini, Julio Noe, and Benjamin Taborga, Carlos Ibarguren, and Julio Irazusta—proclaimed that what was being sought above the ruins of the materialist positivism was "the substantive and hegemonic value of the human personality."[32] This sense of voluntaristic individualism was summed up in the words of Carlos Alberto Erro, editor of the *Revista de América*, who remarked that he would rather deal with a "furiously atheist" Bolshevik than with a "lukewarm liberal."[33] This moral rebellion against the established intellectual truths and the political establishment brought about a new fraternity of passions that transcended doctrinal rigidity.

One of the most significant intellectual figures influencing the new spirit of criticism of positivism in Argentina was the German philosopher Friedrich Krause, whose works inspired Hipólito Yrigoyen, leader of the Radical Party. Krause, a political philosopher unknown in Germany and in most of the Western world, had a great impact on Spain, particularly among liberal thinkers such as Giner de los Rios and Manuel Cossio. They saw in Krause's theory a bridge between a hierarchical society that keeps its sense of traditional communitarian values and the participation of the masses in the political system under a new idealistic and humanist concept of the liberal state. Spanish liberals in particular were influenced by the concept of spiritual liberalism pitted against material liberalism, which they, along with the conservatives, considered alien to Spain. Krause's teachings pointed the way toward a kind of culturally humanist, elitist liberalism. His *Ideal de la humanidad para la vida* (Madrid, 1860), translated into Spanish by Julián Sanz del Rio, was the key book for Spanish liberalism. Krause observed that the most disturbing phenomenon of contemporary history was class struggle and competition. His (Krause's) conception of society was that of a voluntary moral corporation. A solution to social mobilization centered on educating the individual to the "highest callings of human nature," namely, through instruction in art, literature, music, and so forth. (Mass education, rather than serving as a means to social mobilization by elevating the self-expectations of the individual, was supposed to have the opposite effect.) The goal of education was to liberate man from an obsession with material desires, from base passions and appetites. According to Krause, social organization must be based on subsovereign and semiautonomous municipal and professional associations that could help those who participated in them to understand their function in society.[34] This was in fact a sort of corporativist organization of society based on self-education and self-restraint. This elitist liberalism provided an answer to the "absurdity of inorganic democracy." Giner de los Rios, who also translated Krause into Spanish and who was considered as one of the greatest educators of the Spanish-speaking world, analyzed the problems of the masses using an approach similar to the one developed in the 1920s by José Ortega y Gasset, who feared and detested the masses. Ortega y Gasset and the Krause-influenced Spanish liberals were far removed from the Spanish conservative, anti-revolutionary intellectual current, but their delegitimization of the individualistic and materialistic components of liberal democracy made a significant contribution to the development of antiliberal thought as a whole.[35]

The two intellectuals who had the greatest impact on the delegitimization of the utopian ideas of Argentina's political elites, however, and who bestowed on the incipient antiliberal nationalism its most significant themes, were Ricardo Rojas and Manuel Gálvez. These two were among the most talented Argentine novelists at the time of the nation's centennial. In fact, Rojas, a liberal writer who was an active militant in the Radical Party, and Gálvez, an ex-socialist and one of the most important voices inspiring the new integral nationalism, are crucial in understanding the roots of the cultural rebellion of "authenticity."

A significant event for this cultural rebellion was the publication of Rojas's book *La restauración nacionalista* (1909). Written at the request of the Argentine government, which was seeking an educational plan for Argentine schools, it set off a series of public reactions in an ideological discussion that mirrored similar discussions in Europe.

Not surprisingly, the first reactions to the book came from the Spanish intellectuals Miguel de Unamuno and Ramiro de Maeztu. In a series of articles in *La Nación* in 1910, Unamuno wrote that he applauded Rojas's nationalism, since he himself several times had tried to prove that the concept of humanism camouflages egoistic interests.[36] In a series of articles first published in 1910 in London, Maeztu declared that *La restauración nacionalista* would be the key of the Argentine national psyche for years to come.[37]

Rojas protested against the "excessive liberalism that has moved [Argentina] since the beginning of the century to copy the principle of freedom of education of countries which had nothing in common with our situation and our destiny. In England freedom of education did not have to be written: it came from its traditions and customs. In France it was a consequence of revolutionary liberalism. . . . While Britain and France are homogeneous peoples, Argentina is a heterogeneous people, as a result of the immigration policy of the government. That means that adopting the same [political and ideological] system will serve the commerce of adventurers with no homeland . . . and the invasion of imperialist powers."[38] This connection between immigrants and economic and cultural imperialism was a classic formula that motivated the integralist as well as the populist wing of Argentine nationalism.

It is important to note, however, that Rojas complained not against immigration but against sectarian education.[39] Although Rojas did not deny Sarmiento's basic precepts about the necessity of immigration, he sought to exclude "Jewish schools dependent on synagogues and European syndicates."[40] At the same time, however, he protested against those schools "that give us that aristocratic spirit and mundane Catholicism so harmful to our politics."[41] There were good reasons for the Catholic establishment and the oligarchic elite to mistrust the basic conclusions developed by Rojas, who denounced the "anti-nationalism" of Jews and Catholic schools alike. Both, he argued, divide rather than consolidate a national identity.

In his second book, *Blasón de plata* (1910), Rojas rejected Sarmiento's view that the basic conflict in Argentina was between civilization and barbarism, and replaced it with his own theory on the conflict between "*exoticismo*" and "*indianismo.*" His search for the authentic characteristics of the Argentine nationality led Rojas back to the contrast between the authentic and the cosmopolitan, a tendency that was developed further in his book *La Argentinidad* (1916). Rojas made important observations on Argentine history in seeking to determine clearly the nature of the Argentine *Volksgeist*. Rejecting the popular view that the struggle for emancipation from Spain was inspired by European liberalism and was led by the city of Buenos Aires, Rojas concluded that Argentine liberalism, federalism, and democracy were native phenomena and that the authentic leaders of the native revolution came from the provinces.[42] The appearance of the book coincided with the victory of the Radicals in the free elections of 1916. Rojas nevertheless disagreed with the policies of the Radical leader and was not active in the Radical Party until 1930.

In his *El radicalismo de manaña* (1932), Rojas developed a concept of political democracy that was far removed from the ideas promoted by the Radical Party. He supported the Radical Party on some issues, such as antitrust legislation, the social use of private property, and the expropriation of certain key industries. At the same time, from a cultural perspective, he rejected those historical revisionists accompanying the rise of Yrigoyenism who attempted to compare the controversial figure of Juan Manuel de Rosas to that of the figure of José de San Martín, the symbol of national consensus. In his book *Eurindia*, as well as in *El santo de la espada: Vida de San Martín* (1932), Rojas contrasted the national leader San Martín with the figure of Juan Manuel de Rosas. While San Martín was the poet of national consensus, he argued, the myth exalting Rosas contributed to divisions and national conflict.

The Rojas of the 1930s differed from the Rojas of the beginning of the century. In the 1922 edition of *La restauración nacionalista*, Rojas noted that if he were to rewrite the book, he would not include some of the ideas in the first edition. He was referring to some of the ideas that had been adopted by national socialists of all nations: "It is not only a foreign association of Jewish bankers who legislate our country. . . . European parliaments also began to legislate here."[43] Despite this attempt to distance himself from his early assumptions, part of his intellectual legacy was the attempt to associate the images of foreign capitalism, cultural dependence, and the inassimilable Jew. This attitude was shared by most nationalist thinkers at the beginning of the century.

Manuel Gálvez's work should be paired with that of Ricardo Rojas. From a different perspective, Gálvez emphasized some of the same issues raised by Rojas. *El diario de Gabriel Quiroga* (1910) and *El solar de la raza* (1913) became the cornerstones of a cultural renaissance and of a direct attack against cultural cosmopolitanism. The central theme of the novels is the antagonism between the old village and the cosmopolitan city, that is, between culture and civilization. Manuel Gálvez's alter ego is Gabriel Quiroga, who tours the provinces in order to experience the real Argentina. According to Gálvez, the national spirit was not extinguished, but it was hidden under the "thick overlay of cosmopolitanism."[44]

Gálvez's novels show the direct influence of Maurice Barrès's conviction that sentiment is superior to reason.[45] The authentic traditional liberties are rooted in the rural areas. In fact, it is local provincialism, with its love of tradition, its resistance to the foreign, and its New World spirit, that embodies resistance to denationalization.[46] Even more than Rojas, Gálvez represented the spirit of anti-cosmopolitanism embodied in resistance to the central goal of the liberal elites, whose most direct expression was the process of immigration and "civilization." The patriotism of Gálvez differed from that of Rojas, in that Gálvez quickly realized that there was no way to connect patriotism to a liberal concept of nationalism. The new concept of nationalism overturned the entire philosophical construct of liberal democratic culture. "This is a nationalist campaign. Collective ideals . . . represent a traditional value. Today's materialist skepticism is instead a recent phenomenon, because it appeared with the present pursuit of wealth coming from Europe. The immigrant, a winner because of his success in the acquisition of wealth, achieved in the country a new lifestyle."[47]

Only in a materialistic liberal society, Gálvez argued, could the immigrant succeed. His success represented an attack on the collective idealism of society, which is rooted in the spirit of tradition. Gálvez was not an anti-Semite, but to describe the foreigner he used the image of the immigrant Jew. Although he recognized the possibility of Jews adapting to national life, as he could see in his friend Gerchunoff, he was skeptical of that possibility for most of the Jewish community.[48] A negative reaction to the characteristics of immigration in Argentina could also be observed among the liberal elites who had promoted that immigration.[49] Sarmiento himself, the most ardent supporter of immigration, was disappointed in it. The dream of waves of Nordic and Anglo-Saxon immigrants was replaced by the reality of Spanish Italian immigrants, who were Catholic and against whom he struggled, and Jewish immigrants, whom he disliked.

For Gálvez the struggle against immigration represented the struggle for the renaissance of a new culture and conception of race. In fact, Gálvez's opposition to the materialism of modern society was not in itself a rejection of modernization. According to Gálvez, from an ethical standpoint Spain had modernized. Hispanic ethics together with the special energy of the Latin peoples would constitute the necessary formula for progress and morality. "Our energy is not the barbarous and automatic energy . . . that boils unceasingly in the United States of America. Our [energy] is and will be a harmonious energy. A force tempered by Latin elegance, an intelligent impulse, a strength in which action has not destroyed imagination."[50] The rebellion against cosmopolitanism was the seed of a deeper rebellion against the conditions of Argentina's cultural and economic dependency on Britain. Rojas's exalting of the "Argentinidad" and Gálvez's call for the recovery of the Hispanic basis of Argentine nationality cannot be disentangled from a wider demand for national emancipation later promoted by right-wing and left-wing nationalists alike. At the early years of the century this spirit of cultural rebellion against the liberal elites' model of national organization accompanied the rise to power of the Radical Party, the first popular movement embodying not only a demand for political reform but also the outcry of a new nationalist spirit, whose content was defined during the 1930s.

The Origins of a New Antiliberal Nationalism:
From Liberal to Popular Democracy

The Radical movement that took power in 1916 was the first serious attempt at challenging the ideological hegemony of the liberal elite. In order to grasp the ideological synthesis of integral nationalism and populist, anti-imperialist nationalism that would develop, it is important to elucidate the new political and ideological message of Radicalism, as well as the political and ideological consequences of the Radical Party's split into "personalists" and "antipersonalists" in 1924. Developments in the Radical Party furthered the general ideological tendencies that divided the political system into those who supported the liberal democratic model of modernization and those who challenged its fundamental principles.

The historical complexity of the Yrigoyenist phenomenon is still a matter of discussion. Some analysts have defined Radicalism as a popular party rather than a populist movement. Others have suggested that Radicalism attempted to combine liberal democratic aims with a personalist style. Still others have emphasized the fact that Yrigoyenism was the first modern political party in Argentina and that it moved the Argentine government from consensual toward competitive decision-making,[51] leading therefore to a crisis of political legitimization. While I agree with those analyses, it is my contention that Yrigoyenism also represented a new perspective on national identity. In other words, there is a correlation between political institutionalization and cultural and national identity. Yrigoyen's populist approach and his attempt both to redefine the country's cultural identity and to redefine the idea of the nation as a nonpluralist civic community represented the only way to surmount the power held by the oligarchic elites.

Initially, as noted by some of the most influential historians of the Radical Party, the Unión Cívica Radical represented the political expression of an ideal that aimed at rescuing the Argentine people from the materialist compulsions of the conservative regime.[52] While the Socialist Party was a reformist party that accepted the model of national organization promoted by the liberal elites, and thus attempted to improve the social and political quality of formal democracy, the Radical movement expressed a nationalist feeling of cultural and political rebellion against the conservatives' model of national organization to a degree previously unknown in Argentina. On the one hand, the Radicals embodied the struggle for democratization. On the other hand, their attempt to redefine the rules of political democracy and to associate the movement with the concept of the organic nation radicalized, as nothing had before, the existing political and cultural cleavages in Argentina's society.

Born as a popular revolutionary movement in times of economic depression, the Radical movement gave expression in 1890 to the first violent dissent by members of the oligarchic class against the administration of President Juarez Celman, which was regarded as fraudulent. Although the revolutionary upheaval drove Celman to resign, the young movement could not maintain a united front vis-à-vis the new government of Carlos Pellegrini, who continued to uphold the oligarchic approach to modernization. The Radical movement originally consisted of university groups, young sons of patrician families organized in the Unión Cívica de la Juventud, and professional politicians from the province of Buenos Aires who were banned from office. However, even in its early years the party was divided by two different approaches to political practice that would affect the way the concept of the nation was defined.

The "intransigent" wing of the party led by Leandro Alem constituted the Unión Cívica Radical, which represented the caudillo tradition of Juan Alsina and Juan Manuel de Rosas rather than the idea of a modern liberal nation.[53] Opposing it were those sectors of the party that accepted compromise with the political principles of the liberal-conservative elites and that were the forerunners of the "antipersonalists" of the Radical Party.[54]

The "intransigent" line was continued by Hipólito Yrigoyen, whose main concern was the struggle of the Radical movement for the principle of free universal suffrage. "The Unión Cívica does not seek ministries but guarantees of free suffrage."[55] In this respect the new party resembled the Argentine version of the bourgeois struggle for universal suffrage. In the political context of Argentina during the 1910s, however, it represented the contemporary continuation of the populist caudillo tradition that was first defeated in the Battle of Caseros and later expressed in Juan Alsina's struggle against Bartolomé Mitre.

When universal suffrage was enacted with the Sáenz Peña Law (1912), the national elite expected that a "democratic" concession was the way to prevent from the Radical Party from becoming a rebellious "intransigent" movement along the lines of its caudillo tradition, as seen during the rebellions in 1890 and 1905. The oligarchic elite believed that the Radical Party could be turned into a party of the system. In the political calculations of the elite, the new rules of the game would provide a path to legitimization for the new middle class, while the working class, made up of foreigners, would be excluded from the political game. Thus the elite reformers were convinced that they would benefit from the participation of the middle classes pursuing their own economic interests, since the Radical Party did not oppose the economic interests of the agrarian elites.[56] However, the emergence of a new and energetic political phenomenon with a quite different political style was sufficiently worrisome to the national oligarchy, and hence it attempted to confront the new Radical movement in the election process by organizing a modern conservative party. In 1916, Lisandro de la Torre and his Partido Demócrata Progresista (PDP) became the new and last card in the conservative hand. De la Torre represented the spirit of the Roca generation and remained firm in the defense of a formal reformist democracy without populist or caudillo connotations. The Partido Demócrata Progresista included among its founding members some of the figures who played a decisive role in the revolution of September 1930. Among them were Felix de Uriburu, who would lead the coup, José Maria Rosa, a future nationalist historian, and Carlos Ibarguren (the father of Carlos, Jr., and Federico), a key figure of conservativism who also developed the party's leading ideas. As Carlos Ibarguren recalls, the party attempted to harmonize "the present demands of the country with the things that must be preserved, as a form of solidarity between the old and the new generations."[57] Ibarguren admired the moral stance of de la Torre.[58] At the same time it was apparent to this future nationalist intellectual as well as to other colleagues at the conservative newspaper *La Fronda* that the liberal regime could not ensure moral political practices or politics without corruption.

The most important political development, however, had to do with the substance of the conservative coalition that opposed the Radicals in the 1916 national elections. This coalition revealed the future ideological divisions within Argentine politics.

In 1914 Julio Costa, the ex-governor of the Buenos Aires province, defined the conservative position in Buenos Aires as follows: "the Socialist Party is not our electoral adversary, and most of us agreed with most of its social demands."[59] As represented by its slate of candidates, the Socialist Party did not threaten the fundamental principles of the liberal elites' approach to modernization. By contrast, the Radical Party was said to be "one of those factions of creole politics, reactionary as they all are, that expressed Argentine social backwardness."[60]

Despite the efforts of the oligarchy, in the 1916 election the Radical Party led by Yrigoyen defeated the Partido Democrata Progresista of de la Torre, the Socialist Party, the Conservative Party, and a dissident faction of the Radical Party (which, after the electoral results, offered its support to the Radical Party and thereby achieved some access to power). This was a turning point in Argentina's politics. The oligarchy saw in the Radical Party's rise to power the beginning of a new ideological hegemony. The new political speech and style was much more substantive than expected. In fact, the bland, closed manner of the oligarchy was swiftly swept away in a wave of popular euphoria, announcing the age of populist democracy.

The Radical Party's Political Ideology:
Between Populism and Liberal Democracy

Raising the banner of democracy, the Radical Party objected to the oligarchy's system of reserved political privileges. Although the Radical Party's call for democracy was based on the principles of universal suffrage, the Radical's concept of democracy would have major repercussions on the formation of Argentine antiliberal nationalist consciousness.

It is interesting to consider how Yrigoyen attempted to institutionalize this concept of democratic populism at four levels: the federal level, the party level, the level of the working class–state, and finally, the army-state level.

The first sphere where Yrigoyen's paternalistic characteristics were manifested was in his continual resort to federal interventions in the provinces. In principle, the traditional theory of provincial autonomy was the basis of the Radical concept of democracy. During the federal intervention in the province of Buenos Aires in April 1917, Yrigoyen declared that "the provincial autonomies belong to the people, and not to the government."[61] However, starting in 1919, the old practice of federal intervention, by which the national government assumed direct control over the provinces to correct local abuses of power, was restored. The reason for the shift in political practice was that when the Radical Party took office in 1916, the conservative liberal establishment, representing the old regime, continued to dominate the Congress and to govern some provinces. Yrigoyen nevertheless devised a way to exercise central control by intervening in the provincial governments. In an attempt to combine the politics of regional federalism with the constitutional order, Yrigoyen monopolized political power in the provinces in order to create local handpicked regimes subservient to the president, thereby enabling him to control the elections to the National Senate. In principle, federal interventions were supported by constitutional law, which gave great authority to the president and the majority party. However, while acting according to a formal interpretation of the law, Yrigoyen used the law as a political device to a much greater degree than ever before and thus undermined the way the delicate interregional balance functioned under the oligarchy.

At the party level, the new role performed by "professional politicians" displaced the old conservative practice of politics as a marginal occupation. This fit Yrigoyen's ideas of a strong presidency: political partisans depended on the favors of the executive power. Yrigoyen increased his influence through "neighborhood caudillos," particularly in densely populated areas.

The systematization of the practice of patronage divided the leaders of the party. It attracted the support of middle-class sectors of the Radical Party because it opened the political arena for these new social strata. Nevertheless, the party elite realized that the popular leadership created in local committees was a potential threat to their control of the party.

The new political mechanisms and refreshingly new spirit of the Radical party paradoxically allowed a non-charismatic person such as Yrigoyen to become an object of public idolatry. A prominent conservative nationalist, many years later, described Yrigoyen as he took office as "saluting the people . . . impassive in front of this expression of personal idolatry. That cold man . . . did not maintain personal contact with the masses, he never addressed them, he did not have oratorical qualities, . . . he did not prepare, as demagogues used to do, popular demonstrations [systematically]. . . . Even so, the people . . . shouted out his name."[62]

The personal characteristics of this austere man and his moralistic approach in fact frightened those members of the party who could not cope with his personality or with the non-doctrinaire leadership of the Radical Party. In 1909 Pedro C. Molina resigned from the party because of its lack of any political program. "What kind of fundamental ideas will the Radicals develop in their government?" he asked. Yrigoyen's reply in December 1909 was that "the Unión Cívica Radical is the "nation itself . . . it is a conjunction of forces emerging from national opinion . . . and from public demands."[63] The oligarchy, according to Yrigoyen, did not recognize as programs "the high fundamentals of national reconstruction," but it did accept "the list of vague promises, . . . posited as . . . basic foundations."[64]

In other words, while the Radical movement was a nationalistic and moral movement, the oligarchy represented the narrow interests of the privileged. For Yrigoyen, the fundamental problem of the liberal regime was its amorality. He criticized the amoral characteristics of the classic politician, who is the product of the materialistic and utilitarian values of liberal democracy. Although the evils of the old regime are not clearly explained, "the Radical Party does not proclaim seductive and circumstantial platforms . . . because its concern . . . is the sanctity of the vote."[65]

One of the fundamental projects of the Radical Party—based on the claim that "Radicalism is a cultural and political conception responding to a cultural ideal"[66] that is supported by the majority of the peoples— was the University Reform of 1918. Its repercussions were clearly felt throughout Latin America. Responding to the need to democratize the old and static principles of the higher institutes of learning, students in the city of Córdoba launched a revolutionary process that received wide support from the government, which recognized an opportunity to spread a message that would challenge the existing liberal establishment. Indeed, "the citizen's access to national life, due to the Radical Party, as well as the student's access to university life brought about by the University Reform, are two indications of the same phenomenon, . . . the creation of an organic, integral sense of nationality."[67]

Echoing the high ideals embodied in Krausian educational theory and in the new antimaterialist and anti-utilitarian currents, the Radical movement considered the ideals of the student revolt as the ideals of its own movement. "Until 1916 a type of utilitarian education prevailed in the nation and in the university whose . . . falsity . . . originated within the governmental oligarchies: mercantile criteria in politics, and self-centered criteria at the university [and] in public education."[68]

An integrated and organic society was the basis of the Radical concept of democracy, a concept that opposed class conflict as well as the utilitarian and positivist basis of the liberal program of national modernization. This notion of popular democracy challenged the oligarchy's authoritarian barriers to what the radicals called "distributive justice," a concept that in the ideological context of the Radical movement was not inspired either by the European social-democratic principle or by reformist liberalism. Its rebellious spirit reflected the way labor conflicts between the employers and workers were resolved by the state as well as the ambivalence that characterized the movement's economic policies. What is plain, however, is that the Radical movement did not attempt to be a conventional political party representing factional interests. The Radical movement under Yrigoyen's leadership blended liberal and national organic ideas. It promoted the liberal ideals of universal suffrage. At the same time it was reluctant to accept the other facet of liberal politics, namely, the diversification of interests and the building up of democratic consensus between political factions. The Radical concept of politics was organic and "personalist" (based on the leader's moral authority) and preferred clientelist politics to formal democratic procedures.

Yrigoyen's Economic Nationalism:
Populism without Industrial Modernization

Although the Radical movement challenged the ideological hegemony of the liberal elites, it did not attempt to disturb the agro-export economic order dominated by the oligarchic elites. In fact, a striking feature of Yrigoyen's economic nationalism was its lack of any policy on industrial production. The Radical Party in fact represented politically excluded elites as well as the new middle classes. It is difficult to conclude, however, that the Radical movement represented economic interests different from those of the oligarchy. The middle classes themselves were part of the oligarchic production system and dependent on it. The growth of export revenues during World War I led to a period of exceptional prosperity for the meatpacking industry, one that also benefited cattle ranchers, who saw their production increase in value. However, World War I also generated rapid inflation due to the rise in import prices and production costs in Europe and higher international shipping rates. Prices of domestically produced goods were similarly affected because they depended on imported raw material. Consequently, the main task of the Yrigoyen government was to compensate the urban workers and middle classes affected by the higher cost of living without damaging the interests of the exporting landowners who actually benefited from this inflationary period. The patronage system, as noted earlier, was the simple populist answer that opened the bureaucratic apparatus to the middle classes and created a new approach to the working classes. It must be clearly understood that although Yrigoyen did not develop a particular position that necessarily favored the workers in labor disputes, nevertheless, he initiated a new approach to labor-state relations in Argentina. This paternalistic approach was in competition with the Socialist Party approach as well as with the class-struggle approach of the Anarchists, and very soon, sectors of the Argentine syndicalists found in the populist state a qualitatively different approach to managing social conflicts. Yrigoyen's new approach to the relationship between state and labor in fact exemplified the strategic alliance between national populism and antisocialist syndicalism.

Thus a new association was formed between labor (FORA IX) and a national populist government that enabled the state to become involved in labor conflicts.[69] In the Argentine case this trend developed into the future partnership between Perón and labor.[70]

As the Radical senator Ricardo Caballero explained it, "the state is obligated to . . . [serve the function] of regulating the distribution of social wealth, of protecting the dispossessed masses against the relentless advance of self-seeking individual interests."[71] Francisco Beiro of the Chamber of Deputies supported this position, saying: "nor do we accept class differences, or that there are any classes in the Argentine Republic. . . . [and] we do not accept that there is a proletarian or a capitalist class, even if 95 percent of the Argentines were to fall into what in Europe is called the proletariat."[72] The concept of class was denounced as a European idea unsuited to the ideals of a new America. In contrast, the organic state would provide an integral solution to the national workers.

Between June 1917 and February 1918 there were fifteen railway strikes, marking a rise in labor unrest. In most of these disputes, the Yrigoyen administration supported the workers against employers. In the railway strike, as well as in the port strike eight months earlier, Yrigoyen forced concessions for the workers.

The government was criticized by both conservative groups and the socialists, who interpreted Yrigoyen's policies as simple demagoguery that attempted to divide the working class. La Fraternidad members, however, believed that the success of the railway strikes was due to the action of the government, which was the first Argentine government that "tacitly recognized the endeavors of our organization, which before the strikes, were treated with no respect or consideration."[73]

The fact that Yrigoyen approached the workers in a friendly and paternalistic manner did not mean that he ignored the primary exporting interests of the elites. The government took a hard line in those labor disputes where no electoral advantage could be gained, where the state itself was directly involved, or where foreign capital was threatened.[74] An especially harsh stance was adopted when foreign workers linked to the anarchist FORA V were involved, as was the case with the unions of the Berisso meatpacking plants in late 1917. In short, Yrigoyen did not support those strikes that threatened his administration's own interests. These developments led to the railway strikes of 1918 and the metallurgical strikes of the Vasena factories that culminated in the famous Semana Trágica ("Tragic Week") in January 1919, in which hundreds of workers were killed and the country came to a halt. The relationship between the Radical Party and the working class consequently deteriorated. From that point onward, insecurity increased, primarily because of the relationship between the Radical Party and La Liga Patriótica and the Asociación del Trabajo, who were the direct agitators against working-class neighborhoods. La Liga Patriótica was affiliated with the national youth committees, which were originally organized to lobby against the government's position of neutrality during World War I (because they were liberal supporters of the Allies). They collaborated with the government in labor repression by offering their services to Elpidio González, the police chief and close friend of the president.

Yrigoyen's attitude toward "non-national" workers or workers who expressed "class solidarity" is not strange if we heed the type of nation the Radicals strove to create. The Radicals aspired to include the sons of immigrants into the nation, while at the same time they were far from averse to exploiting the latent xenophobic sentiments against new immigrants. Yrigoyen did not repeal the residency laws and other repressive regulations of the old regime directed against immigrants. This attitude was demonstrated on May 22, 1914, following the electoral success of the Socialist Party in elections of national representatives in the capital. The Radical Party reacted by claiming "that the success was achieved with the participation of rootless immigrants."[75] Similar arguments were presented against La Liga del Sur, the conservative progressive party of the Santa Fe province: "It combines the Rosario plutocracy, originally from overseas, and Italian settlers." In contrast, the Radical movement struggled against "the forces that abhor what is native."[76]

This anti-foreigner attitude was not limited to foreigners. The exclusion from the nation encompassed all those who adopt an "anti-national" posture, or who challenged the integrity of the nation, according to Yrigoyen's view of it. The repression of the sheepherders who revolted in Patagonia in 1920 was a clear example of this approach. Indeed, the Patagonia episode became the greatest moral indictment against the Radical government.

Yrigoyen's political ambivalence was manifested in every area of the political sphere, and in general, the social and economic contradictions in Argentina during the 1920s could be not resolved by a unified party. Thus, Yrigoyen's commitment to working-class demands, middle-class access to consumer goods, and the agrarian interests of the elite could no longer be successfully reconciled by the Radical Party's populist approach under constitutional law. More clearly than ever, most political elites arrived at the conclusion that populist policies violated the spirit of constitutional law. The oligarchic class did not turn against Yrigoyen for economic reasons. As discussed earlier, his economic nationalism did not work to the detriment of the primary agricultural sector. Moreover, in order to avoid alienating the oligarchic sectors in the party, Yrigoyen nominated Marcelo T. de Alvear, a member of the patrician group of the Radical Party, as the presidential candidate in the 1922 elections. This tactical move, however, was conceived merely as a means for Yrigoyen to return to office after the fulfillment of Alvear's term as president.

Alvear was a symbol of retrenchment and consolidation, and he enjoyed the cooperation of the aristocratic groups that had caused the government so much trouble during the period of the labor strikes in 1919. The aristocratic groups, however, believed in the possibility—through Alvear—of a return to what they regarded as constitutional legalism. In contrast to Yrigoyen's constitutional populism, characterized by federal intervention in the provinces and by the sanctioning of presidential decree or ministerial resolutions, the aristocratic groups demanded more congressional control and rational management of public funds. Their concern was to dismantle Yrigoyen's patronage system. Alvear was convinced that Argentina's future and the Radical approach to modernization depended upon surpassing Yrigoyen's political style and transforming Radicalism from a populist movement into a party "of the system." Transforming the Radical Party from within, however, was almost impossible for Alvear; he had no personal following in the party. Alvear needed the middle-class elements that had historically provided the rank and file of the Radical Party.[77] Nevertheless, at least until the end of 1925, Alvear proved less committed to middle-class groups than he was to the relief of the landed groups, in that he eased the pressure on credit. His attempt to control government spending quickly led to the collapse of Yrigoyen's patronage system and to a schism within the party, which gave birth to two factions: the populist Yrigoyenists and the Unión Cívica Radical *antipersonalistas*, who opposed the patronage methods of control displayed by Yrigoyen and supported a more rational type of parliamentary rule.

This confrontation between two different political styles soon developed into a wider rift. Ironically, the *antipersonalistas* felt more akin to the conservative parties than to the personalist Yrigoyenist branch of the Radical Party. This was especially clear in the period leading to the national elections of 1928, when the conservatives, antipersonalists, and even some sectors splintered from the Socialist Party joined forces in order to thwart Yrigoyen's run for a second term in office.

In April 1927 a meeting of all the anti-Radical forces was held in the city of Córdoba. The "confederation of the rights" brought together the Autonomist and Liberal parties of Corrientes, the Conservative party of Buenos Aires, and the Liberal parties of Tucumán, San Luis, Mendoza, and other areas under a common front led by Julio A. Roca.

At the same time, the antipersonalist front of Radicalism ordered a national convention in April 1927, which chose Vicente Gallo and Leopoldo Melo as candidates to challenge Yrigoyen in the 1928 national elections. Gallo, who had been interior minister in 1923, had became the leader of the anti-Yrigoyenist bloc within the party. Yet in spite of the support given to the liberal democratic bloc by all of the most respected sectors of Argentine politics, Yrigoyen won the national elections even more decisively than in 1916, by 838,000 votes against 414,000 for the liberal democratic bloc. That constituted the worst of the options for the antipersonalists, who considered any return to the system practiced by Yrigoyen as an obstacle to "the organization of a government of ideas."[78] For the conservatives, Yrigoyen's reelection represented the return of the "tyranny of the mob" or the dangers of a Mexican- or Russian-style revolution.[79]

The Crisis of the National Populist Regime

In spite of Yrigoyen's senility and his penchant for personally directing all government affairs, his second administration, beginning in 1928, proved that he was fully in control of the political situation. He kept his hold until early 1930, when the effects of the Great Depression began to appear in Argentina. Although Yrigoyen did not turn against the primary agrarian interests and their British associates, his relationship with the conservative elite deteriorated. Yrigoyen's regime seemed to many synonymous with disorder and anarchy, and hence incapable of providing a political answer to the new international and domestic political demands.[80] During the Great Depression, when the government appeared to be increasing the burden of the country's external debts to a critical point, the agricultural exporters represented in the Sociedad Rural joined forces with the Industrial Union to demand a reduction in public spending, which was in fact the main source of Yrigoyen's political support.

At the same time, there was growing distrust of Yrigoyen's administration at army headquarters. The army disapproved of his populist consumerism and the lack of a clear industrial policy. However, what

disturbed the professional army officers even more than Yrigoyen's economic and social policies was his continuous intervention in army affairs.

Yrigoyen could not accept a purely legalist conception of the army. He
promoted officers on the basis of partisan allegiance rather than seniority
or merit (and partly to repay his debts to the military men who had supported his attempted coups in 1893 and again in 1905). However, the
rebellious country of 1905 was not the same as the country of the 1920s.
Yrigoyen's attitude was in direct conflict with the army's professional
autonomy. His interference especially in military appointments caused
great instability within the army.[81]

Initially, a central purpose of the military was to prevent officers from
being drawn into politics and to strengthen the sense of military duty. It
was impossible, however, to isolate the army from the ideological developments in the world and in Argentina.[82] The Argentine military was a
microcosm of the country's ideological developments, and it was permeated by the new political ideas demanding the end of the populist rule.

Two important figures who represented the range of ideas behind the
military plot against Yrigoyen were General Agustín Justo and General
José Felix de Uriburu, who was to play a key role in future political developments. The two organized the military coup of 1930 and demanded that
Yrigoyen resign, but they had quite different reasons for doing so.

General Uriburu, an old friend of President Alvear from his youth and
a senior army officer, was a corporativist nationalist and an admirer of
Prussian military discipline, under which he had trained in Germany.[83]
Well aware of the new antidemocratic trends in Europe, he evolved from
serving as a national deputy for the conservative Partido Demócrata Progresista to becoming a conspirator against Argentina's political democracy.
Under the direct influence of the poet Lugones and the new antiliberal
nationalists, whose works he read in *La Nueva República* and *La Voz
Nacional*, he reaffirmed the nationalist corporativist conceptions that he
had learnt in Europe. Uriburu agreed with Nicolas Accame, the Argentine
military attaché in Rome, who commented that "such a pronounced
nationalist reaction [against democracy] can be felt in Europe that to be
nonaffiliated with it is synonymous with being a traitor to the country to
which one belongs."[84] This statement summed up the anti-democratic
spirit of the age. Nationalism implied opposition to democracy.

General Justo, a "legalist" military man of liberal democratic convictions, was director of the Military College during Yrigoyen's first term.
In contrast to Uriburu, Justo's opposition to Yrigoyen was shaped by the
same principle that guided the "*contubernio*" (as Yrigoyen called his
opponents).[85] A military uprising should restore formal democracy based

on the functioning of political parties under a liberal constitution.[86] General Roca was always the model that Justo earnestly attempted to emulate. Roca's political skill, his pro-civilian inclination, and his love of books were some of the characteristics Justo admired. Justo believed that the function of the army was to avoid involvement in social conflicts.[87] He did not accept military corporativist solutions for society, but his proven hostility to "Yrigoyenism" was rooted in his disagreement with the populist, disordered way of offering expression to the masses.

What most plotters were agreed upon was that the structural weakness of the Radical Party made it impossible to reconcile the agro-export economic order and the party's national populist ideology. As described by the prominent nationalist intellectual Carlos Ibarguren, Jr., Yrigoyen's national populism was a product of the liberal democratic rules of the game. "Yrigoyen was, no doubt, a 'caudillo,' but already an anachronistic one. Some of his actions against foreign powers defined him as an interpreter of national pride; but the man began to manage the Republic as a highly partisan committee."[88] The structural contradiction of Yrigoyenism consisted in maintaining an ideologically moralistic stance and a paternalist political system under the constitutionalism of the liberal state. This structure provided the framework for the emergence of a version of nationalism that, without repudiating the basic organicist concepts of Yrigoyen's nationalism, sought to highlight its basic flaws. Federico Ibarguren has described the spirit of the era, when the Argentine republic was paralyzed by its old institutions, as a time when "the world was passing through a truly deep ideological and social crisis." Yrigoyen "was not capable of modifying the status quo of the liberal regime."[89] The primary criticism of Yrigoyen, in fact, was that he could not fulfill his self-appointed mission. The new nationalist intellectuals envisioned a new era and demanded a thorough cultural change. Recalling those years, Carlos Ibarguren, Jr., wrote, "For us—youngsters in the 1920s—bourgeois individualism, skepticism, and egoism, as well as the irresponsible caprice of the majority, . . . sooner or later led to anarchy and social breakdown."[90] The new conception of integral nationalism was initially intended to contest the Yrigoyenist concept of politics. Mario Amadeo, another prominent nationalist, noted that until 1930 Argentina had lived under a clear framework of liberal ideas inherited from the nineteenth century.[91] Beginning in the 1930s, maintained Amadeo, an alternative ideology developed that opposed such ideas and advocated a different model of political and economic evolution. However, the process of ideological delegitimization of liberal democracy began not with the appearance of the integral nationalism that destabilized the Yrigoyenist Radical government, but rather with the Yrigoyenist national idea itself. Yrigoyenism had its origins in the "intransigent" struggle for democracy, but it also represented an authentic expression of nationalism whose traditionalist roots and populist political practices were at odds with the cultural basis of liberal democracy and reformist socialism. Although part of the moral message of the Unión Cívica was popularized by the Catholic press starting in 1882, the Radical movement was the first direct political reaction against the liberal establishment and its positivistic religion.[92] This feature of the Yrigoyenist tradition was later revived by the nationalist right as the myth of national mobilization.

CHAPTER 3

The Origins of the Argentine National Right

The Poet Leopoldo Lugones: From International
Socialism to Military Nationalism

The military coup led by General José Felix de Uriburu in September
1930 could not have been carried out had not the Yrigoyen regime first
been undermined by a campaign in the conservative newspaper *La Fronda*
and the new nationalist newspaper *La Nueva República*, beginning in
1927. The process that started with the overthrow of the populist regime
of Hipólito Yrigoyen was completed in the 1940s with the removal of
constitutional democracy as such in Argentina and with the consolidation
of a concept of nationalism that reversed the path of Argentine political
and economic development. The contribution of the poet Leopoldo
Lugones to this delegitimization of liberal democracy and to the ideological consolidation of the Argentine national right is of cardinal importance.
Lugones was the first and most important Argentine intellectual to claim
that only a strong, hierarchical state led by the military could confront the
new political challenges in a world of imperialist competition. His advocacy of military nationalism stirred strong feelings in the army high command and in public opinion. His was the first public voice in Argentina
calling not only for military intervention in politics but also for an understanding of nationalism that would both oppose the philosophical principles of liberal nationalism and repudiate the sort of constitutional populism presented by Yrigoyenism. Like other intellectuals of that time in
Argentina and elsewhere, Lugones was concerned about the destructive
consequences of mass society and the inability of liberal democracy to

cope with modern social and political developments. Influenced by the ideas of French nationalism and Italian fascism, and then, during the 1930s, by Falangism and Francoism, Lugones and the intellectuals of *La Nueva República* mirrored in Argentina the conservative revolution in Europe, from which they drew inspiration for their own antidemocratic ideas.

This intellectual context was of great importance for Lugones's ideological evolution from socialism to military nationalism. The kind of intellectual development that Lugones underwent was similar to that of other key nationalists, such as Manuel Gálvez, Juan Carulla, and Ernesto Palacio, and was representative of the intellectual process undergone by other socialists in Europe who came to believe that the nation, rather than the social class, would set the course of history as the agent of a new type of productivist 'conservative revolution', the basis of a new synthesis between nationalism and socialism. That conviction was at the basis of the ideological turn, from left to right, of intellectuals such as Oswald Mosley in England, Marcel Déat and Jacques Doriot (a candidate for the General Secretariat of the French Communist Party) in France, and Hendrik de Man, the president of the Belgian Workers Party.[1]

Lugones's ideological turn from left to right was a direct consequence of his disdain for bourgeois politics and for the materialist and rational foundation of socialist and liberal politics. On June 28–29, 1896, the young Lugones represented the Socialist Center of Córdoba, his native province, at the Congress of Socialist Deputies in Buenos Aires. The debates within the founding assembly of the party revolved around two basic positions. One position, proposed by the socialist leader Juan B. Justo, urged an alliance with other bourgeois parties, which were at least theoretically based on the same rational faith in political and economic evolutionary progress. The other position, led by hard-line revolutionaries like Lugones and José Ingenieros, took a moral revolutionary line against any collaboration with the bourgeois political parties.

As early as 1891 the poet from Córdoba had abandoned his positivist faith in progress and the materialist convictions of his youth.[2] By 1896 the main themes of Lugones's socialism were moral, based on the heroic act of the individual, a stance that made him totally averse both to the give and take of democratic politics and to the materialist characteristics of Marxist socialist thought. The mythical basis of Marxism (as Lugones saw it) was its revolutionary moral way of thinking and not its scientific and economic categories. His deep aversion to the bourgeoisie extended to bourgeois civilization as a whole, including its political and philosophical values. Above all, Lugones could not subdue his individualist thinking to comply with party directives and official ideology. His strong individualism led to his first clashes with the Socialist Party. Upon the arrival of the prince Luis de Saboya in Buenos Aires, Lugones published an article in *El Tiempo* entitled "Saludo a S.A. de Saboya," in which he expressed his elitist concept of politics. "I have respect for princes and for great souls. Napoleon and Washington, Torquemada and Garibaldi." He applauded the ideological communion that linked dedicated, passionate people despite their doctrinal differences, and that distinguished between dignity and disgrace, and between glory and infamy.

In words that best synthesized his aristocratic concept of socialism, Lugones affirmed, "My socialism is no obstacle for me to kiss the hand of an aristocrat. It's the hoof of the bourgeois pig that horrifies me."[3] Like most of elitist revolutionary syndicalists in France and Italy, Lugones felt a stronger attachment to the aristocracy than to the liberal or socialist bourgeoisie.

Not surprisingly, Lugones's political positions as well as his temperamental personality were severely criticized by members of the party. For example, Domingo Rosso, a worker and a member of the Socialist Party, published a letter in *La Vanguardia* on July 27 accusing Lugones of monarchical tendencies. In fact, rather than monarchical tendencies, Lugones displayed a total aversion to reformist socialism, which to him was permeated by bourgeois morality. An examination of *La Montaña*, a biweekly magazine co-edited by Lugones and Ingenieros that first appeared in 1897, is crucial for understanding the ideological discussions that characterized the formative years of Argentine socialism as well as Lugones's political evolution. Lugones and Ingenieros criticized those socialists who sought to play down the revolutionary consequences of socialist thought and action in order to attract petit bourgeois elements to the party. "Socialist and revolutionary," Lugones concluded, "are two inseparable qualities."[4] Lugones promoted this conclusion through his regular column ("Los Politicos del País") in *La Montaña*. He criticized the political class of Argentina from a moral perspective. He attacked socialist politicians who played according to the rules of the game of the parliamentary system, their inclination to satisfy their own hedonist pursuits, and their materialist and bourgeois tendencies.[5] Paradoxically, Lugones's ultimate break with Justo was triggered by Justo's demand for the naturalization of party candidates. Justo wanted to make the Socialist Party, which was supported mostly by new immigrants at the time, into a national party, but that ambition clashed with Lugones's early internationalist, prorevolutionary stance. The Centro Socialista Revolucionario de Barracas al Norte, founded by Lugones, rejected in the name of "intransigent Marxism" what it considered to be the party's nationalist tendencies. Together with other political activists like Enrique Leonardi, Ricardo Cardalda, and Angel Balzanetti, Lugones also founded La Federación Socialista Obrera Colectivista in 1899, thus signaling these activists' rupture with the Socialist Party. The break was only temporary, however; all of them except Lugones returned to the Socialist Party in 1900 in order to preserve socialist unity.

Lugones's internationalist and proletarian convictions were confirmed in his harsh criticism of the military repression of the Vasena metallurgical plant workers' protest in 1919. This protest evolved into a general workers' revolt in Buenos Aires, culminating in the Semana Trágica, which constituted the worst outbreak of social violence in the republic since the turn of the century. The Semana Trágica is particularly memorable because of the role played by "respectable" citizens organized in La Liga Patriótica and the Asociación del Trabajo (both of which represented the interests of the employers). Both collaborated with the military in the persecution of the "maximalists," who were revolutionary workers of foreign origin. Of special importance is that these self-styled "patriots," under the protection of the military, also singled out the Jewish community of Buenos Aires and accused it of Bolshevik sympathies, assaulting individuals and destroying its libraries, religious meeting places, and shops.

After informing the Congress that the government was taking all the necessary steps to restore order and to consider the workers' demands, Ramón Gomez, minister of the interior, added that "the subversive action of elements foreign to the nation, which have tried to take advantage of these conflicts for their own criminal ends, have been repressed with the necessary force."[6]

Paradoxically, this announcement was strongly rejected by Lugones. In a letter to Leon Kibrick, a well-known Jewish leader, Lugones wrote: "The persecution [against the workers] also reflected the [police's] hatred for Russians." (Argentines of the time called all foreigners from Eastern Europe "Russians.") In this instance, Lugones expressed his disappointment both with the aggression against workers of foreign origin and with the reaction of the political system against the supporters of the Soviet Revolution.[7] Lugones was referring to the police action and in particular to the repressive activities of the members of the Comité Nacional de la Juventud, who were the promoters of the anti-worker and anti-Jewish riots in Buenos Aires. Yet at the same time that he was criticizing this type of "official" vandalism, he was also expressing his support for a type of moral internationalism more akin to a Kropotnik-style anarchism than to socialism.

Lugones called for a complete cultural and political revolution. Until 1919, his vitalist and revolutionary spirit was manifested in a loose idea of revolutionary syndicalism. In 1919 Lugones wrote a political plan for Argentina that he titled "Revolutionary Argentine Democracy," a radical revolutionary program that called for the replacement of the bourgeois state by a syndicalist one.[8] The plan, submitted to the Federación Universitaria de Córdoba and to the Sociedad Georgista, proposed that the army and the police be disbanded and that the formal judicial processes be replaced by popular trials. Public services would be directed by the workers themselves. Banks and insurance houses would be directed by the state. The church and other religious communities would be eliminated. The plan unquestionably contained an extreme program of socialization. However, it was much more than an economic plan; Lugones was proposing a proletarian and syndicalist state that would give rise to a new culture. Such a heroic and elitist standard made it possible for Lugones to admire both Mussolini and Lenin. He continually repeated Lenin's statement that "the great historical conflicts are resolved by force."[9]

Lugones was influenced by both the Russian Revolution of 1917 and the Fascist revolution of Mussolini, whom he had admired even before the "March on Rome." Both revolutions were targeted against liberal institutions and the concept of parliamentary democracy. Those were heroic acts in themselves, led by heroic leaders who represented the new spirit of the age, challenging the basic philosophical and esthetic tenets of bourgeois society. Echoing Sorel, Bergson, and Spengler, Lugones presented a concept of the heroic life in opposition to bourgeois notions of rational truth and of materialist individualist interests. Life is intuition and virility, and it "does not triumph by means of reason and truth but by means of force. . . . War is natural to man because he is a combat animal."[10] This emphasis on the heroic rather than the materialist features of bolshevism was at the root of Lugones's preference for the fascist rather than the Soviet-style revolution and for Mussolini rather than Lenin.

To Lugones there was a clear distinction between the Soviet political system and the revolutionary act. The revolutionary act of the Russian Revolution was freedom itself, whereas the maximalist program of the Bolsheviks, based on Marxist materialism, was "gastronomic,"[11] concerned with filling bellies. The bureaucratic development of the Soviet state, particularly the concept of the "dictatorship of the proletariat," was also purely materialist and could not be separated from what Lugones considered its defeatist character. The defeatist peace of the Brest-Litovsk Pact convinced him that Marxism had failed. For Lugones, Marxism was a rationalist and materialist ideology, and Bolshevik developments in domestic and foreign policies proved that Marxism brought no message of change to civilization. That is the reason why the failure of Leninism in Europe was contrasted with its successes in the colonial world of Asia and Africa. Indeed, Lugones believed that Leninism, instead of promoting a truly spiritual revolution enhancing European civilization, had turned Russia into an Asiatic country that threatened Western civilization. Lugones would arrive at the same conclusion drawn by most fascists, namely, that Western civilization would be saved only after the complete defeat of the materialist, rationalist, and utilitarian philosophical concepts of liberal democracy and Marxist socialism.

Lugones's decision to abandon socialist Marxism therefore, was not based on the elimination of the heroic and mythic values of revolution; rather it was in keeping with the kind of revolutionary determination that could be attained only through a quite different concept of nationalist socialism or military nationalism.

The Hour of the Sword: Integral Nationalism and Militarism

During the 1920s, Lugones's utopian conception of the pure syndicalist state evolved toward a new corporativist conception of the state in which the real principles of revolution and freedom were found in the nation and particularly in the army as the agent of national unification. Lugones's visit to France in 1921 at the invitation of the Comité France-Amerique coincided with his growing interest in fascism. Prior to the "March on Rome," he was aware of the political advances of the Fascist Party, and saw Mussolini as the leader who could represent the Latin tradition. That tradition, according to Lugones, was the basis of the idea of a popularly supported authoritarian dictatorship that would replace collectivist democracy and decadent parliamentary democracy. Lugones was already convinced that there was no order and no heroism in "majority democracy."[12] In contrast, the military was a disciplined and technocratic body, which would serve as an example of organization and popular mobilization, representing a new, higher, patriotic morality. In fact "the only healthy and clean" institutions were those of the military,[13] and their technocratic qualities, together with the obligations of mass conscription, transformed the military institutions into a higher model of "democracy, more popular, more genuine and complete," enabling them to provide a basis for progress. These qualities marked the difference between a military that protected the tyranny of formal democracy and a military representing the correct concept of democracy, portrayed by Lugones as a disciplined society.[14]

Technological and scientific advances in the natural and social sciences provided Lugones with a new vision of the fundamental changes underway in the world. As one who opposed philosophical passivity, Lugones called for an educational system that would produce businessmen and industrialists rather than philosophers. However, Lugones's concept of the technocratic spirit was not prompted by greed, as it was among the laissez-faire liberals, but by a fascination with national strength. Lugones was clearly a modernizer in the sense that he recognized the virtues of the dynamism of modern life. An aspect of his modernist passion was evident in the early 1900s, when the oligarchy was still in power (under the presidency of Manuel Quintana).

Following the defeat of Spain by the United States in Cuba, Lugones expressed admiration for the United States. Assuming a different attitude than the one taken by the Spanish "Generation of 1898," Lugones became not "*anti-yanqui*" but anti-Spanish. Because he believed that Argentina must be emancipated from the Spanish heritage, Lugones saw in the United States a model of a dynamic and vital society worthy of emulation.

There is no basic contradiction between Lugones's admiration for the United States and his turn to nationalism and fascism. Lugones admired the technical and economic power of the United States that enabled it to become a world power. The United States with its vitality, he argued, was a continuation of pagan civilization and stoic philosophy.

In the case of Argentina, Lugones assumed that only a fascist corporativist system could raise the country to that level. This utilitarian discipline differed from the Catholic concept of obedience, which leads to mediocrity. A rebel like Lugones could not accept Christian morality, which was conducive to the sort of obedience that destroys the vital strength of the individual and of the people. Lugones defended paganism, especially what he understood to be the concept of pagan freedom. It was a freedom of life, instinctive and full of strength, in opposition to the dogmatic imposition of Christian norms. He spoke in favor of "barbarizing the country" in order to emphasize his sympathy for American practical education, which he believed should be adopted in Argentina.

Lugones saw no contradiction between spiritualism, social utility, and a new rebellious vitality. The fascist aestheticization of politics, the ethical state, the cult of power, the elitist theory represented in the virtuous leader, and the anti-materialist idealism that characterized his thought from his early years would lead him finally to nationalism. His oratorical energy resembled the nationalist poet Gabriele D'Annunzio's patriotic rhetoric as expressed in the "March to Fiume." Even though he had no Fiume, Lugones became the Argentine D'Annunzio, who felt compelled to search for the real Argentine national identity.[15] What seemed clear, however, was that Argentina's national identity could never be expressed if the liberal democratic system remained in power.

Lugones explained his rejection of parliamentarism in terms similar to those expressed by Alfred Naquet, a radical member of the Boulangiste movement in France. Naquet called for the revision of the French constitution in 1881, because he believed that in contrast to the republican and revolutionary French traditions, the parliamentary regime was suited to the English traditions based on limited suffrage and on a homogenous political class.[16] Similarly, Lugones believed that the parliament was a genuine Anglo-Saxon creation. Everything is deliberate in the Anglo-Saxon countries, including the principal instrument of their government. The private and public life of the Latin, on the other hand, is conditioned by an aesthetic norm. The Latin is an artist and the Anglo-Saxon is an entrepreneur. That conviction led Lugones to conclude that for Latin American countries, the concept of command is much more suitable than the concept of dialogue, since habits of command and obedience are in the best of their national traditions. Lugones was convinced that

> As opposed to the ideological democracy . . . of the rights of men, [there stands] the reality of the nation. As opposed to government under consent, there now emerges the government under command. In contrast to rationalism, [there stands] discipline. As opposed to the freedom of formulas, [there stands] the well-being of facts. And that because only those who are healthy and strong can be free.[17]

The conclusion was that only a nondemocratic Argentina could survive the challenges of the modern world. Lugones's argument was also sustained in his evaluation of the structural weakness of Argentina: there were no safeguards of national survival other than those provided by international law.

Facing an imperialist world ruled by virtue of conquest and war, Argentina was militarily weak but economically strong (because of its rich land). "The rural republic that we are . . . now, constitutes in fact a sort of colonial state."[18] In order to defend itself and maintain peace along with territorial and economic sovereignty, Argentina had to develop a concept of strength rather than a concept of political representation. In fact, "the keys to peace are of gold and iron" and can be found neither in "parliaments, nor in electoral urns."[19] Neither democratic socialism nor liberal democracy would resolve the problems of national integration in a society like that of Argentina. The nation could guarantee its survival only by being united on the basis of its own strength. Lugones attempted to explain the effects of world imperialism and the international balance of power in two chapters in his book *La organización de la paz,* published in 1925: "Fuerza y derecho" and "El factor económico." Peace in the world could only be maintained through a balance of power and not through universal moral values: "organizing peace must be the work of economists and military men: the technocrats of strength."[20]

In 1924 in Lima, Peru, where he represented the Argentine government at the commemoration of the centennial of the battle of Ayacucho, Lugones publicly expressed this new approach to the function of the army and military authoritarianism. The speech provoked a good deal of commotion among the Latin American intellectuals because it was one of the first ideological justifications offered for military revolutions on the continent. The speech was preceded by four lectures given in 1923 in the Teatro Coliseo, under the auspices of the nationalist organization La Liga Patriótica of Manuel Carlés, whom Lugones had previously condemned. These lectures constituted the preamble for the speech in Peru, entitled "The Hour of the Sword." This speech and a series of essays criticizing the evils of parliamentarism and developing Lugones's concept of power, which Lugones published in *La Nación* from 1927 to 1930, were compiled in a book entitled *La patria fuerte,* published by El Círculo Militar. It served as study material for the new generation of Argentine army officials. Criticism of the "Hour of the Sword" was offered by liberals and socialists throughout the continent who understood the dangers of justifying the use of force and of the concept of nationalism espoused by a well-known poet. Lugones attempted to reaffirm the idea that Latin American emancipation was to be a product of the sword, of heroic military struggle, rather than a product of political arrangements. "From Suipacha to Caseros, from Ituzaingo to Tuyuti, war created [the nation]."[21] A heroic war emancipated Argentina from Spain, while

> For European nations . . . war is a work of generosity inasmuch as its only aim is to establish civilization. Socialists also regard their wars as beneficial in character, because they seek to achieve social justice. Lenin explicitly believes that "no achievement beneficial to humankind has been obtained except through war"—with the famous corollary "Pacifism is a bourgeois prejudice."[22]

In other words, peace must be established by force. Even the struggle for social justice is carried out by violent means, because war is antibourgeois, it fosters morality, and it is the power of will. The ethical and aesthetic aspects of war and heroism which were so important to Lugones found definitive expression in the army and the state as a live organism created by the heroic act, in radical opposition to the cult of fear:

> Pacifism, collectivism, democracy are synonyms of the same empty space that fate is offering the foreordained leader, i.e., the man who commands. . . . Pacifism is nothing more than the cult of fear (or a decoy of communist conquest, which in turn defines it as a bourgeois prejudice). Glory and dignity are twin children of risk; in the ever more frequent conflict between authority and law . . . the man of the sword must stand with authority. . . . The constitutional system of the nineteenth century is in decline. The army is the last aristocracy . . . the last possibility of hierarchical organization remaining to us in the face of demagogic breakdown. At this historic moment, only military virtue achieves the higher life, namely beauty, hope, and strength.[23]

Lugones's conception of ethics was consistent with his aesthetic idea. "In art as in everything else, discipline is the foundation of honor, of personal responsibility accepted . . . and sacrifice."[24] His attack on decadence, or nihilist aesthetics, was consistent with his appreciation of the classicist concept of ethical and aesthetic unity. Lugones admired the integral world of the Greeks in a manner akin to that of intellectuals like Sorel, William Butler Yeats, and others who were disturbed by the disintegrating character of modern life and its aesthetic expression. The struggle against decadence, which in Argentina was characterized by the loss of authenticity and by cultural dependency, was in fact the real struggle waged by Lugones. The important point here is that Lugones made the first linkage between a spirit of cultural and political renewal in Argentina and the role of the army. His political legacy could be reduced to the theoretical justification of military intervention in politics. However, Lugones's support for the militarization of society should be seen in the framework of his own ideological evolution from socialism to a new organic and radical conception of nationalism. Like other early revolutionaries who saw Marxism as a rationalist theory of class struggle that lacked a mobilizing revolutionary spirit, Lugones did not limit himself to the framework of evolutionary socialism or orthodox Marxism, since both ideologies were basically bourgeois. Nationalism represented the new force of social mobilization, and fascism represented the universal spirit of a new, virile socialism combined with the nationalist spirit.

The question that remains is whether Lugones's political ideology made an impact on the group of right-wing nationalists who were appearing first on the pages of *La Fronda* and then, starting in 1926, on those of *La Nueva República*.

The Argentine Maurrasians of *La Nueva República:* Nationalism and Military Revolution

The ideological mentors of the Uriburu movement were the *Nueva República* intellectual contributors. Influenced by Maurras especially, the intellectuals of *La Nueva República* aspired not only to overthrow Yrigoyen's populist regime but also to substitute in place of democracy a new type of authoritarian corporatist system, representing a vision of nationalism severed from the democratic tradition. Despite their admiration for Lugones and the fact that they were as elitist and antidemocratic as Lugones himself, however, they disapproved of his radical atheism and Nietzschean voluntarism. Nor were his views acceptable to the Catholic proponents of the integral nationalism that became the ideological basis for Uriburu's uprising against Yrigoyen's democratic regime.

Rodolfo Irazusta, Julio Irazusta, and Juan Carulla, three of the most important editors at *La Nueva República*, were the principal followers of Maurras in Argentina.[25] Other figures at the paper, such as Ernesto Palacio, Tomás D. Casares, Alberto Ezcurra Medrano, and César Pico, a lecturer at the Cursos de Cultura Católica, were indifferent and even declared themselves hostile to the work of Maurras. Yet his influence could be seen in their political and cultural ideas, their denials notwithstanding.

When it was launched, *La Nueva República* gave expression to a new rebel intellectual generation: those born between 1890 and 1900.[26] Radical Yrigoyenists such as Mario Jurado, former Radicals such as Julio and Rodolfo Irazusta, and conservatives such as the well-known journalist Alfonso de Laferrère (the brother of Roberto de Laferrère) took part in the initial discussions, but not all of them continued to work with the paper after its ideological line had been formally decided.

Juan Carulla added the paper's subtitle, "organ of Argentine nationalism," to indicate that this paper would promote a new nationalist ideology. *La Nueva República* provided an alternative to the old conservative criticism of Yrigoyen's populist administration, which was associated with the newspaper *La Fronda*, founded by Francisco Uriburu in 1919. *La Fronda* criticized the Yrigoyen administration without proposing an alternative ideological formula. Roberto de Laferrère defined this emerging tendency in 1929 in terms of "conservatives . . . [who] began to call themselves nationalists because they wanted to exploit the name but remained far from its true substance."[27] This was a different era, however, and the new Maurrasian currents were in opposition to political conservatism, liberal democracy, and Marxism. The former conservatives and new integralists intended to develop an alternative ideology. Although it never evolved into a clear doctrine, it became the intellectual pillar of a new idea of nationalism that certainly inspired developments in the 1930s and 1940s. The fundamental goal was to give a renewed interpretation to the old values represented by the constitution of 1853. Although these intellectuals were convinced that a new spirit had to replace the positivist culture of bourgeois society, they did not believe that the fundamental principles of the constitution should be transformed. The Argentine constitution of 1853 represented the ideological values of material progress and liberalism championed by Alberdi. However, for the nationalist intellectuals of *La Nueva República*, that constitution offered a republican spirit far removed from the democratic notion translated into the Sáenz Peña Law of 1912. The road to Yrigoyen's populism was the product of the "one-man-one-vote" system, which, according to the *Nueva República* nationalists, was contrary to the elite-oriented and organic spirit of the constitution. "Yrigoyenism" thus was viewed as a direct result of decadent mass democracy and of materialist positivism, undermining the spirit of aristocracy which should be the basis of any great nation.[28] *La Nueva República* distinguished between a national constitution based on the traditional republican traditions of the Argentine nation and a constitution that served as the spiritual foundation of the liberal route to national modernization as characterized by its bourgeois, materialist, and cosmopolitan spirit. Influences from Maurras were evident in the manner in which *La Nueva República* examined these matters. For Maurras, tradition must always be greater and more important than the individual; it does not mean transmission of everything, that is, it could not include revolutionary, humanitarian, or romantic ideas. A distinction must be drawn between those ideas deriving from lower nature and animal instinct and those produced by intelligence. Tradition meant only the transmission of the beautiful and the true.[29]

A republican system led by an enlightened minority and free of foreign influences, in which the concepts of liberty and democracy were integrated into the framework of the community, would become an alternative to the principles of liberal democracy and the constitutional populism of Yrigoyenism. It is important to stress, however, that *La Nueva República*'s elitist republican project was elaborated by intellectuals who came from different ideological backgrounds. Of special importance are those intellectuals who evolved from left-wing socialism to right-wing nationalism. Some editors, such as Juan Carulla and Ernesto Palacio, shared a socialist past and, like Lugones, replaced the revolutionary content of class struggle with a new nationalist revolution. Others, such as the Irazusta brothers, had been active in the Radical Party in their home province of Santa Fe. All were convinced that *uriburismo* would introduce a new nationalist spirit, unlike the bourgeois materialist and utilitarian spirit of the liberal oligarchy and the abstract and parliamentary socialism of the Argentine Socialist Party.

Juan Carulla's alignment with nationalism was inspired by a split in the French CFT (General Confederation of Labor) in 1910, which was provoked by a group of Marxist intellectuals influenced by Sorel. This act was an awakening for Carulla, and it led him to reevaluate the ideological interaction between nationalism and socialism. Indeed, Carulla identified the ideological synthesis of fascism as a blend between revolutionary syndicalism and nationalism. This intellectual awareness was at the root of its own shift from socialism to fascism.

> It is difficult to establish why the Sorelian Marxists joined arms with the monarchists of Maurras' L'Action Française, but for me, that political episode made me become interested in the dynastic theories of that movement.[30]

Carulla's interest was translated into practical action when, together with Dr. Roberto Acosta, he started a syndicalist newspaper, *La Voz Nacional*, which opposed Marxist syndicalism but supported a different type of socialism: national socialism.[31] He admired syndicalists like Aquiles Lorenzo, Julio Arraga, and Emilio Toire, who were "heterodox" socialists, followers of Sorel who read Maurras and who initiated him into the syndicalist tradition that was struggling against traditional socialism and anarchism in Argentina. Carulla was also well aware of the crisis within socialist thought. Pacifist and reformist socialism observed the political and economic rules of the game of the liberal establishment. The discussion between the trade union supporters of a reformist democratic socialism and the partisans of "direct action" was a process whose impact was widely felt within both European and Argentine socialism.[32]

> Are you seeking to abolish class struggle and war? That is the great error of Marxist anti-militarism. Without war, without hunger, without diseases . . . the surface of this planet would be covered by . . . cancer cells . . . which would destroy the genius, and life would lose any superior sense.[33]

Without a doubt, the patriotism of these days of war—which changed intellectuals like the French historian Gustave Hervé from a socialist and an enemy of militarism to a nationalist and a fervent warrior—made Carulla understand the power within this new nationalism, which was waiting for the old liberal materialist and rationalist order to fall.

La Voz Nacional, founded by Carulla, spread this message in Argentina even before the foundation of *La Nueva República*. Although it had a very small circulation, one of its readers was General José Felix de Uriburu. Through *La Voz Nacional* he began to consolidate the nationalist ideology that motivated him to lead the revolutionary action of September 1930.

If Carulla represented the nationalists who evolved from the left to the right, the Maurrasian face of *La Nueva República* was represented by Rodolfo and Julio Irazusta. Both the Irazusta brothers at this time expressed admiration for the classical thought of Dante and Machiavelli. They were also intellectually influenced by the anti-utopian political and philosophical currents of the beginning of the century, such as those espoused by Maurras.

> Croce in Italy and Santayana in the Anglo-Saxon world restored the notions of political realism. The former asserts that the principles of 1789 are theoretically null, although they are passionate realities. The latter concedes [the necessity] of despotism if it is for the good of the community.[34]

Maurras was the first to "restore the eternal truths of politics."[35] Obviously, under the principle of political pragmatism, any kind of political representation and political value could serve national interests, depending on the particular situation.

The contribution of the Irazusta brothers was primarily their attempt to differentiate the concepts of republicanism and representation from that of democracy. They attempted to connect the heroic and emancipatory spirit embodied in the federalist Argentine tradition with a conservative antidemocratic position. While the concept of republicanism implies the primacy of the public interest over the individual, the concept of democracy means "the primacy of private right as it is seen in Herbert Spencer's *The Individual against the State.*"[36] According to the Irazustas, representation cannot be effective if it is not properly applied among people of the same social or professional condition. In other words, if its content is universal and indiscriminate, based on the abstract principles of natural law and universal suffrage, the principle of representation loses its fundamental nature. In contrast to universal and individualist democracy, the concept of republicanism supported by the Irazustas was related to "[f]ederalism [which] is by nature traditionalist, and because of that, it constitutes a barrier against [a central] political power."[37]

Initially, the nationalists of *La Nueva República* shared a similar Barrèsian and Maurrasian concept of nationalism.[38] This new nationalism would retrieve the voice and presence of those who have gone before and would show respect for the land and what is particular about each region. That would be quite at odds with the cosmopolitanism of the city and with nationalism based solely on self-determination.

The confrontation between the real "country" and the cosmopolitanism of the liberal establishment was one of the central issues in the nationalist cultural struggle. This was a struggle for national identity, for the retrieval of real national values, which at the same time would rescue the real value of the "good" government. Critiques of democracy by Argentine nationalists were not based on the defense of human rights and minority rights against the majority. For the *Nueva República* nationalists, the concept of liberty was divorced from the individualist, materialist, and utilitarian foundations of modern liberalism. Maurras himself said that his devotion to real liberty drove him to repudiate liberalism, just as the respect and the love of the people led him to fight democracy. Liberty could only function under authority.[39]

Even in the United States, maintained Rodolfo Irazusta, "Protestant individualism, which shaped liberal doctrine, is countered rigorously by a puritan fanaticism."[40] In other words, the national ideology of the United States was not an abstract ideology. It was in fact conservative and was suited to the pragmatic needs of its people. In contrast to the United States, Argentina of the 1920s was being destroyed by liberal doctrine despite the material progress produced during the second half of the nineteenth century. Material progress was being preferred to the glory and virtue of republicanism. This position clearly illustrates the influence of Maurras. In his *Enquête sur la monarchie*, Maurras asserted that when a republic tends toward democratic forms, it shifts from a regime that encourages national production for the strengthening of the country to a regime that encourages bourgeois consumerism. On those grounds, the *Nueva República* intellectuals criticized Yrigoyen's democratic populism. It was a vicious democratic consumerism rooted in the concept of liberal democracy. The Irazustas did not accept the ideas of Maurras as ideological dogma, and they were aware that the cultural and historical development of Argentina, which had never had a monarchy, was different from that of France. Nevertheless, they admired the Maurrasian interpretation of the monarchy for not being

> a form of unilateral government, but for being a mixed regime, pragmatic rather than systematic, capable of harmonizing the complex social forces instead of opting for one of them against the others, as was done by the political theories that caused the 1789 revolution....[41]

In an article published in *La Nueva República* on January 31, 1928, Julio Irazusta contended that

> all governments are monarchical, aristocratic, and democratic at the same time.... [However] without the collaboration of the people there is no regime that could sustain itself; without the intelligence of diversely qualified human capabilities there is no counsel for the executive power; without a personal agent that can decide quickly, there is no executive will and therefore there is no government.[42]

The task of government must be based on intelligence and popular consent. The anarchic experience of Yrigoyenism and the impotence of liberal democracy proved that the only authentic system that could combine central command with popular consent was an authoritarian system with a clear social agenda. An authoritarian system was the only way to achieve political order in Argentina and to resolve the central problem that most concerned the Irazustas—the economic dependence of the state.[43] During the 1930s, the Irazustas were already emphasizing what they considered to be the central question of nationalism, namely, who represented sovereignty in Argentina. The question was not what kind of political system Argentina had, but which hidden forces of foreign capital were controlling the state. That question was directly connected to the philosophical tensions between liberalism and nationalism. The attack on the philosophical foundations of liberalism and its political application in Argentina was a constant theme of the Irazustas in *La Nueva República*:

> A direct result of freedom of thought is the decadence of all those disciplines directly related to that function of the spirit. The laissez faire as well as the other liberties of liberalism frees the individual from impositions [*trabas*] ... in order to enslave him under the dominion of great monopolies.... At the international level, laissez-faire capitalism will deprive countries lacking high amounts of capital of their ability to

industrialize, and in most cases this leads to indebtedness for foreign capital.[44]

According to Rodolfo Irazusta, this last option was the worst one for Argentina, given the country's process of modernization based on free immigration and free entry of capital. In the early 1920s, one could already discern in the Irazustas the seeds of the anti-imperialism that would fully develop in the 1930s.

Until 1929, however, *La Nueva República* limited its critique to the concept of democracy in general and of constitutional populism in particular. The attack on Yrigoyen became much harsher and evolved from mere editorials to a full-fledged conspiracy against the regime starting in March 1929, when the newspaper kept in close contact with General Uriburu. In early March 1928, Rodolfo Irazusta wrote a fiery article filled with a spirit of political conspiracy against what was considered a caudillo-led democracy. "Nobody wants to risk his position or prestige by confronting them over the authoritarianism of the democratic caudillo. That is the indignity of these times."[45] However, if populist *caudillismo* was an indignity of present times, the return to formal democracy was the worst alternative. What Argentina needed was its own counterrevolution. Ernesto Palacio was the *Nueva República* writer who best represented the counterrevolutionary sentiment in Europe, arguing that Argentina had to rethink the connection between the idea of democracy and nationalism. Using the terminology of the conservative revolutionaries, Palacio held that there was a clear difference between nationalism and democracy.

Formal democracy was the direct result of a corrupted framework of values:

> We have more than half a century of intellectual disorientation behind us. The romanticist sophisms and the French Revolution that disturbed all the thinking activity of several Argentine generations and were an obstacle to our political growth are still the dominant ideology.[46]

The idea of liberal modernization based on the philosophical precepts of the French Revolution was an obstacle to the political modernization of Argentina. Within every democrat lives an adherent of the abstract principles of Rousseau's social contract, which, by direct connection, are a "constant danger to the political reality of the constituted nation." That is why, concluded Palacio, political men can be divided into two groups, those who recognize the primacy of society and consider it "a natural phenomenon, and those who consider it a more or less artificial creation of individuals. The former could be nationalists, but never the latter."[47]

Like other Argentine nationalists, Palacio advocated combining the integral nationalist revolution with a modern concept of order and discipline; the result was military nationalism. Like Lugones and other intellectuals of that generation, Palacio shifted from universal socialism to national-socialism, emphasizing values such as vitality, heroism, and nationalism rather than materialism or welfarism. A new, vitalist sense of living dangerously, of the struggle of will, could attain what pacifist and scientific socialism could not.

> We are not . . . pacifists; we believe that man is a bellicose animal, that war is inextricable. . . . We believe heroic courage is a virtue, that without blood and fire it is impossible to reach the great ideals of life. . . . Violence is right. . . . A people without warrior virtues is a people condemned to disappear. Here is why it is a crime . . . the diffusion of pacifist and anti-militarist doctrines that replaced socialism, and that tend to conform to a generation of the weak, hysterical and cowardly. . . . In spite of the boring prophecies of the theoreticians of pacifism which characterized the last century, it is of no doubt that a new era of violence has been opened for the world.[48]

Palacio was certainly not preparing for war; war was not on the agenda of Argentine nationalism. Although he praised violence insofar as it developed moral qualities, he in fact was echoing the Maurrasian idea that the army must be at the service of a just idea, the principle of order itself.[49] *Uriburismo* was expected to be this combination of a hierarchical national organization with a vitalist and heroic spirit that would guide the country on the long path of modernity and national liberation.

In his memoirs Carlos Ibarguren recalls statements that General Uriburu made to him before September 1930: "My plan is to carry out a true revolution that would change many aspects of our institutional regime. . . . I will not carry out a mutiny on behalf of politicians in order to shift those who govern."[50] Ibarguren was convinced that the ideological endeavors of the *Nueva República* intellectuals had produced momentous results, at least with respect to the leader of the revolution. Echoing the political message promoted by *La Nueva República*, Uriburu was convinced that only a revolution from above could replace the liberal democratic system with a functional democratic system, or in other words, a corporativist system. Not all sectors of the military agreed with Uriburu's corporativist plans. In fact, as General José Sarobe recalls, most of the regular officers supported General Agustín Justo's opposition to the nationalist concept of a political revolution with constitutional changes that would nullify the participation of political parties. Even the military leaders of the revolution understood that without a political compromise with the political class, there would be no revolution. Ernesto Palacio revealed his disenchantment and attacked General Justo's anti-ideological and professional conception of the army. Taking it for granted that the people may rebel against a bad government, Palacio's message to the army was that "the disciplinary obligation is not an absolute dogma; it is defined by fulfilling its essential goal, which is the defense of *la patria*. . . . It ends . . . when the government itself becomes a faction against the homeland."[51]

The nationalist interpretation of the concept of homeland entailed a thorough organization of the state that was by no means consistent with the factionalism of political parties. However, the dominant trend in the army at the time was that of Justo, which was supported by politicians of the conservative sectors, the Independent Socialist Party, and the antipersonalist sectors of the Radical Party. The great difference between them and *La Nueva República* was that the army group simply intended to oust Yrigoyen in a coup, whereas the *Nueva República* group aspired to a corporativist revolution. The conservative politician Matías Sánchez Sorondo convinced General Uriburu to accept the program proposed by Generals Sarobe and Justo. The plan that Justo chose was to carry out the revolution against the government but not against its institutions.[52] The political class was not ready to give up easily, and a coalition of parties called the Federación Nacional Democrática was formed in order to press for a return to constitutionalism, without the rebellious Radical Party led by Yrigoyen. The conservatives of Buenos Aires, the Independent Socialists, the antipersonalist Radicals from Entre Rios, Catamarca, Corrientes, and Santa Fe, the liberals and autonomists of Tucumán, the Provincial Union of Salta, the Democrat Party of Córdoba, and the Liberal Party of San Luis all demanded that national elections be held soon.

Although the *Nueva República* circle accepted some of the political measures taken by the Uriburu regime, especially those directed to repress the workers, it rejected the general thrust of the regime. For example, when martial law was reestablished, and the anarchist- and communist-led unions were suppressed and their leaders arrested or deported as foreigners, the government received the approval of the nationalists. However, their influence was drastically reduced, since what they sought was not only to turn out the Radical Party masses but also to drive out the liberal order.

The intentions of the conservatives were different: they wanted to keep the Yrigoyenistas out of power and restore their own privileges by restoring a "formal" constitutional democracy, which would be controlled by fraudulent elections. The conservatives conceived neither a fascist corporativist government nor a liberal democracy as a political option. The few nationalist civilians who collaborated directly with Uriburu, such as Leopoldo Lugones, Juan P. Ramos, Carlos Ibarguren, Juan Carulla, and Ernesto Palacio, soon lost influence. The great question that remained to be resolved for the conservative politicians in the Uriburu's cabinet was how to return to a state of "normalcy" without falling into a situation that could bring the Radicals back to power. Uriburu was pushed toward elections by the conservative front, in the hope that popular support for the government would confirm the success of the revolution and bring a definitive end to the "Yrigoyenist" popular hegemony. On April 5, 1931, the government called for provincial elections that would result in the election of new governors and legislators from the provinces. However, the return to constitutionality turned out to be a fiasco for the liberal conservative coalition, since it proved that the Yrigoyenist party was still as popular as ever. Contrary to all predictions, the vote in the province of Buenos Aires went against Uriburu.[53] At that point, Uriburu decided to postpone the elections in the other provinces and to reinstate a curfew. The military called for the formation of a new front of democratic parties led by General Agustín Justo, who represented the army opposition to Uriburu. The message was very clear. The only illegitimate political current was the Yrigoyenist one, which enjoyed popular support. In contrast to Yrigoyenist populism, the Radical Party liberal establishment, led by Marcelo T. de Alvear, accepted the new rules of the game and supported the same principles as the liberal bloc known as "la Concordancia."[54]

The new political system after Justo's takeover consisted of the government of the Concordancia, which united the Conservative Party and the Independent Socialist Party, and a loyal opposition composed of the Progressive Democratic Party together with the Socialist Party, who presented a slate of Lisandro de la Torre and Nicolas Repetto. With Justo's victory the Conservatives and the Concordancia had won. The new cabinet imposed upon Uriburu after the revolution of September 1930 clearly reflected the fact that the nationalists did not control the political scene. It represented, as we shall see later, a new coalition of interests between the oligarchic political class and British economic interests. The old economic and political interests of foreign and national capital thus reasserted themselves in a more developed form and demonstrated that the Uriburu regime was not a nationalist revolution.

Yet despite the frustration of nationalists over developments that eroded the spirit of *uriburismo*, the original message of the "would-be corporatist revolution" did not disappear. It lived on in a new type of political expression reflected in and propagated by the newly formed paramilitary leagues.

The Legacy of *Uriburismo,* La Liga Republicana, and the Legión Cívica

The legacy of *uriburismo* was expressed in a wide variety of paramilitary leagues that shaped Argentina's public sphere in the 1930s. The Legion Civica, Legion de Mayo, Liga Republicana, Acción Nacionalista Argentina, and ADUNA (Afirmación de una Nueva Argentina) were semi-military leagues whose style was unique in Argentine politics up to that time. More important than the new political style, however, was the appearance of a political discourse that began to adopt "authentic" Argentine sources expressing the particularities of Argentina's historical development and a growing aspiration to become a movement with popular appeal. In other words, these leagues with their military style also reflected a new political discourse that forecast a synthesis between corporatist integralist ideology and populism.

It must be stressed, however, that not all the nationalist leagues that conspired against Yrigoyen embraced this integralist ideology. For example, the Legión de Mayo represented an anti-Yrigoyenist position that sought a return to the liberal constitution. Founded in August 1930 in honor of the May revolution, the Legión de Mayo endorsed the ideals of the liberal aristocratic order. This goal was out of step with the revolutionary spirit of the integralists of *La Nueva República* and the Liga Republicana, and it clashed with the vigorous martial style of the Legión Cívica, founded by Uriburu.

Uriburu formed the Legión Cívica, which was directly attached to the government, once he realized that his corporativist plans had no future and that the spirit of the military revolution had disappeared. Its purpose was to spread the ideology of the revolution. Uriburu's final political message, through the creation of the Legión Cívica, was that a new sense of heroic nationalism in military organization, order, and hierarchy would be the legacy of the revolution, even though it had lost political power.

Even before the Uriburu military revolution, however, the Liga Republicana, "Les Camelots du Roi" of *La Nueva República*, had begun to display this new spirit of revolutionary energy on the streets of Buenos Aires. The Liga Republicana, founded by Roberto de Laferrère and Rodolfo Irazusta in 1929, set itself the task of spiritually preparing public opinion for the necessity of the revolution. Roberto de LaFerrère, Carlos and

Federico Ibarguren, Rodolfo Irazusta, Ernesto Palacio, Faustino de Lezica, and other Liga sympathizers engaged in a direct confrontation in the streets with the Radical Party militias called the Klan Radical.[55] The style of the Liga Republicana, with its revolutionary slogans, provoked a fierce commotion not only at the Socialist and Radical Party headquarters but also at the headquarters of the conservative parties, which saw in the Liga Republicana a new threat to political stability. The Liga Republicana was in fact the first nationalist movement to use a revolutionary terminology, and that fact was more significant than its call for a coup against the constitutional government of Yrigoyen.

The Liga Republicana's goal was, first of all, "to promote a revolution of spirit" and to develop political action that under certain circumstances could become "increasingly violent."[56] Its central conviction was that there was an "urgent need to oppose the current government and its system."[57] Imbued with a new type of ideological purity, the Liga Republicana, unlike the Legión Cívica created by the provisional government after the military coup, did not believe in compromising ideologically and politically with the current political system. The Legión Cívica was less dogmatic than the Liga Republicana, but it, too, represented the new vitalist and revolutionary feeling. The Legión Cívica took the form of a paramilitary unit with a solid organization modeled on the army, and it achieved a degree of success in terms of popular acceptance. As defined by Uriburu himself, "the Legión Cívica is an apolitical force" that would help carry out the program of the revolution.[58]

The Legión Cívica was organized under a military structure into brigades and divisions, which paraded in columns of eight, usually headed by Colonel Lautaro Montenegro. As noted by Montenegro himself, war, "more than a function of armies was a function of the peoples, and no component of the nation . . . could [allow itself] to abstain from it."[59] The Legión was intended to represent a people in arms. The organization of the Legión reached into the working-class neighborhoods, where "legionaries" were organized into groups of twenty, headed by a leader. The Legión mobilized women and children, who also received military training.[60] As documented by the police investigation, Juan Carulla and the provisional president José Felix de Uriburu himself supervised the military training of children in the gardens of the Hotel de Immigrantes.[61]

The women's organizations (Agrupación Femenina de la Legión Cívica), which promoted social welfare on behalf of the unemployed working class, illustrated the new nationalism's growing concern over the social effects of the economic crisis. In August 1932, the Legión Cívica, using a fascist model, organized its own syndicalist movement, the FONA (Federación Obrera Nacionalista). This was an attempt to occupy an ideological and social space based on a concept of solidarity that symbolized the spirit of organic nationalism. In this spirit, free food and housing were distributed to unemployed workers in various districts of the capital city.

Besides its welfare work, the Legión Cívica engaged in other significant political activities which were reported by the police as follows: "diverse commissions of the organization tour the city in order to push organization members to . . . supervise worker centers and residences of the main Radical [Party] leaders."[62] The police, who in several cases collaborated with the government-supported militia, detected the putschist characteristics of the Legión Cívica, which could be quickly transformed from a citizen group supporting the provisional government into a revolutionary force. In consequence, despite the Legión's direct connection to Uriburu, the federal police services kept its principal leaders, Juan Carulla and Juan B. Molina, under continual surveillance.

Since the legitimacy of the liberal constitution was questioned by the nationalists, the Legión's cooperation with the security forces to maintain order in the cities could certainly be seen as maintaining a "revolutionary order" rather than the existing legal order. Its motto "With the revolution or against the homeland"[63] reflected the totalitarian ambitions of its members and echoed the frustrated ambitions of General Uriburu. The new order promoted by the provisional government could be achieved "by legal paths or . . . by a march on Buenos Aires like the one on Rome."[64] General Uriburu believed that his proposed constitutional reforms could be achieved if "70,000 legionaries would parade in front of the Congress in order to teach it what it has to be done," should Congress refuse to legislate in favor of a constitutional change.[65] This style of politics was manifested in street confrontations and vandalism by the legionaries. These acts were reported by the national press, and it was clear that a spirit of violence was overtaking Buenos Aires and the provinces. In the province of Cordoba, the legionaries collaborated with the local police to close the newspapers *El Dia* and *Córdoba* for criticizing vandalism by legionaries.[66]

The failure and immediate resignation of Uriburu initially seemed to leave the Legión Cívica without its direct protector. That was not the case, however. Uriburu's successor, Agustín Justo, in order to calm down nationalist resistance to the return to constitutionalism, was tolerant toward the Legión Cívica and other nationalist activities. In an effort to eliminate antigovernment operations, the members of the Legión Cívica were persuaded that the most important task was the struggle against leftist communism, which loomed behind the imminent social revolution.

What looked like the Legión's appeasement of the liberal state was suspect in the eyes of the other nationalist groups, who were convinced that the Legión Cívica was accommodating itself to the liberal conservative order. It was evident to these nationalists that "after the September revolution . . . another revolution is unavoidable"[67] and that conviction demanded a more decisive revolutionary action in which all the political and economic institutions of the liberal establishment would be nullified. This was apparently why Juan Carulla left the Legión. In 1932 he founded the Agrupación Liga Republicana de la Legión Cívica, which changed its name to Logia Teniente General Uriburu. In March 1933, in a series of conferences on organizing civil militias given in Buenos Aires at the Lieutenant José Felix de Uriburu local meeting sites, Carulla spoke of the new situation as reminiscent of "the Italian situation before the fascist revolutionary movement" took power. Carulla emphasized "the way in which the march on Rome was organized" and reminded the audience that in a situation in which the professional politicians had been returned to power, the youthful energy of "youth organizations like those in the Soviet Union and Nazi Germany"[68] was the only model that could create the spiritual framework for a political upheaval.

The similarities of ideology and style that Carulla found in the radical movements of left and right expressed the revolutionary synthesis of modern times. New nationalist groups, however, had to grapple with certain issues that were absent during Uriburu's leadership. With Uriburu, a military leader representing the army was in charge. Since then, a vacuum in power and ideology had developed. Solving the dilemma of how to transform the right-wing nationalism into a mass movement became the most important task. In a letter to Colonel Natalio Mascarello in June 1941, when the latter assumed the direction of the Legión, Juan Bautista Molina listed some of the mistakes made by the military revolution of 1930, which made it impossible to reach the masses who were not ready to assume the principles of the revolution. Molina declared that his fundamental concern "is to have the popular masses identify more with the purposes of nationalism." In fact, "without the support of the masses no revolution succeeds and endures." This principle was clear by the end of the 1930s, when "the ideals of nationalism had been invigorated [through] . . . a true Argentinean ideology relying upon a strong popular sentiment."[69] This was not the case at the beginning of the decade, although the Legión Cívica had succeeded in attracting many recruits by mid-1931. There were between 10,000 and 30,000 brigade members through the capital, eleven provinces, and one territory, but that did not constitute a mass movement.

As a matter of fact, no paramilitary league would succeed in attracting mass followers until the appearance in the mid-1930s of the plebeian Alianza Nacionalista. However, by the mid-1930s the new political discourse shaped by the paramilitary leagues had set the stage for the development of an authentic Argentinean fascism that differed from conservative anti-Yrigoyenist movements like the Legión de Mayo on the one hand, and movements mimicking fascist characteristics, like the Partido Nacional Fascista, on the other. Although "fake" fascists like Nimio de Anquin, the leader of the Partido Fascista Argentino, blamed the Yrigoyenist Jacobin tradition of popular mobilization because of its alleged anarchical roots and claimed that "it was our bad fortune to be born under the principles of 1789,"[70] the emerging authentic fascism would aspire to be "national" and would blend the myth of Yrigoyen's national populism with its Maurrasian roots. Finally, there was a clear distinction between the style and ideology of both the Liga Republicana and the Legión Cívica on the one side, and the Liga Patriótica of Manuel Carlés, which was in charge of the great repression of workers in 1919, on the other. The Liga Patriótica's nonpartisan attacks on the left were accepted by the liberal establishment, but those same liberals viewed the Legión Cívica's militarization of society as usurping their own authority and as leaning toward fascism.[71]

In short, the leagues of the 1930s created a novel political style and set the stage for a political discourse that combined at first sight contradictory messages. The seeds of a new corporativist political order blending authoritarian politics with themes of social justice were planted under the flag of *uriburismo*. Hence, *uriburismo* was the first step toward the radical integralist-populist program implemented in 1943 by the next military government.

CHAPTER 4

The Década Infame

The Conservative Restoration
and The Rise of Integral Nationalism

The Historical Setting

One of the most perplexing periods of Argentine history began during the presidency of Agustín Justo. The "conservative restoration" in Argentina opened a period whose characteristics were "fraud and privilege."[1] It was also the period when Argentine economic dependency on Great Britain reached its peak. An ideological synthesis took shape between two types of nationalism which at first sight represented contrasting political views: integralist nationalism and populist nationalism, which emerged from the "intransigent" wing of the Radical Party. The points of ideological coincidence between the right and left began around the issues of historical revisionism and the head-on critique of the approach to nation-building taken by the Argentine liberal elites. In both strains of nationalism, cultural and economic emancipation meant decisively rejecting not only the ideas of political modernity of the Argentine elites but also liberal democratic values and procedures themselves. The differences between the two forms of nationalism stemmed partly from the fascist influence on the integralist right. In contrast, the populist left was rooted in the authentic traditions of the Yrigoyenist party and of Latin American populism. The main concern here, however, is to analyze the ideological connections between the two strains, draw out their political implications, and thereby demonstrate how these two strains of nationalism became the two faces of the conservative revolution against the old conservative political establishment.

It must be borne in mind that Argentine conservatives aspired to restore their oligarchic rule under a democratic constitutional framework. This meant that they wanted a liberal democratic order, but one without the political participation of the only movement that challenged its political rule, the Yrigoyenist wing of the Radical Party, which chose to return to its pre-1912 policy of not participating in fraudulent elections. Its electoral abstention in the early 1930s was both enforced and self-imposed. The party's participation in attempted military uprisings in the early 1930s gave Justo the justification for banning it. Once the party returned to an electoral strategy in 1935, it did well in Entre Rios and Córdoba but was defeated in the province of Buenos Aires by ballot rigging. For the conservatives, it made more sense to thwart the Radical Party through fraudulent elections than to abolish the liberal constitution and install a fascist nationalist state. Their main attempt was thus to set in place a quasi-democratic regime consisting of the government and a loyal opposition, leaving no space for the rebellious Radical party. Overshadowing political fraud during the decade was economic dependency on Great Britain. The 1930s were defined as the "Década Infame" by the nationalist intellectual José Luis Torres because the country was driven into a position of colonial dependency upon Great Britain, a condition that represented a moral decadence more than a real economic problem. In fact, the 1930s were the decade when, despite economic dependency and some minor social dislocations, the traditional economic structures of the country were permanently altered and modernized.

The dependency of the country largely favored the traditional upper class, which controlled the dynamic agrarian export sector represented in the government. However, the economic dislocations wrought by the world economic crisis of 1929 in both the international and domestic economies had a great impact on this primary export sector, resulting in a nonintegrated semi-industrial economy.

Not all representatives of the agricultural export interests opposed industrialization. They rather saw it as a necessary evil. The choice was clear: either Argentina would produce manufactured goods through its domestic industrial efforts or it would be forced to do without. The government chose the import-substitution industrializing option, hoping not only to fill the vacuum of consumer goods but also to expand the internal demand for agricultural products.

In essence, Finance Minister Federico Pinedo's economic plan signified a functional coalition of the cattle-agrarian interests represented in the government with the interests of a new and growing industrialist class, which, rather than attempting to challenge the agrarian interests, had long expressed admiration for the oligarchy's social status and wished to emulate it.[2] This mutual agreement notwithstanding, the conservative representatives of the primary export sector understood that a new era was beginning and that it would have cultural and ideological consequences. They were forced to concede that the ideal of economic self-sufficiency was in the ascendance everywhere. However, what they feared was not so much the drive toward industrialization as the ideological concomitant to that process. In other words, the point was to industrialize while avoiding social and political mobilization that went along with industrial modernization.

By 1934 Argentina had embarked on a process of fairly rapid import-substitution industrialization, favored by the fact that the international prices for Argentine traditional products rose significantly. Between 1935 and 1937 alone, Argentine industrial growth nearly equaled the industrial advance made between 1914 and 1935.[3] Traditional Argentine manufacturing had consisted largely of the processing of primary products (foodstuffs, leather goods, forest products) as well as some clothing manufacturing.

During the 1930s, the emphasis fell on the secondary sector. Textiles, metal and machine production, and chemical and rubber products became the new driving forces in Argentine industrial activity. This process was increasingly characterized by large-scale, intensive production, and the growth of semi-monopolistic organizations in several important industries, the most dynamic of which was textiles.[4] This economic modernization relied on cheap, unskilled labor, a process that eventually created an urban industrial working class unlike that of any previous period in Argentine history. This socioeconomic process was to have a critical impact during the 1940s, when the Peronist movement would give the new masses political expression. Even before Peronism, however, the first seeds of a new social approach could be noted among nationalist intellectuals and their political groups. The social question and a new idea of economic nationalism became the new banners of Argentine nationalism, especially after a series of economic pacts signed between Argentina and Great Britain angered Argentine public opinion.

The Roca-Runciman Pact of May 1933 came to be seen as the symbol of Argentina's surrender to British interests. According to nationalists of both right and left, the pact clearly demonstrated the common interests between the Argentine liberal oligarchy and foreign interests. The pact made provision for a stable but sharply reduced level of Argentine beef exports to Britain (some 65 percent of the 1929 levels), a grain export quota, and a token loan to ease Argentine debts. The pact further promised to reserve 85 percent of the reduced beef trade for British meat-packing enterprises in

Argentina. The remaining 15 percent of the Anglo-Argentine beef trade was allotted to government-subsidized, nonprofit Argentine companies, and had to be carried and marketed "through normal channels" (i.e., British ships and British distributors). This economic arrangement was further augmented by the duty-free guarantees given by Argentina for British goods. More importantly, British capital investments, in both public and private enterprise, were promised particularly privileged treatment. This provision clearly aided British railway and urban transport systems in Argentina.[5] The Roca-Runciman Pact was obviously beneficial to the British, inasmuch as it left almost all bilateral trade between the two countries in the hands of the British exporters. The creation of the Argentine Central Bank contributed to this trend and for that reason was denounced by the nationalist intellectual Carlos Ibarguren, who charged that it made Argentine national sovereignty subservient to foreign interests.[6] In fact, the Argentine Central Bank (included in the proposed legislative package on money and banking), which the administration urged the Senate to approve in 1935, was not controlled by the state and was operated by a directory of fourteen members, eleven of whom were foreigners.

In 1935, under the leadership of Raul Prebisch, the Central Bank was empowered to act as a government financial agent and stimulate demand.[7] Because Finance Minister Pinedo's plans supported economic recovery through foreign investments, the Central Bank and the other national institutions created to implement those policies promoted foreign and oligarchic interests alike. The Mobilizing Institute of Bank Investments was created by Law No. 12,157, primarily to cover poor bank investments. The government was evidently concerned to aid the financial oligarchy and thereby diverted resources that might have profitably been used to serve the broader common good. At the same time, the Production Regulatory Boards for meat, wine, cereal, milk, cotton, and other products served two purposes: they centralized the direction and control of the basic industries of the country in Buenos Aires, and they helped consolidate the existing production and distribution monopolies.[8] Municipal autonomies were abolished, prompting authorities in provinces like Mendoza and San Juan to tax wine, and in provinces like Tucumán and Salta to tax sugar, thus placing constraints on production in these provinces. Great trusts, represented by Bunge and Born, a subsidiary of the Antwerp Trading Company, as well as other major trusts like Dreyfus, La Plata Cereal, and L. E. Ridder, controlled more than the 80 percent of wheat and linen exports. Foreign enterprises controlled 58 percent of the food industry, and the electric energy services were controlled by the Electric Bond and Share Company in the interior of the country and by SOFINA and Motor Colombus, two important international holding companies, in Buenos Aires, the capital. From the standpoint of the nationalist intellectuals, however, the most sensitive economic issue was British control over the railway system, because it served Great Britain's import needs and did not help integrate different regions of the country.

The passage of the "Coordination of Transportation" bill created the Corporation for Transport of the city of Buenos Aires in 1936. The corporation was a monopolistic entity with state support that accorded special priorities to the British urban transport enterprises, to the detriment of the national bus companies. It must be borne in mind that British city railway companies were in gradual decline compared to bus services, which were supported by automotive production spurred by North American interests.

Even though these economic arrangements benefited British interests, the assessment of the British of their contribution to Argentine socio-economic modernization was quite correct. In the opinion of the *Buenos Aires Herald*, "it is no exaggeration to say that British capital has been largely responsible for the phenomenal rise of Argentina. Millions of British pounds have been invested in this country. . . . Argentine railways have been built at the cost of millions of pounds of British money."[9] It is not surprising that the pact was supported by the cattle-raising Argentine exporters. Argentina, in fact, was to keep cattle exports at 1932 levels.[10] According to the Argentine government, this provided the only possible road for development after the Ottawa conference in 1932, when Great Britain and its dominions made a pact by which Great Britain granted preferential treatment to products from the empire. That agreement produced great uneasiness in the cattle-raising circles of the Argentine Rural Society and ultimately drove them to support the Roca-Runciman Pact.

As I have noted, the critique presented by the nationalists in the 1930s, although elaborated in economic terms, was based on social, political, and moral assumptions. In economic terms, the growing dependency notwithstanding, a process of industrialization began during the Justo administration that led to significant social and geographic mobility, evidenced not only by immigration but also by migration from rural to urban areas and particularly to greater Buenos Aires. In social terms, the price of modernization resulted in the appearance of shantytowns which sprang up to disfigure the outskirts of Buenos Aires. The rural areas began to suffer at the end of the easy phase of the agro-export stage of development. Consequently, the rural areas faced the serious threat of population loss.[11] Increased alienation associated with the moral and social consequences of economic development was mingled with a growing search for Argentine national identity at this particular stage of national development. In other words, this period was characterized by loss of identity, the sense of disintegration due to the gap between the bourgeoisie of Buenos Aires and the wealthy landlords of the "Littoral" areas, and the poverty that prevailed in the provinces.[12]

Describing the government in the provinces, José Luis Torres observed that "those who controlled the wealth also controlled the government. And the province was governed, at any level of the party, by the merchants and for the merchants."[13] Torres defined the practical, corrupt political situation that characterized not only the provinces but the whole country. The politicians were lawyers or headed the directories for foreign companies: Federico Pinedo himself was both the finance minister (1933–1935) and a lawyer for the SOFINA company; Miguel J. Culaciati was interior minister (1940–1943) and a lawyer of the Bunge and Born Corporation; Guillermo Leguizamon was a member of the Argentine delegation that drew up the Roca-Runciman Pact and was closely connected to the Buenos Aires South Dock Company and to other large companies. The Justo government's minister of public works, Octavio Pico, headed two oil refineries (the Argentine Company of Comodoro Rivadavia and the Andinian Petrolífera). Pico and Horacio Beccar Varela, the agricultural minister, held shares in the "El Condor" refinery. Ernesto Bosch, the new minister of foreign affairs, was the president of a subsidiary of the Anglo-Persian Petroleum Company. The new interior minister, Matías Sánchez Sorondo, was the legal counsel for Standard Oil, which was the most prestigious function for any liberal technocrat during Argentina's era of easy economic expansion. In this atmosphere, political scandals were common, sometimes accompanied by political violence. Economic and political corruption, for example, plainly lay behind the assassination in 1935 of the Progressive Democratic Party senator Enzo Bordabehere.

This was the setting that gave rise to the question of anti-imperialism. The issues of political morality, the drive for production, and social justice provided the impetus for the development of the nationalist consciousness. Although these issues had been related to Argentina's agrarian-oriented political economy and could be raised without considering the question of Argentina's political identity, in fact economic dependency became a central issue within a broader cultural and ideological revolt. Paradoxically, despite political fraud and the repression of the Communists and other leftist parties, the 1930s were characterized by a significant degree of pluralism and, in general, of political and ideological contestation. Analysts like Carlos Waisman have seen the new period as characterized by relative economic stability and at the same time by economic dependency. Accordingly, the correlation between dependency, economic development, and political development was positive, since it allowed Argentina to diversify its economy and generate the surplus that made possible the growth of liberal institutions.[14] If we accept this interpretation, then the problem of economic dependency does not itself constitute a factor leading to underdevelopment. Indeed, countries under economic dependency may grow and develop as industrial democracies. However, economic and political dependency stirs moral disaffection, especially for nationalists whether from the left or the right. Marxists attack economic dependency from a class struggle perspective, and nationalists from right and left stress the cultural and moral factor of dependency. The response to dependency for nationalists is rather a cultural resistance, in which the values of tradition are pitted against the liberal values that camouflage economic imperialism. The crucial issue thus came to be regarded as the cultural identity of Argentina. The times called not for political and economic reform but for a new path to economic emancipation based on the retrieval of a set of values stemming from the mythical *caudillista* struggle against Argentina's modernizing elites.

The Revision of Argentine History:
The Rebellious Myth against Liberal Modernization

In the 1930s, a nationalistic critique of culture, elaborated by writers such as Leopoldo Lugones (*La guerra gaucha*), Manuel Gálvez (*El diario de Gabriel Quiroga*), and Ricardo Rojas (*El país de la selva* and *Las provincias*), was transformed into political myths. The myth of its rebellious past, dominated by the "gauchos" and caudillo politics, represented authenticity, the landscape, the heroic life, the national myth over against the modernist utopia of the liberal elites. Historical revisionism would enable a new economic and populist notion of democracy to present a cultural and political alternative to the liberal model of democracy. As noted by Diana Quattrocchi, if the historian's discipline can be defined as the established vision of an institutionalized social memory, a counterhistory or historical revisionism is the starting point for a contrary social memory.[15] Furthermore, if we affirm that history is written by the victorious side, then the counterhistory is written by the losers—in the present case by those who have been defeated in the process whereby the elites have organized the nation. In this sense, the counterhistory, or historical revisionism, offers a further clue to political revolution against the hegemonic worldview of the victorious liberals.

We may ask whether historical revisionism is a particularly Argentine instrument or whether it reflects a universal tendency. For European nationalist intellectuals, the essential links between the human soul and its natural surroundings, in the cult of the past, became revolutionary concepts that were used to attack the abstract concept of liberal democracy, which was held to be the cause of social disintegration and national humiliation. Indeed, cults of the past are often transformed into mobilizing myths whose purpose is to transform current reality.

Maurice Barrès attacked liberal democracy by reconstructing a period of French history according to the political norms of a subsequent period. Georges Sorel believed that in order to study the past it had to be made present. Trying to reestablish a historical truth is a question not only of consciousness and pure knowledge, but of practical interest and of immediate utility. Although for Sorel it was the myth of the general strike that mobilized the proletariat for revolutionary action, he emphasized that the power of tradition, which was "the mother of the social instinct," also played a decisive political role. This was far from political romanticism. Carl Schmitt, for example, criticized the romantic tradition in politics as escapist, looking not only or primarily backward into the past, but inward into the self.[16] Although Schmitt rejected political romanticism, he embraced what he called the "romantic politician" as an actor who demonstrates that the self finds its realization not in "lyrical descriptions of experience, but in politics," considered to be a work of art.[17] Cervantes' Don Quixote was an early model of one whose battles were marvelously foolish even though they were struggles in which he was exposed to personal danger. To struggle for values, whatever the values might be, and whatever the chances of success, was a value in itself. Carl Schmitt, Oswald Spengler, Ernst Jünger, and almost all the members of that generation made a cult of action and will in opposition to the rationalization of political conflict. This cult also represented the rediscovery of the inherent values of the heroism of the past, which inspired the organic conception of the nation. The nation is a living organism, and nationalism is therefore an ethic that had to be grasped and boldly acted out by the individual and by society. However, only those who shared the national consciousness shaped over the course of the centuries could be included under the framework of this nationalism. Jews, for example, who were considered a foreign race representing the desert people, were seen as a shallow, arid, and "dry" people, a race embodying all the values contrary to the concept of the nation as an organic entity.[18]

In the Argentine context, as in France and to Germany, the rediscovery of the past by the new nationalist generation had a practical, political, and ideological objective. "Engaging in politics is almost unavoidable when doing history,"[19] said Julio Irazusta. And although Mario Amadeo maintains that historical revisionism could hardly be taken as a "fruit of foreign imitations,"[20] this cultural and historical revisionism in Argentina reflected the same historicist assumptions on which nationalist attacks against the liberal tradition around the world were based. It was the historical myth, the myth of the particular Argentine pre-liberal tradition and its social and cultural configurations, that became the new mobilizing myth accompanying the economic critique of Argentine liberalism.

The revisionist interpretation of the Rosas era thus laid the cornerstone for rebuilding Argentine identity. The myths of the gaucho resistance to modernity and of Rosas's resistance to the great imperial powers—France and England in the first half of the nineteenth century, added to the idea of national unification under an authoritarian and traditionalist regime, were the new values set forth in opposition to the "Europeanized" bourgeois values of the liberal elites. Worth emphasizing is the fact that the myth of Juan Manuel de Rosas reveals the first necessary theoretical link between the rightist and the leftist nationalists. Arturo Jauretche, for example, a leading proponent of the left-wing Yrigoyenist movement FORJA (analyzed in following chapters), admitted that historical revisionism was the legacy of the integral nationalists and that such a perspective on history allowed them to understand the present economic and political situation, in particular.[21]

Despite differences of emphasis between right-wing and populist left intellectuals on a wide variety of aspects of historic revisionism, one of the central ideas that began to take shape was that through historical revisionism not only Argentina's cultural identity but especially its economic establishment could be criticized. Through Rosas, the nationalists of both the right and the left initiated a critique of the history of Argentina's oligarchy.

Juan Manuel de Rosas, whom the liberal political and intellectual elite had attempted to efface from the national consciousness, was considered the personification of the "barbaric" culture. Sarmiento's *Facundo*, Esteban Echeverria's *El matadero*, and José Mármol's *Amalia* were the three principal works that had made Rosas the symbol of "barbarism" and tyrannical rule.

One of the early nationalist intellectuals who first challenged this view and initiated a historical revision of Rosas's time was Carlos Ibarguren. In 1922 Carlos Ibarguren lectured on Rosas during a conference at the University of Buenos Aires, in the process challenging the liberal historical tradition. The conference was published in 1930 as *Juan Manuel de Rosas, su vida, su tiempo, su drama* and became the first in a series of provocative books and articles. In 1935 Julio Irazusta published *Ensayo sobre Rosas: En el centenario de la suma del poder, 1835–1935,* based on the conferences given by the author at the Sociedad de Historia Argentina. This last book continued the provocative line initiated by a book jointly written by the Irazusta brothers, *La Argentina y el imperialismo británico: Los eslabones de una cadena, 1806–1833* (1934). Written at the time of the Roca-Runciman Pact, this book was the most direct intellectual attack on the history of the Argentine liberal oligarchy, inasmuch as it tried to explain the reasons for Argentine dependency upon Great Britain throughout the political and economic development of the oligarchy. The Irazusta brothers admitted that the mistakes committed by the "Roca mission . . . are so huge" that the only way to understand how these mistakes could have been committed by intelligent people is by analyzing the history of Argentina's oligarchy.[22]

The history of the oligarchy was the history of its political and economical association with foreign interests, which led, according to right-wing and left-wing nationalists, to the total surrender of Argentina's national interest. Right-wing nationalists added their particular emphasis. The responsibility for Argentina's economic dependency lay in the hands of "the ones who, illumined by Europe, were allowing foreigners to divide up the wealth of the native people."[23]

In 1939 Ernesto Palacio published another important book, *La historia falsificada,* which added new arguments to the basic thesis advanced by the Irazustas. Palacio believed that the faith in progress that characterized the spirit of the early years of the century was not an unfounded faith. Rather, it had been spoiled by the materialist spirit of that generation, whose interpretation of national history sustained its cultural and economic worldview. It was a time when the world

> seemed to be marching . . . toward universal happiness, without suspecting the future conflicts that derived from the industrial revolution, and from the expansion of capitalism. . . . Under this universal faith the liberal interpretation of our national history was the background and justification for the political action of our oligarchies . . . in other words, of the party of "civilization."[24]

Rosas represented an alternate worldview, one that emerged from his political action and that exalted national integrity, the vitality of the violent and heroic action. Like Lugones, Ernesto Palacio understood that "the anguish of our immediate destiny explains . . . the exaltation of Rosas."[25]

In opposition to the optimistic bourgeois view of progress promoted by the liberal elites, wrote Carlos Ibarguren, Jr., "a spiritualist wave impregnated with neo-mysticism, appears. . . . All the rationalist constructions . . . give way to a 'Bergsonian' conception of exalting the intuition of life that must be lived rather than thought."[26] According to Ibarguren, Argentina needs a new morality rooted in its own "warrior past" myths of popular and heroic vitality.

The image of the gaucho was endorsed by the image of Rosas as the model of a rebellious, modest, and authentic combatant against the foreign, the strong, and the modern. The gaucho represents the image of heroic defeat. The *"patriada,"* which should not be confused with the *"cuartelazo"* (the military coup, a prudent commercial operation with an assured success), is "one of the few honorable chapters of undervalued American history. . . . In the *patriada*, it may be said, failure was guaranteed. . . ."[27] The *patriada* was a form of primitive gaucho warfare, with little likelihood of success. This form of pre-modern struggle requires personal heroism and a complete subordination to the charismatic leader represented by the nineteenth-century caudillo. Participation in the *patriada* is a decision that excludes any rational determination, since one is really opting for defeat.

According to Lugones, the transformation of the bourgeois values of a developing society could be achieved by awakening the heroic instinct hidden in the gaucho soul. Lugones believed that an epic poem is fundamental for a people struggling for national self-identification. However, Lugones was not thinking only in terms of Argentina's own particular development.

Lugones likened *Martín Fierro* by José Hernández to Greek epic poetry. For Lugones, Argentina was part of the new civilization in which aesthetic beauty and heroic values prevail over materialist values.[28] In opposition to the bourgeois concept of rational truth and materialist individualism, the idea of the heroic life forms the foundation of this new civilization. The heroism implied in the figure of the gaucho also implies an ideological stance of respect for humble people, for justice, and for representative governments from a substantive rather than a formal standpoint.[29]

Like the myth of Rosas, the myth of the gaucho was celebrated by both right- and left-wing nationalists, who associated it with the Radical movement's rebellion against the liberal oligarchy. The famous poem by Arturo Jauretche, "Paso de los Libres" (1934), speaks of the frustrated rebellion of the Radical movement in Pomar. In the poem, Jauretche recalls the merits of this heroic act that is properly Argentine.[30]

Arturo Jauretche's myth of the rural world was complemented by a work of Raúl Scalabrini Ortiz, *El hombre que está solo y espera* (1931), which reflected the problems of the urban intellectual. In this work of social psychology, Scalabrini Ortiz presented the central themes that he later developed in his political and economic essays, in which he denounced Argentine economic dependency upon Britain. The alienated intellectual and the dominant classes are jointly responsible for the nation's surrender to financial imperialism. Scalabrini's rejection of the cosmopolitan intellectual represents the other face of the image of the rebellious gaucho rooted in the homeland. The intellectual does not carry with him the spirit of his land and hence is disconnected from his "people." But Scalabrini did not believe that this situation could be maintained. There was hope for a cultural resurrection and a real national liberation even though the gaucho rebellion had been lost from the outset.

This hope distinguishes Jauretche and Scalabrini from intellectuals like Eduardo Mallea and Ezequiel Martínez Estrada, who were pessimistic about modernization[31] and deplored the demise of an "invisible Argentina," a country whose Roman virtues of creative labor, authenticity, and idealism had been supplanted by the shallow materialism and ostentation of a "visible Argentina."[32] Furthermore, Martínez Estrada was sharply critical of modernity, which could offer no hope of liberation for a country like Argentina. In his bestseller, *Radiografía de la Pampa* (1933), Martínez Estrada expressed the conviction that spiritual poverty is a direct result of economic growth. In fact, he speaks of a kind of society rendered helpless by "birth defects" that hindered any attempt at political change. Estrada did not deplore the *loss* of civic virtue or national direction, because he believed they had never existed. Scalabrini Ortiz and Jauretche challenged this existential fatalism. Their optimism impelled them to struggle politically for economic independence, a struggle that could produce an alternative path to modernization. The search for the authentic self, as represented in the gaucho, constituted a critique of the abstract, universalist, alienated intellectual—and on this point intellectuals of left and right were in agreement. In an age of cultural upheaval, magazines like *Sur* and *Claridad* drew together intellectuals of left and right whose common goal was a radical opposition to bourgeois politics. The old world of the politicians was dismissed in favor of a new world and a cultural renaissance. A new nationalist right and left were to evoke the revolutionary myths drawn from the pre-liberal, rebellious, and antimodernist past, the basis of which was a new "third force" revolutionary ideology. Between 1936 and 1939, nationalists like Ernesto Palacio and Ramón Doll, and Catholics like Leonardo Castellani and Leopoldo Marechal, collaborated on the magazine *Sur*, an anti-Catholic, agnostic magazine whose editor, Victoria Ocampo, was a liberal.[33] Their contributions were published alongside articles of agnostic literary figures such as Jorge Luis Borges and Louis Ollivier, who represented the pro-Communist group L'Ordre Nouveau. This cultural renaissance, which constituted the framework for the nationalist attempt to refashion Argentine history, was understood as the start of an independence process that would have political and economic implications. As defined by Lugones, the anti-positivist reaction began as an aesthetic initiative and represented a second emancipation, characterized by the rejection of "imported liberalism, whose adoption . . . composed the systematic negation of our own self." However, in order "for the nation to find itself again, [it] must begin by defining itself. That is the contradiction of ideological man and of positivist humanity . . . [which is] an abstraction of rationalism."[34]

National liberation thus entailed a cultural rebirth and an escape from the worldview imposed by liberal or socialist patrons of what can be defined as "dependent modernization."

From Traditional Federalism to a Republican Populist Democracy

Ramón Doll, an important intellectual whose incisive ideological and political commentaries were published in the nationalist press (e.g., *Crisol*, *El Pampero*, *Alianza*, and, starting in the 1940s, *Nuevo Orden*), attempted to distinguish between the implications of European and Latin American interpretations of right- and left-wing ideologies. He understood that the categories used in Latin America must be defined in terms of the confrontation with "the liberal oligarchies who represent the Europeanizing action against the Americanist and national reaction."[35] The ideological error committed by the liberal historians was to analyze Rosas in "Europeanizing" categories. Some regarded Rosas as a dictator who governed against the popular will, while others attempted to refute this notion using the same terminology. In commenting on Julio Irazusta's essay on Rosas, Doll admired the historic categories used by Irazusta, which were themselves a kind of emancipation. The Irazustas accused the school system of educating students "against the classic caudillismo of Hispanic origins. The reason for that was that [for the oligarchy] . . . democracy has to accept the principles established by liberalism, therefore it must be lay and progressive."[36] According to the Irazustas and Doll, however, a liberal constitutional regime was the refuge of the national associates of liberal plutocratic nations. From a historical perspective, claimed Doll, the concept of a constitutional democracy used by the "Europeanizing" historians does not correspond to the reality of Rosas's era, which had to cope with the unification and defense of the nation, a task that was accomplished by the people who responded to his charismatic power.

According to Doll, Rosas succeeded in bridging the gap between the "extreme rationalist enterprise of Rivadavia . . . and the habits of the colony,"[37] between the city and the farm, between "Europeanizing" centralization and peasant federalism. In any case, the notion of popular consent, interpreted in a communitarian antiliberal perspective, was basically accepted by both modernizing and traditionalist nationalists. However, this issue was not free from controversies, inasmuch as it affected ideological and practical discussions among the nationalists about the characteristics of the nationalist movement.

Two different approaches to the interpretation of Rosas's "traditional leadership" were evident. Manuel Gálvez, for instance, attempted to equate the old concept of federalism with the democratic populism of the Yrigoyenist movement. In his critical response to Gálvez's book on Rosas, Federico Ibarguren rejected the theoretical association of the concept of federalism with that of popular democracy. The federalism of Rosas was associated with the essence of Spanish colonial rule "because in those heroic times we, the inhabitants of the Rio de la Plata, kept almost intact the original Catholic-Hispanic form of life."[38] The basic fear of some nationalists was that the struggle between federalism and centralization of the Rosas era would be projected onto the struggle between Radicals and Conservatives in their own time. Nationalists like Federico Ibarguren could not accept the new tendency represented not only by Gálvez but also by the Irazusta brothers and Doll, who considered national-populist Yrigoyenism as the real embodiment of Rosas's traditionalist rule.[39]

According to the most conservative advocates of Argentine nationalism, the epic of national emancipation had to be freed of association with modern populism as well as with the democratic values emanating from the French Revolution. Indeed, according to the conservative interpretation, the leaders of the independence struggle drew inspiration from the Spanish traditionalist resistance against the Bourbon model of modernization based on a highly centralized state. For Federico Ibarguren, Latin American emancipation was achieved in the name of tradition. With the Bourbons, he claimed, religion was transformed into solely a matter of state.[40] The attack on something considered as basic as traditional Spanish regional liberties was one of the fundamental issues considered by Juan Donoso Cortés in the nineteenth century and Ramiro de Maeztu in the 1930s. From this Catholic traditionalist standpoint, Argentina's emancipation from Spain was not comparable to that of the Massachusetts separatists, with their early talk of self-governing independent kingdoms and commonwealths. As Richard Morse asserts, the "Hispano-American" revolt was within the framework of the Thomist patrimonial state.[41] Rosas's *caudillista* and federalist past was associated with a type of patrimonial government. Hence, even though Rosas governed in a centralized and dictatorial manner, his authoritarian dictatorship was perceived as a form of government opposed to that of an enlightened centralized state. Support for this view was further developed in newspapers and magazines like *Crisol*, *Sol y Luna*, and *Baluarte*, whose message was the need to restore the Spanish traditionalist spirit as an alternative to modern Western models of political development and civilization. Liberal democracy was different from Thomist "democracy." According to one writer in *Crisol*, when we talk about the government of many we are talking about St. Thomas, "who did not speak in the name of the government of all as in our democracy."[42] For the most radical antimodernist Catholics, the Rosas myth should not lead to any sort of democratic populism that would remind them of Yrigoyenism, but rather to a pure, traditional, hierarchical order.

Quoting Gaetano Mosca's *Elementi di scienza politica*, Hector Sáenz Quesada attempted to explain mass support for Rosas. "The common people are a necessary instrument in almost all . . . the revolutions, and that is why we frequently see men of a superior social condition standing at the head of these popular movements." According to Quesada, Rosas shaped the necessary modern relationship between the aristocracy and the masses. In Spain, the "democratic" traditional resistance against the modern innovators differed from the modern concept of Jacobinic "populist" democracy or from a liberal constitutional democracy based on rationalist utilitarian and materialist principles. "Sometimes, the opposite phenomenon happens: that part of the political class that has the power in its hands, resists the innovative currents and receives support from the lower classes which are loyal to the old ideas and the old social type. Such has happened in Spain after 1822 and until 1830."[43] The popular consent that characterized the authoritarian Rosas regime contradicts the foreign, modernist, democratic concept supported by Sarmiento and the liberal elites. Sarmiento's legacy was one of intolerance toward ordinary people and poverty. As stressed by Quesada, poverty is a direct result of "the Protestant and Anglo-Saxon ideologies."[44]

In short, for the antimodernist members of the nationalist right, Rosas synthesized a sort of aristocratic caudillismo. At the same time, an alternative interpretation that endorsed Rosas to the national populists began to take shape. Unlike the Catholic antimodernist right-wing nationalists, Julio Irazusta did not claim to be "using the example of Rosas in order to dream of dictatorships based on the precedent of Rosas."[45] The alternative interpretation was not merely a case of severing the link between Rosas and the concept of a conservative dictatorship. The most important ideological development generated by the revision of Argentine history involved a reappraisal of the nationalist character of Yrigoyenismo, defined as an offshoot of the Rosas tradition. The Irazusta brothers, Gálvez, and Doll arrived at the conclusion that the "radical" Yrigoyenist tradition was part of the authentic nationalist idea because the Radical movement was characterized by its federalism. "National unity in (the radicals) is much more solid, since it derives from the popular consensus, in accordance with the provincial caudillos."[46] In *Vida de Juan Manuel de Rosas* (1940), Manuel Gálvez connected the federalism of Rosas to populist democracy. In *Vida de Hipólito Yrigoyen: El hombre del misterio* (1939), Gálvez clarified the parallel between Rosas and Yrigoyen: both leaders defended the economic and cultural independence of the country, and they were the only leaders in Argentine history who had worked for the people. Aware that Rosas and Yrigoyen had to be adapted to the new era and to its challenges, Gálvez did not use the Rosas legacy as the myth to rescue an old and inexistent traditional hierarchy. Rather, he connected the Rosas myth to a rebellious nationalist populist movement—with a new social and political message— which, according to Gálvez, had some features in common with fascism.

The retrieval of the Rosas myth was directly connected to the adoption of an anti-imperialist and populist position, and thus it represented the nationalist movement's search for its own identity. For most Argentine right-wing nationalists, however, this attempt at cultural revisionism and elaboration of a right-wing concept of cultural and economic anti-imperialism was directly connected to the fascist revolution. Most Argentine nationalists believed that it was impossible to separate a critique of Argentina's liberal model of national organization from the alternatives inspired by the fascist model of modernization.

On this point, however, the Argentine integralist right was somewhat divided between those who set Catholic doctrine first and those who endorsed the more modernizing and populist sides of fascism. Both groups admired Rosas and admired fascism. However, while the Catholic

integralist right endorsed fascism to Catholicism, only the latter succeeded in endorsing fascism to economic anti-imperialism and the Yrigoyenist tradition.

The Catholic Right and the Fascist Question

Fascism, as Lugones observed, offered not only a political formula but an
intellectual framework "to build that which is ours, out of that which is
ours and is not English-speaking, German, or Russian ideology, but Latin
American reality."[47] For Lugones, fascism was an intellectual and spiritual framework rather than a political project that should be imposed,
whereas nationalism was the real political movement that embodied the
message of a new world order in local cultural reality and its political
myths. Most Argentine nationalists of the right agreed with this notion,
but the majority, who, unlike Lugones, were fundamentally Catholic,
believed that the question of fascism had to be considered in close relationship with their Catholic cultural experience. Fascism both threatened
liberal democracy and was competing directly with the interests of the
church. Yet Catholic nationalists could hardly scorn the communitarian
solution to the social question propelled by fascism. They could hardly
ignore the fact that during the interwar wars, fascism, its radical secu-
larism notwithstanding, was part of a political tradition that combined
communitarian values and a modern approach to politics. Both the
greatness of the nation and its historical success were linked to its loyalty
to the church; secularization became a threat not only to the church but
also to the nation.[48]

Gustavo Franceschi, Leonardo Castellani, Julio Meinvielle, and laymen
like César Pico were Catholics, nationalists and were an integral part of
the church establishment. With the exception of Franceschi, they did not
constitute the dominant current within the church hierarchy, although
they set off an intellectual and ideological debate that the hierarchy could
hardly dismiss. They were aware that the old conservative democratic
equilibrium worked out by the liberal state and the Catholic Church did
not respond to the needs of the hour.

As already noted, Argentina's liberal elites, like those of other Latin
American countries, had been influenced by the republican ideas of the
French Revolution. They attempted to erase those Hispanic traditions
that were inherent in the church itself. At the same time, with the decline
of Ultramontanism, the church had been "made safe" sufficiently for liberal conservatives to begin to value it as a means of social cohesion. In

other words, despite its secularist zeal, Argentine liberalism stopped short of separating church and state and expelling the church from the public sphere, as had occurred in France. Church and state had retained a link not unlike that of the Church of England.[49] Starting in the 1870s, however, ecclesiastical elites in Argentina began to chafe against the complicity of the agnostic state in fostering the anticlerical spirit[50] promoted by "Masonic lodges" and the liberal press. Newspapers like *La Unión*, published by José Manuel de Estrada, and *La Voz de la Iglesia* reflected the debate on education among the rank and file of the church. Intellectuals such as Pedro Goyena, Emilio Lamarca, Navarro Viola, and Estrada himself, who—his own laicist convictions notwithstanding—was opposed to the anti-Catholic initiative of the government, contributed to *La Unión*. They sought to achieve a viable consensus between the secular and religious currents in the country.

More radical tendencies began to be heard during those years. *La Voz de la Iglesia* echoed Vatican Council I (1870), which offered a harsh critique of modernity. The question involved not only opposing secular education, but proposing a social alternative to liberalism. Resistance to secularization was a first step in a long struggle in which Catholicism would propose a comprehensive response to liberal secular modernization. With Leo XIII's *Rerum Novarum* (1891), the Catholic Church laid down the guidelines for resolving the social question. *Rerum Novarum* identified both liberal capitalism and socialism as inclined to twin abuses: the absorption of the state by sectors of the economy, and the absorption of the economy by the state. The basic idea of the church, therefore, was that labor should not be subject to the law of the market. Drawing on Thomist philosophy, Leo XIII affirmed that property should be both personal and social. Thus the church was seeking to recover the practical role attributed to the state by the scholastic tradition, namely, defending the defenseless and intervening to bring about a more just distribution of wealth. The new developments in Catholic thought offered Argentine Catholics a further field of struggle in addition to the long-standing struggle for Catholic education.

The Círculos de Obreros Católicos, founded by the German priest Federico Grote, was the first step in propagating an alternative social vision to that of socialism. Between 1892 and 1912, seventy-seven workers' circles were founded throughout the country, comprising around 23,000 members. In 1898, the first congress of Catholic workers laid the foundation for a federation of workers' circles. The workers' circles bore similarities to the French bourgeois Cercles established by Albert De Mun, and were a mixture of mutual aid society, research organization, and promoter of social doctrine. It must be emphasized, however, that these developments in the church did not imply a rejection of democracy. Important Catholic associations led by lay people, like the Liga Democrática Argentina, were democratic. They identified with Christian Democratic ideals.

There were important reasons for the failure of social Catholicism in Argentina to develop into a major political movement and constitutional party, as it did in Italy. In Argentina the higher clergy—selected and controlled by a special privilege granted to the Spanish state—served as guardians of "national" values, especially when they shared liberal-conservative anxiety about the left. The labor conflicts of 1917 and 1922, which, like the conflict over university reform, drew inspiration from European democratic revolutionary ideas, placed the ruling classes on the defensive. In contrast to progressive Christian Democracy, the tendency in Argentina was toward a conservative corporativism devised to protect the political control of the liberal elites. That tendency attracted leading church figures, among them Monsignor Miguel de Andrea, a popular figure within the Buenos Aires upper class. His public sermons were typical of the liberal-regalist *"Católicismo de conciliacion,"* in which the church was regarded as an institution within the liberal state like the army. Indeed, in the 1930s and 1940s the church stood equidistant from communism and fascism, socialism and capitalism, liberalism and totalitarianism.[51] It was thought that neither an army gathered around the cross nor a Christian Democratic party would achieve the profound reform demanded by the church's social doctrine.[52] The Unión Popular Católica Argentina created by Miguel de Andrea represented an attempt to unify the various social Catholic initiatives under an umbrella organization closely tied to the hierarchy. In 1919 he worked with the Liga Patriótica in its campaign against communism and after 1923 his name was associated with the Federación de Empleadas Católicas, a new type of gender-based labor union, which included, among other activities, the foundation of the "Hogar de la Empleada," a project for housing homeless working women. De Andrea was primarily associated with a radical anticommunist stand and with the hierarchy's efforts to preserve a balance between the conservative political establishment and the church. In other words, patriotism and anticommunism were part of a sound nationalism which coincided with the interests of the oligarchic authorities.

The Justo regime expressed that delicate equilibrium in a variety of ways. The church was generally well disposed toward the liberal Justo regime, which embodied the success of the liberal establishment and its model of political modernity. The ecclesiastical authorities could not ignore the aid given by the regime to the organization of the great Eucharist Congress that took place in Buenos Aires in 1934 (it was expressly applauded in *Criterio*). The congress, which included the participation of Cardinal Pacelli, the future Pope Pius XII, became a demonstration of strength by Argentine Catholics. This was one of the most decisive religious and political acts by the Argentine Catholic establishment and marked one of the most important successes of Argentine Catholicism. On October 11, 1934, after years of popular indifference to Catholicism, people of all social classes gathered in Plaza de Mayo in a public mass led by Pacelli, an unforgettable event which from that point on indicated that Catholicism was resuming a leading position in Argentine political culture. This act exemplified more than anything the equilibrium between the church and a liberal regime that stressed its opposition to communism and populism.

The church's attitude toward more radical Catholic nationalism was rather ambivalent. It admitted that the nationalists had played a key role in stimulating President Justo to reject support from the liberal establishment and to find it within Christianity.[53] At the same time, church authorities remained suspicious that the nationalist aspirations would jeopardize the traditional equilibrium between the church and the regime. There were good reasons for that suspicion, since the new brand of young Catholic integralists—Franceschi, Castellani, and others—began to question the whole liberal Gallican conception of "tradition" and the "patriotism" of democratic political parties. According to their views, these groups represented "merely electoral interests."[54]

The Década Infame laid the domestic political and economic foundation for ideological change. For the new Catholic elites, however, the old formula that combined nationalism and liberalism and the political interests of the conservative elites and the church was evil. Groups like Acción Católica Argentina, Restauración, and the Cursos de Cultura Católica, as well as publications like *Criterio* and *Sol y Luna*, began to echo the new voices of protest. No doubt the latter's intellectual and political groups were also virulently anticommunist. However, they aspired to complement that vision with the elaboration of a more complex nationalist approach and with an anti-imperialist discourse. The weekly *Criterio*, for example, published some of the early national Catholic socioeconomic critiques against the liberal oligarchy. The failure of the Ortiz reform program and the Pinedo economic plan, according to one article, had proven the obstinacy of Argentine liberalism, which sought to preserve the unjust social order through fraudulent elections. The article called for military authoritarianism as the only defense against the despotism of the masses.[55] A key idea was that an overt identification with the church did not prove that the state was deferring to church cultural authority. To claim to stand with the church, as liberal conservative governments tended to do, was insufficient.

Nevertheless, just what the political alternatives to the liberal regime might be remained an open question. The dilemma was between support for a conservative type of authoritarian regime that would demobilize the working class and protect the old conservative elites, and support for another type of nationalist revolution (military or not) that would mobilize the people and neutralize the old political elites. Arguments for and against these positions were presented openly, not only in theoretical debates but also in discussions on organizational issues, such as those that took place around the creation of a socioeconomic secretariat for Acción Católica Argentina (a movement that in 1934 had over 25,000 members all around the country). This initiative was rejected by important intellectual figures of Catholic nationalism, such as Tomás D. Casares, one of the founders of the Cursos de Cultura Católica, and also by Monsignor Filippo Cortesi, the papal nuncio. They rejected the movement's future plans to establish a socioeconomic secretariat as a means for advancing social legislation and reaching the working class. Cortesi and Casares argued that the most urgent problem for Catholicism was the threat of communism. One group that held this position was the CPACC (Comisión Popular Argentina contra el Comunismo). CPACC, led by the Catholic nationalist Carlos Silveyra, was always praised by the church for its activities of opposition to the aim of the Justo government to open diplomatic relationships with the Soviet Union. According to Cortesi and Casares, social legislation was useless—the real alternative was to shift the liberal system toward authoritarian corporativism. Other groups, like Restauración, founded in 1937 by Hector Bernardo and Alfredo Villegas Oromi, held a similar position. In its Declaration of Principles, Restauración raised the possibility of using some kind of violence against the real violence, "which is spiritual and social disorder."[56] The violent response to social disorder would be a military authoritarian regime.

Taking a different stand, Father Gustavo Franceschi rejected the authoritarian type of solution and searched for a nationalist "third way" that would be neither left nor right. He expected that a social secretariat would undertake the role of mobilizing and educating the people. Obviously, such education would be antiliberal, but the message was that Acción Católica should perform a role of "democratizing" the counterrevolution, rather than expecting anything from a military coup. In any case, the difference in emphasis did not change the basic result, which was described in a new terminology of corporativist nationalism, far from the idea of Christian democracy.[57]

This debate was extended in more theoretical terms in the Cursos de Cultura Católica, led by Casares and Atilio Dell'Oro Maini. One of the central questions posed in these courses was to what extent fascism could be blended with nationalism and Catholicism. It must be stressed, however, that the debates within the courses were opened to a wide variety of Catholic and non-Catholic ideas and were published in the magazines *Criterio*, *Sol y Luna*, and *Baluarte*. These also published articles by writers such as G.K. Chesterton, Hilaire Belloc, Charles Péguy, Nicolas Berdyaev, Giovanni Papini, Thierry Maulnier, Jacques Maritain, and Reginald Garrigou-Lagrange. Some of those intellectuals, such as Maritain and Garrigou-Lagrange, were invited to Argentina by Casares and lectured at the "Cursos," while Belloc, Papini, Maritain, and Ramiro de Maeztu contributed to *Criterio*. Despite the open-minded character of the intellectual debates, the dominant line of thought was that supported by Casares, Dell'Oro Maini, the brothers Ibarguren, and the well-known anti-Semitic writer Gustavo Martínez Zuviría (Hugo Wast), advocating a more politicized church with a clear stance against the liberal democratic establishment. Yet an antiliberal stance did not imply that they shared a common view on the new political order. Some favored establishing an authoritarian regime as the way to best serve the interests of Catholicism. Others advocated a nationalist integralist "third way" as a response to the new developments of modern times. Paradoxically, that would entail an approach focused on mass mobilization and would be closer to the fascist concept of national revolution than to a conservative authoritarian response to the communist threat. Both methods were grounded in the same intention to control mass mobilization.

"Hispanismo," Nationalism, and Fascist Totalitarianism

The claim of fascism to represent a universal revolutionary spirit[58] did not fully meet the expectations of the Catholic nationalists. In a speech to the Real Academia de Italia on December 17, 1930, Gioacchino Volpe, a prominent Italian historian, asserted that Latin America occupied an important place in what Volpe called the age of fascist classicism and Latinity. Volpe argued that Latin America's historical process had been shaped both by its Hispanic elements and by spiritual Latin elements. By "Latinity" Volpe meant not merely a cultural concept but also what he took to be the institutionalization of fascism, as illustrated by the parallels between the Latin American emancipation tradition and the Italian Risorgimento. According to Volpe, a gradual movement toward new unified, centralizing, and autocratic forms of state power was underway.[59] Carlos Ibarguren, one of the most important nationalist intellectuals, welcomed this modernizing message, which was not accepted by the Argentine conservative politicians. According to Ibarguren, "the evolution of society has been much faster than political changes . . . [and we in Argentina] have the same political structure created more than a hundred years ago by that individualist ideology that developed from the romantic to the bourgeois age."[60] The solution did not require a return to the model of the past. The concept of Argentina as a part of the new world that would rise from the ruins of the liberal world order corresponded to a modernist message, rather than to a reactionary one, according to Ibarguren. Juan Carulla was even more forthright in stating that fascism was the solution for modern times. He asserted that "never had the doctrines of positivist liberalism and of . . . Marxism, suffered such a contrast . . . [provoked by] the fascist triumph."[61] Most Argentine Catholics also believed that fascism was the ideological framework available for confronting the liberal democratic state. In 1928, even before the publication of the "Doctrine of Fascism" defining the Italian concept of the universality of fascism, Juan Carulla had already recognized that fascism represented the new principle, "the new framework of values for opposing democracy."[62]

Of course, the fact that the nationalist movement had a natural affinity with a particular ideological framework did not necessarily mean that it accepted that ideology. As Amadeo argued, "the defense of sovereignty in international matters . . . the issue of economic recovery . . . and historical revisionism . . . are not the fruit of foreign imitations"[63] because they are proper to Argentine problems. Like most fascists worldwide, the nationalists did not belong to a fascist international. All of them stressed their country's particularities. Yet their vision of the basic problems of society and the formulas to solve these problems often had a great deal in common with fascism, and were clearly influenced by it.

Carlos Ibarguren quoted Georges Roux's article in the *Nouvelle Revue de Hongrie* of April 1933, which stated that "the influence of fascist ideas is being felt everywhere. Many do not admit it and others received it without being aware of it. But fascism, Hitlerism, and Bolshevism are phenomena with particular forms in each country that cannot be copied by others." Ibarguren also referred to Pierre Dominique's analysis of French fascism, in which the author concluded that "democracy is dead, the number of French people who think like me is growing; we are going to replace it by another regime. Which? Neither Bolshevism nor fascism, but something that will be French."[64] Ibarguren in fact, reached the same conclusion regarding Argentina—that French "something" would be a type of French fascism, and Argentine nationalism is likewise a kind of local fascism.

A key event that contributed to the convergence in Argentina of the position of the nationalists toward fascism and toward their own Catholic cultural identity was the Spanish Civil War. The Falange helped resolve the conflict between political fascism and Catholic spiritualism. In their own way, the Falange and Franco were creating a different kind of totalitarianism. "This is the fascism that was underway in Spain, with the blood of the martyrs, [that is the fascism] . . . to which we adhere."[65] This was the synthesis of fascism and Hispanidad.

The idea of "Hispanidad," underscored by the Falangist struggle in Spain, was adopted and advocated by Argentine Catholics after the arrival in Buenos Aires of the Spanish conservative Ramiro de Maeztu in 1928.[66] Because of his support for Miguel Primo de Rivera's military dictatorship, Maeztu was appointed ambassador in Buenos Aires, where he frequently met with the group of intellectuals associated with *La Nueva República*. They especially appreciated his *Defensa de la Hispanidad* (1934), which they regarded as his most important book because it presented the idea of a religious Spain at the center of the ideological struggle against the secular, democratic, and liberal processes in Spain and Latin America. The idea of "Hispanidad," originally introduced by Marcelino Menéndez y Pelayo in his book *Historia de los heterodoxos españoles* (1880–1881), was advanced by Ramiro de Maeztu because it presented a clear and specific conception reflecting the Hispanic cultural renaissance that began with the Spanish generation of 1898. "Hispanidad," which according to Maeztu was most radically expressed by the Spanish Falange, was able to stand up to the two great enemies of the continent: "Russian communism and North American economic imperialism."[67] In other words, the answer to liberal democracy and international communism was rooted in traditional Spanish sources. Hispanidad had to do with a cultural community which must gradually develop its own political and social institutions, while all foreign ideological models, such as liberalism and socialism, must be removed from its political body. In *Nueva Política* and *Sol y Luna*, intellectuals like Marcelo Sánchez Sorondo, Hector Llambías, and Hector Sáenz Quesada adopted this central thesis. While Ramiro de Maeztu was advocating *hispanismo*, however, he was disappointed by what he considered to be the lack of authenticity of the Argentine nationalists—a paradox especially evidenced in their unconditional acceptance of inspiration from Spain.

During his years as leader of Acción Española, Maeztu criticized the Argentine nationalists for their absolute cultural dependency on Spain. "The salvation of the Hispano-American peoples must be accomplished first of all by their own work and not by the work of Spain."[68]

César Pico, a bacteriologist by profession and a lecturer in metaphysics at the Universidad del Salvador in Buenos Aires, and one of the most influential figures in the Cursos de Cultura Católica, thought along similar lines. As a writer in *Sol y Luna*, Pico developed the concept of Hispanidad based more on the exigencies of Latin America than on the Spanish yearning to recover a lost cultural empire. Echoing Maeztu's message, Pico did not call for a return to a pure cultural dependency on Spain but for Spanish renewal according to the necessities of the present age. Such a renewal was the real substance of *hispanismo*, according to Pico. If Spain fails, "against our deepest feelings we will have to find inspiration in other European models."[69] Pico's message was aimed at both Argentina and Spain. Hispanidad was the fundamental tie connecting the cultural roots of Latin America to the European world through Spain. In other words, Hispanidad was primarily something proper to the Americas rather than to Spain. Inspired by Ortega y Gasset's synthesis of authenticity and modernization, Pico echoed the philosopher's preoccupation with the Spanish and Ibero-American future in the modern world. Europeanization meant modernization, and Spain had to understand that the concept of Hispanidad was meaningless unless it served as a vehicle and an expression of Europeanization.[70]

Fascism as a political modernizing experience could offer an appropriate solution for both the Spanish and the Argentine path to modernization. However, as noted, the totalitarian and secular character of fascism prevented the Argentine nationalists from fully defining themselves as fascists. As Father Gustavo Franceschi observed, "there is no possible reconciliation between totalitarianism and Catholicism."[71] The Argentine nationalist intellectuals who gathered around the Cursos de Cultura Católica were introduced to this problem through the debate between Jacques Maritain and Charles Maurras. In 1926, during the conflict between Rome and Action Française, Maritain, who defended the autonomy of philosophy, held that Thomist philosophy could and must be applied in different ways, according to time and place, and was entirely independent of political opinions that any Thomist might profess in a contingent manner. Maritain held that Thomism did not necessarily have to be authoritarian. Although Maritain admired Maurras for his nationalism and critique of democracy, he was less rigid and restrictive. The Argentine nationalists partially accepted Maritain's position on the nonpolitical character of Thomist philosophy. Explaining the conflict between Action Française and the Vatican, *Criterio* said that the Vatican condemned "neither the monarchism [of L'Accion Française], nor its struggle against . . . the republic." It condemned one principle of the political school that the Action Française represented, the "subordination of religion to politics"—*politique d'abord*—"which is not justifiable even as a tactic."[72]

Yet the Argentine right-wing nationalists found Maritain's pluralist interpretation of Thomist philosophy unacceptable. That interpretation provided the philosophical basis for Maritain's support of the Republican cause in the Spanish Civil War. The philosophical tenets expressed in *L'humanisme integral* (1936) turned Argentine Catholics against Maritain. In an article in the *Nouvelle Revue Française* of June 1936, translated in *Sur*, Maritain pointed out that although anticlerical excesses by Spanish Republicans or their supporters were "infinitely deplorable," these events in themselves were "not sufficient to transform [the Spanish conflict] into a holy war, or rather into a war . . . consecrated by God."[73] In a response to Jacques Maritain in 1937, César Pico synthesized previous discussions on the relationship between Catholicism and the new revolutionary totalitarianism. In his "Letter to Jacques Maritain," Pico interpreted the rise of European fascism as a way of coping with the secularist liberal threat to Christian society. Pico again tried to justify fascism, which, according to him and despite the message from Rome, was not necessarily totalitarian and was actually at the service of Christianity:

> Although several historical movements have been no more than the expression of doctrines that had been realized at that time, fascism in contrast . . . emerges as a reaction against the calamities ascribed to liberal democracy, socialism, and capitalism; a reaction which in its origin is instinctive and that seeks a doctrine to justify it. In fact, at times that doctrine had been wrongly formulated and supported a totalitarian posture. . . . Neither Oliveira Salazar, nor Dollfuss, nor several fascists in Italy . . . nor the nationalist movements in Spain and in Latin America could be classified as totalitarian. In those areas where the influence of Catholicism was more evident, the reaction had been reconciled with a traditional [conception] of law.[74]

Pico's interpretation, which was accepted by most of the Catholic nationalists, was based on the Catholic conservative vision that the Protestant Reformation began a long, downhill slide continued by the Renaissance spirit of individualism. As Father Julio Meinvielle added, this process of destruction of the natural order was inspired by three great revolutions: the Protestant revolution, the French "bourgeois revolution" of 1789, and the Russian Revolution. The "naturalist," "rationalist," and "classical" age was begun by Protestantism and was continued by a purely materialist and positivist age following the French Revolution, whereby man lost his rationality "and . . . limited himself to corroborating . . . and collecting facts, which means positivism."[75] Pico, Meinvielle, and the other Argentine Catholic nationalists attempted to present fascism as another facet of the long confrontation with secular modernization. In *Baluarte*, Pico responded to a letter sent by French intellectuals to *Criterio* rejecting both the communist and the fascist alternatives to liberal democracy. Pico wrote: "Without [assuming] that our support of the fascist reaction is an unchangeable commitment, siding with fascism is appropriate because it is the only historical alternative to [impede] the breakdown of . . . society."[76]

It was no coincidence that César Pico translated Thierry Maulnier's articles during the years of the Popular Front in France. Maulnier's concept of spiritual fascism, seen through his attempt to present fascism as an intellectual answer to the materialism of bourgeois society, was crucial for the Argentine nationalists' reaffirmation of their own particular place in the universalization of the nationalist fascist phenomenon—indeed, the cultural values of Hispanidad and Catholicism were supranational. Nationalism and fascism were a step toward this supranational feeling of *hispanismo*. Argentine nationalism was the local manifestation of a larger ideological and sociological process that first appeared in Italy under the name of fascism, seeking to provide solutions in the face "of the inadequacy of the liberal solution and the falsity of the Marxist solution."[77] Catholicism would provide fascism with a doctrine, while fascism would provide Catholicism with a new spirit of political action.

As explained by Father Gustavo Franceschi, the world was entering a new and dangerous era that called for a new mentality, a new approach by which Catholicism had to adopt the fascist motto that "life must be lived dangerously," if it aspires to have significance.[78] Life, in all its authenticity, depends on rescuing the value of "natural things." It is the primacy of natural culture over the rationality of civilization. Franceschi's position was of central importance because it attempted to emphasize the independent and antidoctrinaire characteristic of the "third-force" movements, thereby legitimizing similar ideological groups from right and left in Latin America. He was clear about the radical characteristics that the nationalist movement needed; it had to be socially revolutionary, but without internationalist connotations. For example, Franceschi called attention to those "young communists of Germany . . . [who] strive to get away from Russian communism in order to create a proper Germanic communism."[79] He did not disagree with a proper national socialism as long as it did not depend on foreign interests. "In the same way that the Bolshevik central committee demanded that local leaders in France, Spain and other places submit to Moscow's authority . . . in Argentina, those who attempted to realize a strictly national communism were excommunicated by . . . Marxist orthodoxy. . . . The 'Soviet' is eminently nationalist in Russia, but internationalist abroad. The Popular Front—which includes communism— is antipatriotic and anti-Argentine."[80] In other words, Franceschi believed that a new sort of nationalist socialism was the revolutionary formula needed for meeting the problems of modern society. If fascism lost its secularist doctrine it would be the most radical exemplar of a national socialist tendency, which is revolutionary and yet is not contrary to the spiritual doctrine of Catholicism. Franceschi assumed that "third way" movements should offer an alternative to old conservative movements that were combating Yrigoyenism and communism but that "lacked any [ideological] orientation and that unknowingly became the guardians of the antiquated liberal conservatism."[81]

José María de Estrada, lecturer of philosophy and contributor to the nationalist publications *Sol y Luna* and *Nueva Política*, who was also influenced by Pico, Maulnier, and Ortega y Gasset, pointed to the authentic existentialist formula produced by the fascist revolution. While the rationalist revolutions represented the triumph of rational abstractions and removed the "ontological sense of the law," Mussolini rescued the politics of the intuitive act.[82] Estrada interpreted the meaning of the fascist revolution as a revolution "without concrete programs," which, "by accepting the reality of things [creates] a new order that remains very much the old and true order."[83] In other words, rationalist absolutism is a direct attack on the natural order and the real "value of things," according to the expression popularized by Ortega y Gasset. However "a restoration of total order in values and things cannot be carried out without the acceptance of . . . the world's redemption by Christ."[84] From a political standpoint, any attack on rationalist and materialist ideologies had to be welcomed by Catholics, even if this attack was not based on specifically Catholic sources.

Estrada attempted to draw a unifying line between the fascist and the Spanish revolutions. The Spanish revolution, besides possessing all the characteristics of a fascist movement, is "truly metaphysical and is undoubtedly a complete revolution."[85] At the time, Franco's triumph in Spain confirmed the possibilities of the political success of an authentic sort of Hispanic conservative revolution, wherein "Falangismo," which blended Catholicism with fascism, was seen as the real expression of a holy war. The Reconquista implied the removal of communist and liberal ideologies and the rejection of any kind of pagan state.[86] Moreover, the Reconquista brought back the idea of an old type of communitarian socialism and an old sense of social justice embedded in the Middle Ages, which has reappeared in modern times in contrast to Communist state socialism or any type of democratic socialism.

Federico Ibarguren, a lawyer and lecturer in history who had taken part in the Cursos de Cultura Católica, following the lead of Charles Péguy, examined the differences between the Marxist socialism of Jean Jaurès and Péguy's form of socialism. Ibarguren admired Péguy's socialism, which differed from that of Jaurès on two fundamental points. While Jaurès's socialism was rational and materialist, Péguy's socialism was of the Sorelian type; it was antirational and moved by social myths. Péguy's socialism was not against "the concrete man made of body and soul." It admired "the . . . warrior traditions of his people, who strove for the glory more than any welfare . . . produced by the good distribution of wealth."[87] Moreover, Ibarguren did not view Péguy as opposed to social justice. "Identified with the oppressed . . . and the poor, Charles Péguy believes . . . in the just war against evil as the only way to put an end to individualism."[88] That was neither a call for violence along the lines of Sorel, who transformed the doctrines of violence into a "philosophy of history,"[89] nor a signal of acceptance of the cowardly pacifism of deserters. Although Federico Ibarguren did not idealize the Middle Ages, he agreed with the view held by César Pico and most members of the Cursos de Cultura Católica that the Reformation was a revolt of the rich against the poor, since it laid the foundation for liberal capitalism. He also drew on history for support: "Since becoming part of Christendom, Spanish America has taken on the renaissance of the strongman through the conquistador, and the idea of social justice through the action of the priest."[90]

Only fascism in its Catholic version could provide a concept of real social justice and a corporativist solution for society that would not fall into state socialism. "State socialism is the dream of the disillusioned. . . . Under fascism, the state occupies the function of a high controller of the political and economic process of the nation without directly intervening."[91] But what is the function of the state in the corporativist system?[92] The answer is very clear: social and economic activity, which are the natural activity of a society, must be regulated by the corporativist organization based on a spirit of Christian solidarity. The state should simply aid the traditional corporations (or guilds), "promote their foundation, favor their functioning, and sanction their statutes and convictions."[93] This Catholic interpretation of corporativism seemed to find a middle way for the state, as regulator of social activity without directly intervening in it.

Gino Arias, a fascist economist who lectured in Buenos Aires in 1934, stated that a distinction had to be made between the "social function of property which is deduced from its moral end," as it is in Thomist philosophy, and the "monist identification of the individual with the state which denies the right of private property," as happens under communism.[94] That distinction would respond to the main concern of Argentine Catholics, namely, the preservation of the traditionalist framework of society, which the modernization process threatened to destroy. This idea, which echoed trends in Vatican thinking since *Rerum Novarum*, became a central component of an integral concept of nationalism. "Against . . . the freedom proclaimed by liberalism, [the corporation] invoked the right of association for the worker, in order to defend him from capitalist exploitation. Against the socialist principle of struggle between capital and labor, it demands the collaboration of one with the other, to the benefit of the working class itself."[95] However, for most nationalist Catholics, especially those who developed a more pragmatic and political posture, the corporativist conception served as the political basis for an alternative model of national modernization, and entailed endorsing modernizing industrialization of some kind. Hence, a new ideology of technological modernization had to be placed above the idea of the restoration of the old antiliberal order. In contrast to Julio Meinvielle, who held that in an "ordered economic regime, agrarian production should have a primacy over the industrial production,"[96] Hector Bernardo, a coeditor of the weekly Catholic paper *Baluarte* (and an admirer of La Tour du Pin's traditional corporativism), had something else in mind. He believed that the attempt to "conform to a medieval corporativist phenomenon is to ignore the real conditions . . . of the modern capitalist world."[97] In other words, there is no way to escape from modernity. In the modern world, the social question must be resolved under Catholic inspiration, but the modern instrument for doing so is a national version of fascism. Although the Catholics feared that "inasmuch as nationalism is essentially a political reaction, it would give to the political (field) a significance that is not proper to it,"[98] the final path of nationalism was to be political. Thus, nationalism as a mobilizing political movement was not necessarily fascism, but at that specific time it could be hardly separated from its fascist connotations. Franceschi founded

Renovación, a group whose purpose was to elaborate a timid non-fascist "third way." When it had to respond to World War II, Renovación rejected the national-integralist type of "pro-Axis" neutrality, but it also rejected the "semicolonial" status assigned to Argentina by the United States with its Pan-Americanism. There was no easy communion between fascism and Catholic nationalism. Meinvielle, Castellani, Franceschi, and other integral nationalists held that under the current crisis of civilization, no political space was left for other political alternatives. In other words, the nationalist "third way" at that special time was associated with national socialism in its different configurations. The ideological track opened by Franceschi was followed by Ernesto Palacio, the Irazusta brothers, Bruno Jacovella, and others. It was a formula that differed from both conservative authoritarianism and social democracy. In contrast to social democracy, it supported a non-egalitarian type of social justice. In contrast to pure anti-mobilizationary authoritarianism, it promoted the fascist way based on popular mobilization under authoritarian control.

CHAPTER 5

The Integralist Right and the Populist Left

Anti-Imperialism, Productionism, and Social Justice

The Productionist Right

The Catholic sectors of the Argentine nationalist right remained suspicious of fascist modernization, but the more modernizing sectors believed that fascism established the framework for a new theory of political mobilization under authoritarian control. To the latter, the domestic ideas of cultural and economic anti-imperialism were akin to the fascist critique of plutocratic imperialism. Furthermore, under fascist inspiration they conceived of an alternative type of productivist national modernization.

Argentine right-wing nationalists were especially conscious of Argentina's status as a wealthy country with a large immigrant population that, nevertheless, could not become an economically and culturally independent country—a "regional power," Lugones called it. This constituted a real and concrete problem for those Argentine nationalists who also understood that fascism presented a concept of imperialism radically different from that of the liberal "plutocratic" countries. Mussolini stated that "in the doctrine of Fascism, Empire is not only a territorial, military, or mercantile expression, but also spiritual or moral."[1] This conception of "cultural imperialism" did not differ from José Antonio Primo de Rivera's idea of Spanish cultural empire based on Spain's cultural and political hegemony in the Americas. The new spiritual hegemony presented an intellectual framework to counter the prevalence of the materialist, utilitarian values that formed the philosophical basis for the "liberal" economic imperialism of the plutocratic powers. In the view of the Argentine nationalists, the "plutocratic" state powers and the plutocratic bourgeoisie shared common cultural and economic interests. The Italian proletariat nation and the dependent nations of Latin America suffered from the consequences of a national oligarchy, a weak industrial bourgeoisie, and dependency on foreign capital.

In the late 1930s the deepening international crisis served as a framework for this attempt to bring together the common interests of dependent nations struggling against financial capitalism and proletarian nations struggling against imperialist competition. A strong proponent of this view was Enrique Osés, director of the newspaper *Crisol* and one of the most extreme nationalist intellectuals. Osés supported the "imperialism of poor nations" as well as Argentine anti-imperialism directed against the Western democratic powers. He fervently believed that Argentina should be part of the fascist revolutionary international, given the logical international alignments of the new era. The "society of nations is revealed . . . as an instrument at the service of capitalism and other hidden international forces, in order to maintain the supremacy of certain imperialist [powers]"; thus it opposes the fascist alliance to which both proletarian nations like Italy and dependent nations like Latin American countries should belong. Therefore, in order to confront both the Wilsonian concept of self-determination and the Communist International, it was "necessary and urgent to perfect . . . a stable organization of a huge worldwide and European alliance open to all national corporativist movements of different countries."[2] Osés represented the current in Argentine nationalism that believed that, in addition to ideological inspiration, rich but dependent nations shared a common struggle with nations such as Italy, Germany, and Japan, which "lacked the most elementary basis for living,"[3] namely, honor and economic viability. For him and for many other right-wing nationalists, Germany, Japan, and Italy owed their political crises, inflation, and social unrest to the wealthy nations they eventually fought against, who had deprived them of the basis for proud and independent development.

Not all nationalists accepted the validity of direct political collaboration with fascism. Moreover, since anti-imperialism was supposed to be a distinguishing feature of Argentine nationalism, some Argentine nationalists underscored the particularities of the Argentine situation. Their focus was on those in Argentina who directly contributed to the country's growing economic and political dependency. The nationalists identified liberalism as a political system that was most useful for the development of shared interests of the national oligarchy and foreign capital. The nationalists thus feared that "our oligarchy's internationalism might make us the victim of universal capitalism."[4] For them it was clear that the plutocratic countries and the unproductive, non-nationalistic oligarchy shared responsibility for the dependency and slavery of "new countries" like Argentina. Neither developing countries nor dependent ones could afford to adopt a liberal democracy, since the political apparatus of liberalism led to "indebtedness, taxation, subjugation, and economic enslavement."[5]

Although determined to limit their criticism to local problems, the nationalists attacked directly the philosophical foundations of those theories that lauded the virtues of "commercialism and ideological progress."[6] The Irazusta brothers were the first Argentine nationalists to invoke the concept of foreign "plutocracy" in a vein similar to that of fascism. Plutocracy "dominates the economy and national finances, governs . . . through liberalism and democracy. . . . The plutocracy owns the railways, the freezers, part of the banks, the grain concerns, and the commercial press. . . . The plutocracy is foreign as is the capital of all those institutions."[7] This concept of plutocracy appeared in the introduction to a book by Julio and Rodolfo Irazusta, *La Argentina y el imperialismo británico: Los eslabones de una cadena, 1806–1833*, which became a key source for nationalists of both the right and the left.

As I have already noted, historical revisionism was reflected in criticism of both the national oligarchy and British imperialism. In their book the Irazustas also articulated a theoretical distinction between liberalism and democracy and stressed the economic consequences of that distinction. As they explained, in the early years of its power the oligarchy repeatedly sought to suppress every "popular uprising." More importantly, this cultural and political approach, according to the Irazustas, would foster dependency and underdevelopment, because the liberal political system was based on agricultural production, thus favoring the oligarchy and its British partners. "The pastoral economy makes us dependent on Great Britain. . . . Great Britain reserves its right to follow its laissez faire imperial policies, while we do not reserve any corresponding right to resist with protectionism or economic nationalism."[8] In the words of Ramón Doll, this represents "subordination of the sovereignty and national dignity [of the country] to the interests of the factory."[9]

Benjamin Villafañe, a devoted conservative and a deputy and senator from the province of Jujuy, added his voice to that of the Irazustas, Palacio, and Ramón Doll by asking, "Wasn't [the reason for the] . . . May revolution [war of independence] to save us from the Spanish monopolistic tyranny to which we were subject?"[10] He answered, "Emancipation from Spain gave rise to another form of modern slavery. We were freed from the Seville contract house only to fall into the hands of the speculators at the London and New York stock exchanges."[11] These symbols of economic liberalism represented a modern and sophisticated form of slavery.

Even before the appearance of the Irazustas' book, anti-imperialist criticism had been expressed in the ideological declarations of principles by nationalist paramilitary leagues like the Liga Republicana, Guardia Argentina, Legión Cívica, and Alianza Nacionalista. Roberto de Laferrère of the Liga Republicana, for example, said in his ideological manifesto of May 1933 that foreign capital was responsible for "widespread and growing misery."[12] In fact, foreign capital was directly related to social injustice, which gave rise to social hatred and communist subversion. According to Laferrère, this was the social basis for the decadence that could not be halted under the system of political parties. The ideological radicalization of the Liga Republicana was reflected not only in the theoretical importance given to the concept of revolutionary "direct action," but particularly in its economic and social positions of categorical rejection of foreign capitalism. The same revolutionary spirit could be seen in the Guardia Argentina. Its political program, as formulated by Lugones, bore witness to the same ideological and economic trends. For Argentina, liberalism symbolized a way of life based on an import-dependent economy. "We have nothing left [for ourselves] but our existence, and that is the existence of a colony under economic liberalism."[13]

One thing clear to all right-wing nationalists was that the anti-imperialist struggle by itself was not enough—it had to be accompanied by a production-oriented ideology, an ideology of industrialization that would transform the economic structures of the nation. This new line of thinking raised several questions. The most obvious was how to combine the quest for autarkic industrialization with the fact that Argentina was an agro-export nation. How would a nationalist industrialization strategy be distinguished from a "non-nationalist" or "liberal" import-substitution approach?

The question of industrialization was not the concern of the nationalists alone. It preoccupied some of the most important political and cultural figures of the liberal elites at the beginning of the century. Political leaders such as Carlos Pellegrini, Roque Sáenz Peña, Victoriano de la Plaza, and Luis Duhau, the president of the Rural Society Argentina between 1926 and 1928, and industrialists such as Luis Colombo were the most radical proponents of industrial modernization. All these individuals were economic liberals and political conservatives. They promoted industrialization within the framework of a liberal constitutional state. Moreover, the idea of import-substituting industrialization did not appear particularly undesirable to some of the most important representatives of the interests of the oligarchy, including Federico Pinedo, one of the leaders of the Independent Socialists, and many cattlemen in the 1920s and 1930s. Even Duhau, one of the political figures most directly involved in the Roca-Runciman Pact, announced his conversion to protectionism.[14]

Furthermore, during World War I, the Sociedad Rural and other leading Argentine proponents of free trade discovered that certain kinds of import-substitution very much suited their own interests. They supported the industrialization of what they considered "natural industries," which processed local agricultural raw materials and produced shoes, leather goods, and woolen textiles, but they saw no need to industrialize the "capital goods" sectors, which required further investments.

Most right-wing nationalists, however, considered the import substitution promoted by the liberal oligarchy as subservient or dependent on the dominant economic powers. In contrast to the industrialist approach advocated by the conservative elites, the nationalists advocated an approach to industrialization that entailed changing the liberal democratic state to an authoritarian one.

The consequences of dependent industrialization became clear during the second half of the 1930s, when economic hegemony passed from Great Britain to the United States. Beginning in 1938, the newspaper *Crisol*, edited by Osés, focused its attacks on U.S. geopolitical interests in the region, most notably on American economic priorities, which were at odds with Argentine interests. Brazil, which had been a traditional consumer of Argentine wheat, now switched to American products. According to Osés, the United States' policy was not only to penetrate the region but also to create an "economic and moral subjugation of these American nations."[15] Whereas the Irazustas and Ernesto Palacio directed their anti-imperialist broadsides at British economic interests and the agro-export bias of the national oligarchy, Osés considered U.S. policy to be much more dangerous and aggressive—particularly when the liberal Justo government began to promote a new stage of "import-substitution" industrialization. "Uneven" industrialization took place as the result of the acquisition of obsolete American equipment and technology: "The United States . . . sells old planes to our army . . . providing jobs . . . and rare scholarships to our ruling class pseudo-intellectuals."[16] In other words, while the agrarian national economy—guided by the liberal oligarchy—had created the framework for dependence on Great Britain, the resulting industrialization was now producing economic and psychological dependence on the United States. An industrialization process under conditions of dependence was impossible. Many were convinced that anti-imperialism and national sovereignty were preconditions for industrial modernization and for the social and political reorganization of the country. This argument was set forth by some of the most prominent advocates of integral nationalism, including the editor of the newspaper *Nuevo Orden* and *La Voz del Plata* (starting in 1940). Most of the Argentine nationalist groups—such as Guardia Argentina, led by Lugones, Liga Republicana, led by Laferrère, the Acción Nationalista, and the Legión Cívica—also held that economic sovereignty was a precondition for national emancipation.

No Argentine intellectual presented the links between fascist modernism and Argentine "need" to become a modern industrial regional power as a precondition for regaining true sovereignty better than Leopoldo Lugones. His view was complemented by that of Alejandro Bunge, who, although not a fascist, also understood that only an authoritarian rule could provide the basis for autarkic industrialization. Indeed, Bunge and Lugones were the most important theoreticians of the blend between industrialization and authoritarian regimes, and their ideas had a direct appeal to army officers.

These two contrasting figures, Lugones and Bunge, offered proposals for industrial modernization that were different but no means contradictory. Their different ideological paths notwithstanding, they both believed that industrialization was a prerequisite for economic independence in Argentina. The writings of both were read by the military establishment, and both influenced the developmental and industrialist attitudes of the army. While Lugones felt that the military served a moral, spiritual function, representing the heroic myth of the homeland, Bunge, a dyed-in-the-wool technocrat, regarded the army as merely an auxiliary body supporting the work of the political technocrats. Both men rejected the populist social-welfare measures promoted by Yrigoyen and his followers.

Alejandro Bunge, a civil engineer who had received his degree in Germany in 1903, became a leading economic thinker in Argentina after 1914. From 1919 to 1943, no one was more closely identified with both conservative politics and economic renewal than Bunge. Although he held a variety of positions—university professor, director-general of statistics, head of the Argentine national census, minister of finance and public works for the province of Santa Fe—he was particularly renowned as the editor of *Revista de Económica Argentina*, founded in 1918.[17] Bunge and his followers saw signs of stagnation throughout the Argentine economy, which, they said, was devoted to raising cattle and crops on the pampas.

According to Bunge, Argentina could recapture the impetus of its pre-1914 economic growth only by diversifying its agricultural production and deliberately promoting the growth of industry.[18]

Bunge did not expect anything from the Radicals, especially Yrigoyen. Populism belonged to the realm of petty politics, which was antithetical to rational, technically based management. Bunge believed that there were good politicians in Argentina, but that "being bound by democratic tactics and bureaucratic procedures undermined 'real' decision making."[19] An authoritarian solution was therefore quite acceptable to him. Comparing Argentina with France, he said that Argentina had "not yet reached the stage of political demagogy or materialism and of dangerous weakness of life, as heroic France [did] between 1934–1938." This catastrophic state of affairs was denounced by Marshall Petain. His *"Revolution Nationale"* with the help of the Nazis supposedly corrected those sins.[20]

Opposing the Popular Front's reformism and political demagoguery, Bunge advocated "invigorating" (*vigorizar*) the nation. Only an organized society full of vitality could "drastically obliterate everything that provokes hatred and class struggle . . . [and] tends to divide society, [and] . . . restore our social and political precepts, [which are] the . . . concepts of discipline, hierarchy, and individual duty."[21]

Bunge's conclusions did not differ from those of Lugones. Both were convinced that the liberal democratic political system had to be eliminated so that Argentina could recover real economic independence. Lugones shared Bunge's concern for the country's low demographic profile and his belief that although Argentina was an agricultural country, this fact should not hamper the urgent process of modern industrialization. Neither Bunge nor Lugones advocated the destruction of the old agrarian-based economic order. According to Lugones, however, the old orientation could be combined with a far-reaching process of capital-goods industrialization. He considered increased production to be the most important factor for the nation's survival, and he pointed to the links between Friedrich List's theory of the "national system of economy" and Heinrich von Treitschke's popularization of Hegel's theory of the nation-state, whose essence is power. Therefore he believed that a liberal regime was incompatible with the promotion of autarkic policies, especially for countries like Argentina. Lugones believed that an authoritarian government could aid the industries that produced wealth and that could be accommodated after the establishment of an internal market. Argentina should rely on policies promoting production "even if at the beginning our products will be more expensive than those coming from abroad."[22] Lugones's books *La grande Argentina* (1930), *La patria fuerte*

(1930), *Política revolucionaria* (1931), and *El estado equitativo* (1932) were seminal works for nationalist theories on how to increase Argentine production. Along with the Irazustas' *La Argentina y el imperialismo británico*, these were the key works uniting the concepts of national strength and economic independence.

Lugones's productivist ideas encompassed both a strategy for long-range production and a strategy of import-substitution conceived to create consumer industries.[23] At first glance, policies of import-substitution and the "deepening" of industrial production are contradictory, because the former process actively inhibits the investments needed for the latter. Yet Lugones believed that the country must produce capital goods in order to survive in an imperialist world. He anticipated the use of the chemical industry for national independence: "Modern war had made chemicals crucial to national defense."[24] If Argentina was to be prepared for this era of conflict, it had to produce cheaper and better-quality exports. "Our production is expensive and deficient because it depends on imported raw materials."[25] If Argentina produced its own raw materials, the basic contradiction between emphasis on increased production and developing the internal market could be resolved.

The production approach required the financial "backing of the necessary industries for our economic autonomy, particularly those needed for national defense."[26] Since there was no aggressive national bourgeoisie in Argentina, the corporate state, headed by the army, would have to implement the process of economic modernization. Lugones also admired other types of industrial modernization, which suited other societies. The industrial vitality of the United States and its economic model were based, as Lugones understood them, on a model of integral productionism. Lugones did not consider the United States as a symbol of doctrinaire liberalism, but rather as a pragmatic symbol of national strength and conservatism. "The United States, a conservative, capitalist, nationalistic, and perhaps bellicose country, [is based] on hardworking people, in whom the only thing deep-seated is ownership of land."[27] The spirit of private property was based on the spiritual strength of the nation. This was not the materialist individualism of the bourgeoisie, but a production-oriented conception based on the needs of the nation. Lugones was accordingly led to think that the fascist model was suited to the Argentine Hispanic and Latin spirit. He shared the belief of Giuseppe Bottai, the secretary of the Italian Fascist party, that "in our regime the economic order identifies itself with public order."[28] He also understood that such a norm could be promoted only by an authoritarian state. The Italian Fascist concept of power and the path of the United States to military and economic strength were based on the same pragmatism: "Power is at times a product of the people, at times a product of a qualified minority, sometimes of a consensual institution. For the essential thing is not the prosperity of an ideology or a political system, but to save the nation."[29]

Italian and other proponents of fascism around the world undoubtedly agreed with this proposition. Fascism did not deny the social and productive value of private property, as long as it was useful to the nation and the state.[30] The reality of the state depended on its capacity for survival, which in turn required a strong, disciplined nation.

This fusion of industrialization and authoritarianism was promoted in several lectures given by high-ranking army officers in the Círculo Militar even prior to the 1930 revolution led by Uriburu.[31] However, industrialization received a real impulse only after the world financial crises of 1929 and 1932, when the problem of economic independence changed from an abstract ideological issue to an immediate preoccupation of the Argentine army, due to the Chaco War on the Argentine border and military and political developments in Europe. The nationalist-industrialist military coalition that began to emerge in the late 1920s became a reality in the 1930s.

The military believed that Latin America had not "been contaminated by the virus that had turned the whole of humanity mad but . . . it was a refuge for humanity because of its fruitful lands and unknown wealth," and that if Latin American nations were united and achieved a certain economic and industrial self-sufficiency autarchy, they would be able to assert their convictions. The day would come when "Latin American thought [would] be taken into account."[32] Captain Ricardo Marambio, an army engineer, declared that Argentina could and must become a regional power. Such was the spirit of the discussions held within the Círculo Militar, which became more radical as the degree of dependence on England intensified. This line of thinking was also supported by Alejandro Bunge's conservative followers. His conclusions were similar to those reached by the Unión Industrial Argentina in 1933, which advocated protecting national industry and praised the political economy of Fascist Italy.[33]

Gustavo Martínez Zuviría, in the preface to a book by Lieutenant Juan Lucio Cernadas, *Estrategia nacional y política de estado* (1938), summed up a common line of thought in the late 1920s. Condemning the bourgeois concept of pacifism, Zuviría embraced Cernadas's ideas, which formed the basis of the ideological attempt to transform Argentina into a regional power. Politics based only on justice, he wrote, "without the necessary strength to support it, is worthless, and the principles that comprise its national doctrine will remain an . . . aspiration."[34]

In 1931, after the establishment of the Justo government, a manifesto appeared entitled "Acción Republicana," signed by Leopoldo Lugones, the Irazusta brothers, Ernesto Palacio, César Pico, Lisandro Galindez, and others. It proposed an alternative nationalist political and economic plan. While the institutions of the "bourgeois order," based on models of "old, overpopulated countries,"[35] helped to produce the professional politicians and the communist reformers, the new order would be production-oriented and corporativist, requiring the participation of the entire nation. A plan for the development and protection of industries was proposed specifically for the chemicals industry. This was to be accompanied by the reorganization of labor unions, and by the "implementation of military exercises in public schools . . . under the direction of army officers."[36]

The same spirit was expressed by Guardia Argentina, the last attempt by Lugones to create a unified nationalist movement. It supported an aggressive policy of economic expansion through the protection of national industry.[37] A new effort to promote a production program inspired by these principles was made by the Liga Republicana. It tried to organize a "Congress of National Recovery" with the participation of all the nationalist groups, just prior to the nationalist military revolution of 1943. Its program called for public services to be gradually nationalized and for industries to be supported with national capital.[38] The aim was to transform Argentina into a regional industrial power.

One of the most important of the theoretical tensions that were not resolved until Perón took power was how to combine the drive toward production, which demands sacrifices from people, and populism, which emphasizes redistribution. One right-wing integral nationalist criticism was that Yrigoyen's policies were focused on distribution rather than production. The evolution of the latter to populism was based, however, on the conviction that under a corporativist regime a country like Argentina could combine autarkic industrialization, based on a mystique of production, with a "nationalist" social justice, based on policies of redistribution. It may be asked whether there were any substantial differences between nationalism and fascism in this area, or whether the nationalist emphasis on social justice was akin to fascist efforts toward national integration. Social justice in this context was based on the idea that workers should be integrated into the nation rather than on the idea of equalitarian right. Fascism rejected democratic egalitarianism but promoted national solidarity under a hierarchical state.

There were substantial differences between Argentina and Italy that allowed a country such as Argentina to combine a productionist ideology with social justice. Italian fascism accorded the highest priority to the political destiny of the nation and the *Volk;* Argentina could add to this formula a strong element of social justice. The nationalists' assumption was that a country like Argentina could produce an economic "surplus" sufficient for economic distribution and thus could confer on the working class social rights as an integral part of the nation.

This position, distinct from the social democratic tendency toward egalitarianism, was clearly manifested in Lugones and the rest of the nationalists, despite the fact that they did not agree on the weight that social justice should have in the productionist formula. Lugones himself leaned toward the classical formula of fascism. Instead of a democratic state, Lugones called for an authoritarian state based on a concept of equity consistent with hierarchy, rather than on egalitarianism. The state was "an entity that represents production and labor organized . . . into responsible guilds." Only when "there [was] nothing in the state higher than the state [would] the government impose equity."[39]

For Lugones, as for fascism, there was a strong connection between growth and welfare. In fascism, however, that growth was associated with different objectives, such as the exaltation of the nation or the ability to pursue an independent policy even to the extent of waging war. Thus, the two central programmatic themes of fascism were the development of the nation's maximum productive capacities and the collaboration of all productive classes. The proponents of fascism agreed with Wilfredo Pareto's argument, put forth long before World War I, that the problems faced by most nations of the world had to do with production rather than distribution.[40]

Most of the other Argentine nationalists, however, stressed national integration and social justice rather than industrialization alone. In fact, because of the easy growth of the Argentine economy during the first decades of the century, it seemed that production-oriented policies involving industrialization and control of labor could be easily meshed with redistribution. In other words, the populist thrust toward redistribution and social justice went along with the emphasis on production. This was a principle endorsed by "those who, like ourselves, start from a social view of the nation and of a fair and equitable society."[41] The Argentine nationalists firmly believed that eliminating the liberal democratic political regime would bring

a renewal of values and systems led by the government, aimed at implementing the social principles of nationalism, nullifying Marxist class struggle, destroying the predominance of the conservative class, and seeking a harmonious arrangement between capital and labor that would represent true social justice for the working class.[42]

The supreme aspiration of right-wing nationalism was, in fact, social justice based on a nonegalitarian concept of equity. The Argentine nationalists sought both material and psychological rewards for workers. They were convinced that fascists were sensitive to social conditions,[43] and the purpose of their pro-labor approach was to achieve social harmony and class collaboration in the framework of a nationalist revolutionary program. In an article entitled "Liberal Democracy, Individual, and Society: Three Serious Questions," published in *Criterio*, Falco Testena, editor of the Argentine paper *Giornale d'Italia*, responded to Gustavo Franceschi's widely circulated claims that only a Christian regime could contribute to social pacification. Although Testena did not reject this claim, he raised the political issue that Catholic nationalists in Argentina were forced to confront: a regime based on Christian principles could not survive "this selfish humanity, so radically anti-Christian."[44] For the problems of our times, he said, "there can be no solution other than the socialist one."[45] The socialism he had in mind, however, was not the socialism embraced by the Socialist party organ, *La Vanguardia*, "which if it had been socialist instead of democratic . . . would have considered the indisputable fact of the fascist economy."[46] Testena claimed that the new socialism was more closely related to nationalism and the spiritual message of Catholicism than to the rationalist materialism of Karl Marx. He undoubtedly felt that the ideological synthesis of nationalism and socialism was the answer to the egoism of bourgeois society.

During the world financial crisis of 1929, the importance of a strong state to manage the economic and social process was obvious. The "plannist" ideology (enthusiasm for government planning), essentially socialist in origin, rejected Marxism in favor of a modernized, national, authoritarian socialism, getting rid of liberal democracy for the sake of social justice, but especially for the sake of efficiency and technical economic progress.[47] Only a nationalist state could protect the worker against the pressures exerted by foreign interests and the national oligarchy.

The Argentine nationalists were persuaded that an industrialist policy could be implemented only if the rights of the workers were protected under a strong, corporativist system. The corporativist state could therefore be implemented only when the nationalist ideal of strength and sacrifice for the homeland included all social classes. For example the nationalists opposed Yrigoyen's populist policies on political and economic grounds,[48] but they were not satisfied with his social policies, either. The reformist policies that introduced the eight-hour work day and the minimum-wage system undermined production, according to Julio Irazusta. "In a country like ours with a labor shortage, putting limits on the work day is not useful for production . . . [because] an underdeveloped country needs far more than simple reformism."[49]

This anti-reformist attitude, which reflected the nationalists' hostility toward Yrigoyenism, changed radically during the 1930s, although it did not soften their opposition to reformist populism. If Yrigoyenist populism were modernized, they argued, it would give rise to a new concept of inclusive corporativism that would complement the emphasis placed on production by Lugones.

"In our country—perhaps more than in any other country in the world—the struggle for the homeland and the struggle for social justice are inseparable. The social drama is intertwined with the national drama."[50] In other words, national liberation meant social liberation. Since the joint interests of the unproductive local bourgeoisie and foreign capital were seen as the cause of underdevelopment and social injustice, the key to national productivity and social justice was national emancipation. Moreover, since the Argentina of the 1930s was characterized by a significant but moderate upsurge of labor activity that in no way resembled the major wave of general strikes in Italy at the end of World War I, the local nationalist fascist movement could concentrate on problems of national emancipation.[51] That emancipation was seen as linked to a comprehensive liberation from the cultural and political patterns of the old rationalist ideologies. Ernesto Palacio wrote,

> We live in a revolutionary era. But this is not a struggle between the notion of an authoritarian government and the notion of the defense of certain individual liberties . . . but rather between a concept of life based on individual profit and another based on social justice. Not between democracy and dictatorship, but between a hypocritical plutocracy . . . that uses the mask of liberty to oppress the people, and the people themselves, who congregate around their caudillos in order to be emancipated from their oppressors and to install a regime of equitable redistribution of the common wealth. A socialist regime . . . but free from . . . Marxist materialism."[52]

The nationalist press gave voice to the new concern for social justice and the needs of the people displayed by Argentine nationalists. They agreed that only a corporativist organization of society could satisfy the people's demands. In other words, a syndicalist, corporativist state represented true democracy, by means of which the negative aspects of capitalism and industrialization could be offset. "We are not enemies of the workers. . . . Solutions to the workers' problems have not yet been given by socialism"—and, in the nationalist view, could not be given by socialism in the future, either. The only path was "classic syndicalism, that can mediate between workers and employers, [and] that would certainly be developed into the corporativist state that binds and harmonizes."[53]

To the nationalists, it was clearly necessary to transform the regimental basis of the liberal democratic state into an authoritarian state which could preserve harmony and social justice. "The unjust capitalist regime must be transformed," proclaimed *Combate*, the publication of the Legión Cívica. "Most of the political adversaries of nationalism consider it a conservative movement . . . whose aspiration is to ensure the establishment of a social class, while abandoning the people who produce." Nevertheless, the nationalist movement did favor social improvements, "since the capitalist system operating in [this] country and in most of the world's nations is . . . unjust and inhuman."[54]

This moral denunciation of capitalism gave rise to a conclusion unthinkable in the early years of the decade: "the proletariat of the present era has no homeland. How can they talk of a homeland, men who have had no bread in their motherland?"[55] The target of this criticism was the liberal democratic state, whose individualistic attitude was indifferent to the life of the worker and to any social justice. "Within the present liberal democratic regime, under the presidencies of Yrigoyen and General Justo . . . this capital problem [of the workers] . . . is of no interest to the pseudo-representatives of the people." The reason was that in structural terms, democracy did not provide for state intervention in the private market and industrial enterprises to bring about a redistribution of wealth. Nationalism based on an organic conception of society, on the other hand, favored the worker, since its basic vision was collectivist and not individualist, and because "equity and social justice, without unjust concessions which provoke warranted reactions from the masses,"[56] were necessary for the development of a strong nation.

Thus, in the liberal democratic state, "which is a bourgeois creation for the defense of privileges, the right to strike is justified."[57] This was by no means an endorsement of the values of free society in the liberal state, but rather an attempt to make the point that in the national state the economic and social aspects of society played a central role, while in the liberal state they were relegated to the sidelines.

Corporativism and the Tension between
Stimulating Production and Social Justice

Most of the ideas on political corporativism and social justice were expressed in the Legion Cívica, the Liga Republicana, and other groups like the Alianza de la Juventud Nacionalista, which appeared in 1935. They portrayed the message of national syndicalism, which was the basis of fascism. Argentine nationalism was an "essentially economic movement" that sought "to set up in the country a new system of government reflecting a true democracy that [would] improve the people's condition."[58] It was to be a democracy of the working people. If nationalism was accused of "attempting to establish a class government," the retort was expressed in the nationalist newspaper *Combate:* "we say to them: yes, a government... of the class that works."[59] This was the class of producers, which differed from the Marxist concept of the proletarian class.

Capital and labor could not oppose each other in Argentina. Therefore *Bandera Argentina* supported the protest by business organizations against the reform of law 11,729, "the destructive, anti-social and antinational law that gives all rights to the employees ... and denies them to the employers."[60] The nationalists regarded a democratic social justice, rooted in Marxism, as flawed, but a nationalist social justice—based on "equity" rather than equality, and one that defended not only the worker but also useful, productive capital—was appropriate for a modern industrialized world. This was a social justice as promoted by the corporativist organization of nationalism, a social justice that could be meted out not by politicians but by a nationalist movement that transcended political parties.

In 1931 and 1936 two interesting experiments in corporativist organization in the provinces of Córdoba and Buenos Aires illustrated how the nationalists would try to resolve the social question. In 1931, Carlos Ibarguren was sent by the provisional president of the republic, Félix de Uriburu, to the province of Córdoba to implement the corporativist ideas of the military revolution at the provincial level.

With his two sons, Carlos (Jr.) and Federico, as assistants, and accompanied by a group of young activists from the Liga Republicana, Ibarguren went to Córdoba, where the nationalists were very active. After broadcasting a stirring speech to the nation from the Indarte Theatre in Córdoba, the new governor proceeded to implement political and economic reforms by means of regulations that would protect society's weakest members. A balance was achieved between different economic interests in the province. The goal of the Economic Executive Council was to carry out the ideal of "the state, with the collaboration of the representatives of the economic forces, intervening to lower the basic cost of subsistence for the average worker, and especially farmers."[61]

This focus on improving the living standards of the weak drew criticism from liberal politicians, who accused Ibarguren of being a fascist—although he could also have been accused of communism, since the old-line political establishment could not comprehend this new ideological synthesis which was neither right-wing nor left-wing.[62] An even more serious corporativist effort was carried out in the middle of the decade by the governor of Buenos Aires, Manuel Fresco. Fresco, a highly controversial figure among Argentine nationalists, had been a conservative deputy in the province of Buenos Aires since 1919. He was a member of the national congress between 1932 and 1934 and became governor of Buenos Aires in 1936, following fraudulent elections in 1935. Although he advocated British interests in Argentina, he was also a fervent admirer of fascism. His visit to Italy in February 1935, when he was president of the Chamber of Deputies in congress, convinced him of the effectiveness of the Italian corporativist system, and in his own government in the province of Buenos Aires, he headed an experimental administration based on the socioeconomic corporativist example of Salazar's "Estado Novo" in Portugal.[63] Using the slogan "God, Fatherland, and Home," he commissioned public works in the province on an unprecedented scale, thereby solving the unemployment problem for the region. At the same time, he implemented reactionary measures in education and politics, instituting religious education in the schools and banning the Communist Party. These steps gained him some admiration among the nationalists, although he was considered a controversial personality whose morality was questionable given his ties with foreign interests.[64]

Fresco unleashed harsh repression against the radical left, even though he considered it to be politically impotent. In the chamber of deputies, Fresco defined the Socialist Party as "a conglomerate of the bourgeoisie,"[65] limited to parliamentary politics. Fresco viewed parliamentary procedures as obsolete, and he defended what he called "patriotic fraud" and "patriotic violence" if they led to the nationalist social reforms that were needed. He wanted to prove that while communists and socialists of the 1930s concentrated on the formation of a democratic popular front against fascism, the nationalist movement's attention was focused on solving the social problem within the framework of the nationalist corporativist state. Even after he was removed from office by President Ortiz, Fresco was still considered an important political figure, whose call for a "civilian dictatorship" alarmed the political establishment.[66] He remained a unique figure among the nationalists, despite criticisms that he was the promoter of a different "populist" style, exemplified by his social reforms. This new style was recorded minutely by the investigative officers of the federal police, who continued to track his political activity even after he left office. The people who attended Fresco's political meetings in 1941, the year he founded the Unión Nacionalista Argentina, were mainly from the poorer classes.[67]

The social character of Fresco's corporatist state was expressed in the conviction that the working class must have a system of representation in which unions would be granted recognition by the state and would be required to submit their demands to state-run compulsory arbitration, which would have a pro-worker orientation. These norms were codified in the Organic Labor Act of 1937. In presenting the bill to the provincial senate, Roberto J. Noble, a provincial government minister, argued that the economic and social policies of fascism and socialism were essentially similar. He insisted—on Fresco's behalf—that the Socialists had betrayed their own doctrine by converting to parliamentarism. Fascism instead promoted "individual freedom within order, collective freedom based on discipline and hierarchy."[68] Yet because he was seen as practicing "patriotic fraud," Fresco was controversial. His ideology failed to inspire confidence among those nationalists who did not want to preserve conservative rule, and who defined him as a displaced conservative.[69] However, Fresco's corporativist efforts at the provincial level, the introduction of religious education at schools, and the proscription of the Communist Party gained the support of several nationalist circles, especially those linked to the newspaper *Bandera Argentina*. The key point is that the political attempts by these groups to establish an authoritarian agenda that was very regressive in terms of liberal rights and social egalitarianism, yet modernizing in terms of popular mobilization, social justice, and anti-imperialism, were to give right-wing nationalism its new face. No single group or intellectual figure combined the theme of anti-imperialist social justice with a stress on production—particularly the latter, which was the special emphasis of Lugones and the movements inspired by him. Some of them emphasized Catholic values and others tilted toward modern populism. Some were fascist-oriented while others, like FORJA, focused on the question of anti-imperialism. Overall, however, the prevailing nationalist line toward the end of the decade was that Argentina's national sovereignty could be rescued only when economic liberalism would be replaced by a corporativist society defining the roles of the active productive forces of the country. Political liberalism as understood by Argentine conservatives was rejected because it was based on political fraud, and liberal ideology in general was also cast aside because, as analyzed in this chapter, nationalists of all tendencies agreed that liberalism was an imperialist tool. They were thus in agreement that Argentina needed a national revolution, a revolution that would restore authority, reinvigorate the nation's productive capacity, and provide social justice.

The Anti-Imperialist Populist Left

The other sector of the nationalist anti-imperialist front in Argentina was represented by the "intransigent" wing of the Radical Party, most notably FORJA (Fuerza de Orientación Radical de la Juventud Argentina), a group of young rebels who broke away from the Radical Party in 1934. These young heirs of Yrigoyen's Radical Party made a distinction between popular democracy and liberalism. For FORJA, a liberal constitution and a parliamentary system enabled the oligarchy to entrench itself in power. The idea of populism, on the other hand, implied popular mobilization without liberal constraints and a concept of social justice based not on universalist ideologies but on a nationalist ideology. Their sole complaint against Yrigoyen was his reliance on the principles of a liberal constitution. For FORJA, a populist movement should not stay at the edge of liberal legality but should throw out the liberal constitution, a move that Yrigoyen did not dare to make.

Its most important members were Luis Dellepiane, the son of a former minister of war under Yrigoyen, Arturo Jauretche, a revolutionary Radical who was its leading thinker, and Jorge del Río, a left-wing socialist journalist. Raúl Scalabrini Ortiz, though not a member, was its economist. Together they raised the romantic flag of the old revolutionary tradition against the "normalization" of the liberal democratic political process within the party and in the nation itself. The FORJA group became the voice of rebellion, the voice of an authentic populist nationalism.

The event that led to the emergence of FORJA was the failed Radical revolution led by Colonel Roberto Bosch in Paso de los Libres in 1935. That attempted uprising, which had won the approval of various military officials, was not supported—for obvious reasons—by Marcelo T. de Alvear, the leader of the antipersonalist faction of the Radical Party. Alvear represented the faction that wanted to play by the rules of the existing political order and that sought to transform the Radicals from a rebellious movement into a legitimate party observing the liberal democratic rules. As related by Juan José Hernández Arregui, FORJA arose out of the meetings of old Radical veterans like Manuel Ortiz Pereyra, Gabriel del

Mazo, and Juan B. Fleitas that took place following Bosch's abortive revolt. The "Strong Radicals" issued their manifesto during the national convention of the Unión Cívica Radical which ended the period of abstention from national elections.[70] While the national oligarchy applauded the party's return to constitutional politics, FORJA raised the flag of rebellion. The end of abstention from the electoral process also signaled the end of the revolutionary and moral appeal of the Radical movement. Like Ernesto Palacio and the Irazustas, the FORJA intellectuals pointed to the ideological and economic common denominator between the national oligarchy and the interests of foreign capital. This was the central focus of their criticism and the basis for the ideological manifesto of the Strong Radicals.[71]

Initially, FORJA did not formulate an articulate, coherent ideology. Its intellectual roots traced back to the University Reform of 1918, and it was influenced by the Latin American and populist ideologies of Manuel Ugarte, Haya de la Torre, and the Peruvian party APRA (Alianza Popular Revolucionaria Americana). A major indication that FORJA's nationalism was authentic was the fact that it had no theoretical allegiance to any European ideology. Arturo Jauretche noted that its analytical method was to view the world from an Argentine perspective and not through imported ideologies. Extrapolating from the principles he had put forward in his book *Política y ejército*, Jauretche observed that FORJA's fundamental task was to liberate the Argentine people from the "weight of its mental colonialism."[72] Most of the non–Radical Party political forces in Argentina, he claimed, viewed the Argentine situation from a "foreign" perspective. In other words, they "systematically refuse[d] to present the conflict in Argentine terms."[73] Accordingly, FORJA developed an ideology based on Argentine and other Latin American sources and directed against both British and North American imperialism. FORJA fiercely attacked the Roca-Runciman Pact, exhorting its countrymen to "reconquer economic sovereignty in Argentina and in the other Latin American nations by abolishing all contracts . . . laws or court rulings, by which concessions to foreign enterprises were granted."[74] This embryonic idea was further developed at FORJA's constitutive assembly of June 29, 1935, where the movement's political priorities were initially presented. The people's struggle against the national oligarchy, which served as the agent of imperialism, was described as a campaign that must first seek to achieve popular sovereignty. FORJA's slogan was: "Through Radicalism to popular sovereignty, through popular sovereignty to national sovereignty, through national sovereignty to the emancipation of the Argentine people."[75]

In various pamphlets and publications, such as *Forjando*, *Cuadernos de FORJA*, and *Argentinidad*, young Yrigoyenists glorified the function of the people, who they believed were worthy of finding their own expression in a different kind of democracy. Such a democracy, an alternative to liberal democracy, was a precondition for national liberation, in the old tradition of the Radical Party: "There is no democracy other than the Radical one. There is no Radicalism other than FORJA. There is no nationalism other than the Radical one. There is no Radicalism other than FORJA."[76]

FORJA represented the "intransigent" nationalist side of the Radical Party in its purest form. There was to be no confusion between "the defense of people's sovereignty and the defense of the institutions" of the regime. According to Arturo Jauretche, the real government of the people was centered in the traditional federalism maintained by regional autonomies. On the basis of Yrigoyen's principles, Jauretche was convinced that the regional autonomies belonged to the people and were therefore independent of the government. This traditionalist concept of democracy was suited to the Yrigoyenist caudillo-style politics of popular mobilization.

The interesting development, however, was that both Jauretche, who was an Yrigoyenist, and Ramón Doll, a fascist-influenced intellectual, judged Yrigoyen's policies by similar standards. As noted by Jauretche, Yrigoyen's great mistake after 1916 had been his failure to resign from the liberal democratic regime.[77] Both Jauretche and Doll saw a contradiction between democracy and the legal apparatus of the regime, but not between nationalism and democracy. The confusion between these terms had been "created by the propaganda instruments of our rulers."[78] This conceptual confusion, which divided the Argentines into "nationalists" and "democrats," was the major focus of Jauretche's criticism, a criticism that was later translated into the FORJA lexicon as "the legal expression of colonialism." Argentina was being robbed by the legal mechanism of colonizing the minds of the nation. Jauretche's position was similar to that of integral nationalists like the Irazustas, and that of his associate Sccalabrini Ortiz insofar as he was indicating the direct link between political liberalism, the history of Argentine oligarchy, and economic dependency. As Scalabrini Ortiz said, "Everything is British in this region . . . [Argentine] servitude has been total since the second decade of the last century."[79]

In September 1935 a popular manifesto was published in the weekly journal *Señales* under the heading, "We are a colonial Argentina. We want to be a free Argentina." The manifesto, consisting of a preamble and eighteen sections, analyzed thoroughly the process leading to Argentina's colonialist status, putting specially emphasis on indicting the main economic institutions through which dependency on Britain was implanted. The manifesto accused the Central Bank of being an institution serving the economic interests of the British. It did not pay taxes for transactions and provided credits only to companies negotiating in favor of the British. The manifesto also indicted the activities of the new Mobilizing Institute of Bank Investments (Instituto Movilizador de Inversiones Bancarias), whose role was to compensate foreign banks whenever their scope of business failed, as well as protecting debtors of the landlord class. FORJA sought to create public awareness on these issues and others during its two periods of political activity.

During the first period, from the movement's inception in 1935 until 1940, FORJA was led by Luis Dellepiane, Arturo Jauretche, and Raúl Scalabrini Ortiz. Dellapiane was the most pragmatic, whereas Jauretche and Scalabrini were determined to develop a doctrine and make it available to the masses.[80] After 1940, certain differences emerged between those who wanted to continue working within the party and those who began to feel that the party was a heavy burden for them since the new era demanded new political symbols.

The most extremist wing of the group decided to abandon the term "Radical," since it felt that the Radical movement had lost touch with the people, primarily as a result of the policies adopted by Alvear. Accordingly, they did not think that membership in the Radical party should be required as a condition for membership in FORJA; such a requirement was actually an obstacle to the young, and also to those Argentines who were deserting the other political factions in droves. Jauretche was aware of the new economic and sociological developments in Argentina that eventually gave rise to Peronism. Although FORJA did not reach the working classes, and although it had never developed a theory of industrialization, it certainly realized that the older political parties, including the Radicals, were being abandoned by the "hidden Argentina." This "submerged Argentina" could only achieve its goals with the help of a national doctrine, which FORJA sought to provide as a central rallying point.[81]

According to Hernández Arregui, the FORJA program, based on the earlier Yrigoyenism, called for protection of the nation's natural resources. Its ideology represented the intermediate and lower levels of the university middle class and had no links to the growth of national industry, but FORJA also criticized the agrarian sectors of Argentina, asserting implicitly or explicitly that the only road to economic nationalism was through industrialization. This implied the nationalist corporativist solution developed and proposed by some of the integral nationalists. Such a solution would necessarily entail real change in the political structures to allow for the emergence of a mobilized society. Only within a new political framework could the old flag of economic nationalism, initially raised by Yrigoyen, be kept flying in the face of the challenges to economic development. The nationalist proposal to bring about state control of key industries and develop national resources had implications for reform and distribution in addition to production. The state would guide the process of economic modernization by means of a policy of nationalization and redistribution. The nationalization of resources constituted an easy, painless road to industrial development that would not disturb the old ideal of class harmony. In fact, the Radical "intransigents" favored the nationalization of resources—including state control of oil production—not only for reasons of national pride, but, more importantly, because it offered a long-term solution to the increasingly critical problem of Yrigoyen's dependent, urban, middle-class supporters. Oil exploitation depended on a policy of heavy spending, and the nationalization of this sector would open up a new range of managerial positions for the middle class in the industrial sector rather than the state bureaucracy.

The issue of nationalizing oil, transport, and electricity also became the spearhead of the Yrigoyenist Radical Party's battle against the common interests of the liberal oligarchy and the British. This fundamental struggle was reflected in particular in a problem related to resource nationalization, namely, the elimination of the transport monopoly that English companies had hitherto enjoyed in Argentina. The British, it will be recalled, introduced the railway to Argentina in order to serve the agro-export economic system. Under the Roca-Runciman Pact, Argentina was obliged to protect the interests of British companies in Argentina, especially the public transportation company known as Compañía Anglo-Argentina. Yet at the same time the British transportation service found itself competing with the new automobile industry, since buses and tracks were more efficient and provided cheaper services than the railway companies.

Alberto Gutíerrez Ruiz, a young member of FORJA who edited the *Cuadernos de FORJA*, one of the most famous propagandistic publications, claimed that the regulation and coordination of transport services approved by the chamber of deputies for the federal capital constituted blatant state intervention on behalf of private interests, and that it restricted the competitive ability of an existing transport service. Citing Scalabrini's book on the links between the creation of the railway system and British imperialism, he said that the history of the railway system illustrated the history of the country's exploitation "in the usual manner [by] financial and plutocratic imperialism." The "plutocratic" nations were blocking the "opportunity to emancipate the Argentine state, an opportunity contained in the technical progress of the motorcar, which operates with [the aid of] two specifically Argentine things, the roads and . . . oil."[82]

Indeed, in contrast to the view of observers like Hernández Arregui, who downgrades FORJA's industrialist approach, FORJA proclaimed several times its position in favor of industrialization and succeeded in highlighting the differences between what its members considered a liberal and a nationalist type of industrialization. FORJA, for example, criticized the socialist leader Dr. Nicolas Repetto for embracing industrialization from a very non-nationalist position. His ambivalent policies, they maintained, depended on his shifting loyalties. At one time he was loyal to Great Britain and did not support industrialization. Then he became loyal to the United States and shifted to support for industrialization. FORJA support for industrialization, however, was based on a nationalist perspective. It did not depend on foreign loyalties. Jauretche proposed a democratic ideal that would lead ultimately to the

> submission of the forces of finance to the collective interest. . . . Not the totalitarian state whose goal is to draw men for its own self-realization, but the state that draws men away from the tyranny of money for their own realization as human beings.[83]

In practical terms, Jauretche favored the suppression of the free press, because it represented the "liberty" of the "plutocracy" (controlled by foreign financial centers). Without developing the concept of the "proletarian nation" as opposed to the "plutocratic nation," Jauretche correctly observed that the problem of the plutocratic nation was a purely domestic issue that had to be resolved by the internal productive forces. In Argentina, however, it was "related to the existence of authentic national sovereignty," since the concept of plutocracy was directly related to international capitalism.[84]

Writing years later, Arturo Jauretche linked the problem of colonization of the mind to the antinationalist right and left. In his view, the "enlightened" intellectuals who espoused liberal democratic modernization and the left-wing intellectuals who applied the Marxist analysis of class struggle to peripheral countries were all in error:

> The struggle for emancipation and social justice cannot be won separately by different social classes. Moreover, the class confrontation was one of the most effective techniques used by British policy. . . . The

proletarian revolution as an instrument of national realization had been abandoned by the national movements long ago.[85]

Nationalism meant class union rather than class struggle. Although Jauretche did not elaborate the concept of the corporativist state as the nationalist integralists did, he did endow populist democracy with a mythical quality. However, other than loosely referring to traditional populist democracy, he did not define any formal political organization that would express the sort of democracy he had in mind. What seems clear is that ultimately FORJA was seeking a strong, mobilized, nationalist state, utterly different from political liberalism or collectivist Marxist socialism—the alternatives implied by the economic critique of dependency. Yrigoyen's constitutional corporativism had already been buried. Since FORJA sought to be an authentic nationalist movement, it did not explicitly adopt any formula based on ideological developments in Europe. The nationalist state was to be popular and corporativist.

These issues brought out the parallels between the nationalism of Ramón Doll, the Irazustas, Ernesto Palacio, and Manuel Gálvez. In a letter to José Benjamin Abalos, who had been a cabinet minister under Yrigoyen, Jauretche spoke clearly of the old and new national functions of the Radical Party, and he criticized those Radical Party members who had abandoned the party's revolutionary mission.

> Nowadays there are Radicals who can hardly accept that the Unión Cívica Radical is not a political party but the civil union of all Argentines in order to realize the nation. They define [this] idea as totalitarianism. . . . That was a perfect definition, and I find that there has never been a nontotalitarian revolutionary force . . . ; the May Revolution was totalitarian, as were the French, Russian, German and Italian [revolutions].[86]

FORJA published Jauretche's letter in its entirety and disseminated it widely, thereby demonstrating the ideological importance the movement accorded to Jauretche's thinking. There was a clear conviction that a corporativist popular revolution was underway—a national revolution that owed more to fascism than its members would admit. Although FORJA did not take extremist Lugonean positions, such as the need to become a regional power, Scalabrini Ortiz, who was not a member of FORJA (as noted earlier) but still expressed its ideas, argued that the economically and culturally emancipated state would transform Argentina into a healthy, powerful nation.

The foreigner wants us to be a people imbued with false values so that we will become a fundamentally weak nation, a primitive country, without industries, an immense meat production farm . . . without political will, without international influence, without an army or a strong navy. Therefore, any expenditure by the nation on arming itself is the object of strong opposition propaganda. . . .[87]

Anti-imperialism also meant the development of the "third position," and a strong army and mobilized population were essential if Argentina was to compete in the imperialist world as an equal power. Young officers should not be educated as a "caste" but as leaders of popular armies. The first goal was to protect national resources, and that required army officers who had "returned to the military ethic of the great national tradition, and rebuilt the technical consciousness of the study of the implementation and defense of continental plans."[88] Although FORJA could not get along with the elitist and traditionalist sectors of integral nationalism or with the advocates of *uriburismo*, who saw themselves as the real defenders of national and economic sovereignty,[89] it was certainly able to coexist with the other populist groups that evolved from *uriburismo* to national populism. FORJA and these groups both gave a positive new value to the figure of Juan Manuel de Rosas and acknowledged one another's role in the anti-imperialist struggle. Scalabrini's book was praised by most right-wing revisionists. As noted by the Irazustas, "it was the most important contribution to an Argentine intelligence conceived in order to form a national consciousness."[90] Both would likewise recognize that there should be no separation or opposition between civilians and military, because that would cause the nationalist movement to languish. Their slogan was "to radicalize the revolution and to revolutionize the Radical movement."[91] There were differences, in the sense that for FORJA members the idea of populist mobilization should not based on hierarchies. "On the one side is the entire nation without distinctions and hierarchies, on the other there are the foreign exploiters and their local representatives."[92] For the integralists, popular mobilization should take place under a hierarchical authoritarian state. Yet despite differences in the articulation of the content of popular mobilization, the integralists and the populists agreed that liberal democracy was an impossible combination, and they rejected the notion that individual and civil rights were intrinsic to democracy, because liberal democracy itself was a sign of foreign imperialism.

The actual form that anti-imperialism and the struggle against the liberal state apparatus should take was an issue that divided right-wing and left-wing nationalists and the followers of Marxist-Leninist ideologies. Since the liberal oligarchy had created the political system that produced dependence on imperialism, and the Marxist parties were preoccupied with the increasing strength of fascism worldwide, the nationalists considered themselves the sole defenders of national interests. One right-wing nationalist wrote bitterly, "What remained of the anti-imperialist struggle of the Communist Party? Have the economic conditions that moved the Communists to [anti-imperialist] campaigns changed? Consequently, have the Communists changed their ideological direction?"[93] Such was the question posed to the political representatives of an ideology that was said to defend the anti-imperialist struggle and promote social justice. The same writer continued:

> [The] Communist International had taken new roads since the Seventh World Congress. The anti-imperialist struggle was followed by the anti-fascist struggle. Open struggle for social revolution was followed by a sharp turn toward the popular fronts, which defend corrupt democracy.[94]

These views provided ample justification for the ideological confrontations that took place during World War II. While the Socialist and Communist parties concentrated on the struggle for democracy, questions of national emancipation and anti-imperialism were abandoned to the nationalist right and left.

CHAPTER 6

The Integralist-Populist Synthesis and the New Order

The Shifting Ideology

In the late 1930s the most prominent intellectuals of the integralist right had nearly completed the intellectual shift from a counterrevolutionary to a nationalist revolutionary ideology. The final ideological development occurred when this important sector of right-wing integralists resurrected Yrigoyen's nationalist tradition, thereby making possible an ideological rapprochement with the populist left and the creation of a synthesis of right-wing authoritarianism and left-wing populism that was adopted by the military regime of 1943.

As noted earlier, prior to 1930 these nationalists had rejected liberalism as a theory of individual rights and as a framework of political democracy in general and scorned the Yrigoyenist version of popular democracy. Nevertheless, in the 1930s the brothers Irazusta, Ramón Doll, Gálvez, and others evolved toward a populism that was expressed in terms of mobilization, anti-imperialism, and social justice in a manner similar to that of the populist left.

The questions here are why this ideological synthesis matured at the end of the Década Infame and why it was important ideologically and politically.

We must bear in mind that by this time the Argentine conservative regime had lost political legitimacy as a result of political fraud and its ties to British imperialism. In a situation quite different from the one prior to the 1930 coup, the nationalists now identified the enemies of the *patria* not as populists or immigrants but as the conservative establishment. In terms of domestic politics, the right-wing integralists reached the conclusion that the Justo regime, though relatively benign toward the nationalist movement, was no longer acceptable. The question was what type of regime should be installed to replace the conservative oligarchy. None of the nationalists wanted a liberal democracy. While some nationalists believed that the solution to democratic decadence should be military authoritarianism, others believed that a national populist "revolution" would combine the conservative and modernist sides of the fascist revolution. The latter believed that it was important to combine forces with the most antiliberal sectors of Yrigoyenism in order to consolidate a fascist nationalist front. The seeds of this new attitude toward Yrigoyenism had been planted in the first years of Agustín Justo's rule, when nationalist rightist like the Irazustas, Gálvez and Doll were reluctant to collaborate with Justo in his attempt to delegitimize the Yrigoyenist branch of the Radical Party and to ban it from taking part in the political process.

In 1935, after the frustrated revolutionary attempts of military men like Lt. Col. Attila Cattaneo (1932) and Lt. Col. Roberto Bosch in Paso de los Libres (1933), Yrigoyen's supporters gave way to a new electoral strategy. That year the Radical Party agreed to take part in elections with the hope of organizing a congressional opposition to check the high-handedness and impunity with which the government handled every aspect of federal and provincial administrations, and to begin occupying positions in the legislatures so that when the party took power again it would have practical administrative experience. One of the most important figures leading this change of attitude of the radicals was Amadeo Sabattini, a new Radical Party leader who had been elected governor in the province of Córdoba. Sabattini and young members of the Radical Party stepped up their activities in the provinces of Córdoba, Buenos Aires, and the Santa Fe, and on several occasions they joined forces with Lisandro de la Torre's Progressive Democrats and with CGT (Confederación General del Trabajo) union leaders.

Proof of this joint action was the collaboration given by intransigent Radicals to the CGT massive demonstration in Buenos Aires on May 1, 1936. Leftist and democratic parties together with the intransigent Radicals gathered on this day to condemn Uriburu's coup on September 6, 1930, which had restored the power of the conservative oligarchy. The immediate reaction of the conservative parties to this commemorative protest was to publish a "manifesto of the right" on June 1, 1936, drafted by the Independent Socialist minister Federico Pinedo. His intention was twofold: to press for electoral reform in order to block the Radical Party, and to unify the nationalist forces against the "populist" forces. The conservative liberal right was clearly trying to bring the antiliberal right into its camp, defining their common enemies as communism and the old Radical Party. An example of this trend was the proposed law against communist activities debated by the Senate in 1936. This law continued the anticommunist campaign begun in 1932 by Uriburu's followers. The draft proposed in 1932, which had never been considered by the Senate Legislation Committee, was included in an extraordinary session in 1936.[1] Although the nationalist antiliberal right approved of the anticommunist campaign, they refused to collaborate with the liberal right. The clearest indication of this attitude was Roberto de Laferrère's communiqué published in June 1936, which rejected the possibility of an alliance with the liberal right. According to the communiqué, the national right-wing front was another manifestation of the conservative forces of the Contubernio (as Yrigoyen labeled them in 1928), of the Frente Unico of 1931, and of the Concordancia of 1932. All of these were political expressions of the corrupt liberal establishment.[2] Under the headline "El nacionalismo argentino al pueblo de la nación" (Argentine Nationalism to the People of the Nation), the communiqué rejected any political collaboration with the Justo government or the "National Front," which "was another attempt to prolong the sad history of the defeated political parties."[3] However, the growing opposition of the integralist right to the liberal right did not hint at converting to democratic practices.

In a circular letter distributed to army officers in July 1936, Laferrère called on the army to fulfill its national and moral commitments and take power: "A Popular Front government would be a difficult experience for our country. . . . A National Front government would be even worse. It would preach high principles which would be put at the service of . . . crude capitalism."[4]

The only way to prevent a return to political anarchy and do away with the liberal Justo regime was to organize a military movement to resurrect the themes of *uriburismo* and enrich them with the basic ingredients of Yrigoyenist nationalism. Meanwhile, however, the nationalist movement grew in numbers and attempted to distance itself from the conservatives, who referred to themselves as nationalists while "keeping themselves distant from its content."[5] The "true" nationalists insisted on playing the role of a moral force in Argentine politics, and more than ever felt that they represented the new Argentina against the old liberal establishment and the communists.

This stance was further aggravated under the presidency of Roberto Ortiz, an antipersonalist Radical who took power by fraudulent elections in 1937, after once more frustrating the attempt of the Unión Cívica Radical (UCR) to reach power by democratic means. In 1936 the UCR had made an alliance with the Socialist party and the PDP bloc and nearly won a majority, but the fraudulent elections of 1937 brought to power the Conservative coalition under the leadership of Roberto Ortiz. Although Ortiz tried to offset the repudiation of his coalition by attempting to conduct clean elections, thus making it possible for the Unión Cívica Radical to achieve a larger presence in Congress in 1938, his attempts at reform were cut short when he became ill. Neither he nor his successor, President Ramon Castillo, could ever repair the damage done by the moral decadence of the conservative regime.

Two important nationalist newspapers, *Crisol* and *Bandera Argentina*, whose editors Juan Carulla and Enrique Osés were self-confessed fascists, presented the political alternatives to any form of conservative authoritarianism or any compromise with a liberal democratic regime. Osés rejected the possibility that the nationalist movement would compete for power under the rules of the democratic liberal state. He believed that the nationalist movement should be revolutionary, claiming that "to accept a compromise, an instrument, a practice, which is contrary to the . . . [principles maintained] . . . is nothing more than . . . to participate in the mistakes of the regime."[6] This hard-line position was rejected by other nationalist intellectuals, who saw the electoral process in tactical terms. Carulla maintained that the anti-election nationalists chose to ignore the fact that Italian nationalism had developed into Mussolini-style fascism, which later would participate in national elections, whereas Hitler's German nationalism had begun at the end of World War I as a political movement seeking mass support: "How much intelligence, how much energy, and how much blood had to be spent before the final triumph! And how many half-won or lost elections! These great world movements had sought popular ratification."[7]

This was the crux of the problem: wooing the people in a political struggle that was conducted according to the liberal rules of the game. This constituted a new and important ideological development because it was an alternative to the dominant view that the country could be saved only by a military dictatorship.

The nationalists had been convinced since the early 1930s that they had to become a political movement with popular appeal, and to that end they sought to achieve political unification and ideological coherence. Does this imply that the nationalists were preparing to play a democratic game? The answer is hardly positive. As noted by Carulla, elections can simply be one tool among others for those whose basic goal is to overthrow political democracy.

On August 12, 1933, the Liga Republicana, Milicia Cívica Nacionalista, Legión Cívica Argentina, and Legión de Mayo agreed to join forces under the name of Guardia Argentina, with the poet Leopoldo Lugones as leader. Guardia Argentina was, in fact, the final political action of Lugones— unsuccessful, inasmuch as it was eventually dissolved. Another unsuccessful attempt to unite the different nationalist groups into one political movement was ADUNA (Afirmación de Una Nueva Argentina), the new name taken by Acción Nacionalista Argentina, an organization founded by Dr. Juan P. Ramos, a lawyer and lecturer at the University of Buenos Aires. Ramos was less passionate and more scholarly than Lugones and had achieved academic distinction. His knowledge of Mussolini's Italy (gained during a visit there) and his friendship with General Uriburu made him acceptable to the nationalist camp. Nevertheless, his attempt to consolidate and unify the nationalist movement was just as unsuccessful as that of Lugones regarding ideological and strategic proposals. All the nationalists accepted ADUNA's social and political ideals, which were aimed at transforming the state into one "that regulates the vital forces of the country" by means of a hierarchical political system.[8] The Liga Republicana, however, was opposed to the strategy of gradualism, which meant participating in the political game of the Justo regime; the Liga denounced both "pacifist" and "legalist" political solutions.

The most striking ideological development was the mounting conviction that fascism represented an attack against democracy but not an attack against the people. Moreover, some of the integral nationalists were now prepared to admit that the idea of the "people" in Argentine politics was directly connected to Yrigoyen's nationalist populism.

As discussed in previous chapters, many right-wing nationalists who had helped oust Yrigoyen from power in 1930 were akin to Yrigoyen's followers in their reexamination of Argentine history, and that also promoted the reexamination of Yrigoyenism. Beyond the debate over history, however, the political and ideological issue at stake was whether the Yrigoyen legacy could be adapted to a nationalist movement that was not about to give up its admiration for fascist authoritarian methods. This central theoretical question was undertaken by the two major right-wing nationalist journals that appeared in the 1940s, *Nueva Política*, which continued the reactionary views raised by Catholic *hispanistas*, and *Nuevo Orden*, which devoted itself to merging fascism with (Yrigoyen's populist) nationalism. For *Nuevo Orden*, military authoritarianism by itself was not enough; it had to be combined with popular mobilization. In other words, most of the nationalist intellectuals of *Nuevo Orden* were convinced that during the 1930s the time was ripe for another type of nationalist revolution, one based on anti-imperialism and popular mobilization. Whereas an authoritarian state without popular mobilization would serve the interests of the oligarchy, a nationalist authoritarian state based on popular mobilization would serve the interest of the people. The old motifs of the right were not put aside, but the new emphasis was on assaulting the old conservative order and its model of national organization. This was the political context within which the integralist right was able to bridge the ideological gap separating it from *yrigoyenismo*.

Revision of Yrigoyenism and the Fascist Order

Although both currents of nationalism embodied in *Nueva Política* and *Nuevo Orden* drew inspiration from fascism, *Nuevo Orden* clearly followed the line that attempted to "nationalize" it, whereas the opposite line, taken by *Nueva Política*, attempted to "fascisize" the nationalist movement. The crux of this ideological dispute was the question of whether to legitimize Yrigoyenism as a national movement and a nationalist ideology. In theoretical terms, this question concerned the new characteristics that the nationalist movement was to assume. What was clear was that from the mid-1930s onward, right-wing nationalists, whether pro- or anti-Yrigoyen, would no longer support the political goals of the old conservative establishment.

Nueva Política attracted those intellectuals who considered the Yrigoyenist movement the ideological bedfellow of the old liberal conservatives, since "both are . . . liberal and anti-traditionalist movements."[9] For this reason Nimio de Anquin, the Catholic intellectual founder of the Partido Fascista Argentino, attacked any possible collaboration with Yrigoyenism. He asked rhetorically, "what kind of Christian could collaborate with the preservation of liberal society? . . . Such an attitude . . . must be attributed to liberal infiltration."[10]

The *Nuevo Orden* intellectuals, on the other hand, saw the retrieval of the Yrigoyenist concept of nationalism as a key to winning over the masses. In their words, "Nationalism will be popular or it will be nothing."[11]

The resurrection of Yrigoyenism coincided with the attempt to popularize nationalism. At the same time, the *Nuevo Orden* intellectuals tried to identify in the Yrigoyenist movement some of the elements that characterized the new modernist nationalist movements worldwide:

Yrigoyenism was synonymous with popular mobilization, economic nationalism, traditionalism, and neutralism in world conflicts. In other words, the new political developments in Argentina and the world made it necessary to restore Yrigoyenism as a form of nationalist traditionalism in Argentina in order to constitute a national front against the oligarchical supporters of liberal democracy. The Radical movement was useful to the country as long as it remained faithful to its mission of restoring the rights of the Argentine people [rights hitherto obstructed by a foreign-oriented oligarchy] and while it maintained an . . . instinctive distrust for the advances of financial power.[12]

Ramón Doll described the Yrigoyenist movement as quasi-totalitarian, a characteristic of the Radical Party until it was betrayed by the Alvearist wing. The Radical Party was not, in fact, a political party like others but rather a movement that "had a historical mission to fulfill, a mission that transcended the political parties."[13] The people, according to Doll's interpretation, had voted for the Radical Party not in order to play the usual liberal democratic game, "but in order to take power, to dismantle all obstacles that were keeping it from governing,"[14] while limiting the political power of the other parties. Vigorous and anti-dogmatic, Yrigoyenism actually represented the spirit of revolt against liberalism. Bruno Jacovella, who wrote for *Nueva Política* but later left it because he detected anti-populist tendencies, said, "the totalitarian movements of national and popular emancipation are completely democratic and proletarian."[15] Yrigoyenism was a popular movement of national emancipation and fascism was a popular totalitarian movement. In this sense Yrigoyenism could be equated with fascism. Ernesto Palacio made the significant observation that until that time the integralist right had been composed of elitist groups but that now it should be more receptive to the authentic and austere "protest of the original Radicalism extended in the proud international politics of Yrigoyen, in his love for the exploited people and in his hatred of bankers and financial exploitation."[16]

In short, according to Palacio, Argentina's right-wing intellectuals should have learned from Yrigoyen the meaning of real nationalism. Under Yrigoyen the Radical Party was faithful to its own tradition and to its "own mission of reasserting the rights of the Argentine people, which were violated by the foreign-minded oligarchy. In his zeal for protecting Argentina's sovereignty. . . . Yrigoyen was a follower of the nationalist ideological current."[17] Thus, in the eyes of the *Nuevo Orden* integralists, the rehabilitation of the nationalist side of Yrigoyenism had brought the social and mobilizing values of fascism into Argentine nationalism.

Bruno Jacovella, like Manuel Gálvez, attempted to salvage Yrigoyenism's nationalist message because it was populist and anti-imperialist. These were the qualities that Argentine nationalism needed in order to be properly fascist.

Gálvez was more direct, declaring that Argentina needed a real fascist movement; in doing so he was by no means stating a disapproval of nationalism. Radicalism in Argentina, like fascism, was a loose, mythical ideology for him, as well as being overly mass-oriented. Nor were the Radicals opposed to violence—Gálvez maintained that "an authentic Radical is not far from being a fascist: he is a nationalist, he thinks he must work for the people, and he sympathizes with direct and violent means."[18] Gálvez shared with other nationalists a quest for authenticity in the context of the new worldwide ideological revolution. His predilection for the populist and socialist aspects of fascism led him not only to regard Radicalism as the real fascist movement in Argentina but also to think of his old comrades at *La Nueva República* "as more dictators than fascists."[19]

In spite of this favorable view of the Yrigoyenist populist movement, the *Nuevo Orden* nationalists noted that the nationalist movement could not prosper without formulating its positions and establishing its doctrine, those being the weak points in Yrigoyenist nationalism. In a world at war, where a new, international ideology was overturning the old liberal order, Yrigoyenism needed renewal. The new Yrigoyenism

> should declare the end of the Radical era [something that the members of FORJA accepted], just as the Radicalism of 1891 ended the Rosas era, without denying . . . the historical affiliation [of the movement]. . . . In politics the most important issue is the present. The past can be used as a guide, but without attempting to stop the spontaneous evolution of current opinion.[20]

Rodolfo Irazusta was in agreement with Gálvez's attempt to associate fascism with populism, adding to Gálvez's assessment his conviction that fascism in all its variants contributed to the war against imperialism. Fascism, national socialism, or even Falangism for Irazusta "had the same purpose, to liberate their respective countries from imperialist domination . . . from plutocracy and communism. Each of these movements was not democratic but populist."[21]

The *Nuevo Orden* nationalists saw the synthesis between the fascist "new order" and an authentic national-populist social movement as established political fact, particularly in the early years of World War II, when a fascist victory appeared to be an imminent possibility. Newspapers like *El Pampero*, *Clarinada*, and *Cabildo*, which put their faith in fascism, expected the Axis forces to win the war. Their political content clearly reflected those expectations, while at the same time they were strengthening their advocacy of populism and social justice. With a daily circulation of 75,000, *El Pampero* published many articles favoring the economic nationalism promoted by the *Nuevo Orden* and FORJA writers, together with anti-Semitic and fascist articles.[22] Bruno Jacovella, who had been prominent at *Nuevo Orden* and was now one of the main editors of *El Pampero*, incorporated into *El Pampero*'s editorials the ideas already developed in *Nuevo Orden*, which had been popularized among the Argentine public during the debate over neutrality. An Argentine variant of fascism, combining an integral conception of nationalism with a populist approach emphasizing social justice and anti-imperialism, was already flourishing. The struggle for neutrality was the basis of the struggle for the new order. While fascism around the world was struggling to impose this new order, in Argentina the nationalist forces were awaiting the leader or military movement that could transform the inclination toward fascism into a political force with broad popular appeal. The ideological synthesis, however, had already been achieved. In an interview many years later, Jacovella spoke of the appeal that fascism had for Argentine nationalists. "We weren't fascists . . . you know . . . but anyhow fascism was—how can I explain it to you—fashionable." Jacovella captured the spirit of the times. He noted that Argentina was blessed by the appearance of the type of nationalist intellectuals fascinated by fascism during those years. Jacovella also pointed out that Argentine nationalism was home-grown, and he criticized those who took fascism too seriously, assuming that they even confused "fascism with a military regime." Referring to some of his colleagues whom he called reactionaries, he admitted that they lacked a "popular consciousness." "Rosas, Yrigoyen, Perón, represented the nationalist synthesis," and in those "years the comparison with Mussolini was obvious."[23]

Marcelo Sánchez Sorondo, who was on the *Nueva Política* editorial board, represented the opposite pole from Jacovella. In an interview in 1989 he called on the nationalist movement to turn to politics, so as to create a movement of public opinion rather than expecting anything from the military regime. He insisted that "we wanted a different type of politics . . . not the politics of political parties."

Question: Do you think that there is another type of democratic politics? *Answer:* We had the model of the army. . . . It represented the best model of the new type of antiliberal democracy. . . . We were living under a universal crisis of ideas, obviously . . . but the Argentine case was a unique case within a broad frame of fascist nationalist revolution.

> *Question:* Here I have an article you published in *Nueva Política* in June 1940, in which you maintained that you had been conservative although at the same time revolutionaries. . . .
> *Answer:* Yes, we were revolutionaries against the liberal order, we wanted some of the elements of the old order in a similar way that Maurras wanted it. We did not expect a monarchy, but the social order of the monarchy.[24]

However, Sorondo as well as the other intellectuals of *Nueva Política* were basically afraid of the possibility of mass mobilization. They could not accept the ideas used by Jacovella to define the new populist era. The *Nueva Política* intellectuals turned fascism into a rigid, static political ideology. By the same token, they portrayed Yrigoyenist nationalism as a mere ideology of consumerism different from fascism.

Yet both types of nationalists understood—despite the differences in their analyses of the past and in the different content they gave to the concept of *reaccionario*—that the liberal order must be surpassed. Moreover, despite their differences over *yrigoyenismo* and the content of populism within fascism, both supported fascism in the world confrontation because fascism represented the universal vitality of the nationalist resistance against liberalism.

Debate on Neutrality: The Clash between Nationalists and Democrats

No local or world development had contributed more to the consolidation of two contrasting political and ideological political cultures in Argentina than World War II. The arguments for and against neutrality in the world conflict ultimately represented a broad debate about Argentina's national identity. At the early stages of the debate, however, there was no correlation between ideological stances and political and economic interests on the issue of neutrality. Hence it is not surprising that Argentina's position of nonintervention was especially supported by liberal conservative politicians, particularly those associated with agrarian interests and connected with Great Britain. Although Argentine conservatives and liberals were ideologically sympathetic toward the Western democracies, they were proneutrality, openly joining the ideological struggle initiated by right- and left-wing nationalists. Similarly, the bulk of the British business community supported what was considered traditional Argentine neutrality, because keeping diplomatic relations with Germany was a precondition for safe maritime interchange in the Atlantic Ocean. Any other position would have jeopardized trans-Atlantic trade of Argentine products. Similar positions were held by significant sectors of the state bureaucracy and the agrarian upper classes, who believed that a neutral position would be the safest policy for a peripheral nation like Argentina. However, after Pearl Harbor, when the Americans pressed the British to stop encouraging Argentina's neutral position and demanded that Argentina join the other South American nations in a common effort against the Axis, no pragmatic interests could be counted in favor of neutrality. After that point, neutrality became a matter of ideology directly connected to the struggle for Argentina's national identity.

Those defending what could be defined as a "pro-Axis" neutral position in the world conflict generally scorned Argentine liberalism and were contemptuous of political liberalism in general. While differing over the characteristics of the new order, they shared a common conviction that Argentina must shift its path of development from liberalism to autarky and political corporativism. For them fascism, in its struggle against democracy, contributed in more than one way to national emancipation. They believed that by combating the democratic nations, fascism was serving the cause of national emancipation. Those opposed to the fascists were not all necessarily moved by a democratic spirit. Within the antifascist coalition were Communists who under Moscow's direction joined the struggle against fascism after the German invasion of the Soviet Union, along with socialists, conservatives, and antipersonalist Radicals. The ideological conflict in Europe led most of them to view Argentina as divided along ideological lines similar to those in most European countries. These were not the old divisions of the bourgeoisie against the proletariat or of liberal and conservative parties against the Communist left. This time, the political conflict was a conflict over civilization. Liberals, socialists, conservatives, and antipersonalist Radicals belonged to the democratic camp. They viewed Argentina in terms of Western democratic countries and basically despised populism. The antiliberal nationalists were neutralist for different reasons. However, they coincided in their common hatred of liberal democracy.

The antiliberal nationalists of right and left were thus divided into doctrinal fascists, fascist populists, and national populists. However, in the context of World War II they worked with the same ferocity toward overturning the liberal world. The intellectual context of the right-wing nationalists was set by the weekly magazines *Nuevo Orden* and *Nueva Política*. They proposed different, but not contradictory, ideas about what could be defined as Argentina's insertion in the new "world order."

In short, neither position was neutral toward the world conflict. They were convinced that the world conflict would bring about the defeat of the liberal state. They differed over the characteristics of the future nationalist state in Argentina, and they differed on the definition of the new role Argentina was to play in the new world order. At *Nueva Política*, intellectuals like Marcelo Sánchez Sorondo, Hector Llambías, and César Pico presented an ideology centered on doctrine, using Maurrasian and Catholic categories. As opposed to those focused on doctrine at *Nueva Política*, Ernesto Palacio maintained that the nationalist movement "is a political movement, not a philosophical school."[25] Yet Palacio could not deny that the nationalist movement was guided by a doctrine "accepted by everyone to one degree or another, explicitly or implicitly."[26]

The *Nuevo Orden* intellectuals pointed to the rebellion of the real country, the motherland, against the abstractions of rational political thought and the abstractions of a formal concept of liberty, in order to present a definition of democracy and liberty different from that of rationalist ideologies. The democratic and populist tone that they used was an attempt to set them apart from the *Nueva Política* intellectuals. The doctrinaire and elitist approach developed at *Nueva Política* was, according to those associated with *Nuevo Orden*, complementary to the liberal and conservative concepts of the political and economic order. For the intellectuals of *Nuevo Orden*, the new world order should contribute to popular national liberation. Rodolfo Irazusta tried to define the situation this way: "As they chose their course, some evolved to Fascism, which allowed them to live together with the minorities and unpopular oligarchies. We chose to ally with the popular forces which at that time were persecuted."[27]

Rodolfo Irazusta was referring to the intellectuals gathered around *Nueva Política*, who were old comrades in the nationalist movement, and who did not adopt the same populist democratic positions to which he, Palacio, Gálvez, and Doll had been led intellectually. Their different perceptions of the real meaning of the new world order was directly connected to their differences over the substance of Argentine nationalism. The *Nueva Política* intellectuals believed that Argentina was not one of the front-line states in this new order, because the central European states were setting the ideological terms.

> We know to what extent the Americas simply serve Europe for raw materials, that the Americas were bestowed on Europe and Christendom to be integrated into the universal unity of culture. Without Europe or in opposition to Europe, the Americas by their own choice place themselves on the road to betrayal and madness.

We heirs of Spain and Rome are situated at the far edge of the southern world, to protect Europe's flank, and it is our mission to reproduce the family image of our race.[28]

The *Nueva Política* intellectuals were quite doctrinaire—they could scarcely agree that in the new century there could be any other variants to what they considered a pure restoration of the spiritual traditions of Spanish traditionalism. Any kind of tactical or ideological disagreement was considered as a kind of betrayal of the central cause.

Rodolfo Irazusta occupied a different position. He held that there was no "international" of nationalisms, even less so if such nationalism was in any way ideologically dependent on sources outside Latin America. He was not thereby denying that at a time of a world ideological conflict between the "plutocratic" imperialist order and the new national socialist one, the latter suited the Argentine nationalists of *Nuevo Orden*. Indeed, "if the Iberoamerican nations' interests could in certain way be identified with somebody, it could not be in any sense with the (liberal) European nations or with the United States, [whose interests] are contrary to ours."[29]

The neutralist assumption adopted by the nationalists of *Nuevo Orden* should be seen in this light. This neutrality, however, arose out of a purely authentic and nationalist attitude, responding not to pure pragmatism but to a general ideological struggle against liberalism. This was why the *Nuevo Orden* intellectuals believed that their own neutrality differed from that of the conservative regime and *Nueva Política* members, which represented a confluence of interests between the pro-British conservatives of the government and the "Germanophiles" at *Nueva Política*. In the view of *Nuevo Orden*, "neutrality" in itself was not to be sought as a political end unless it entailed a strong feeling of independence and a strong popular appeal accompanied by a revolutionary political action. "Our official neutrality is merely passivity."[30] In other words, advocating the defense of neutrality without a nationalist conception aimed at destroying the old regime was ineffective.

It was no accident that one of the principal contributors to *Nuevo Orden* was the French fascist Marcel Déat, who embodied the national-socialist populist formula that separated the *Nuevo Orden* intellectuals from those at *Nueva Política*. Déat's ideas reflected the line that *Nuevo Orden* attempted to follow domestically and internationally. The idea of a synthesis combining a new anti-Marxist socialism and a new nationalism with combating Bolshevism and the liberal state, was suited to the conditions of the nationalist movement in Argentina.

"To assure the triumph of true European socialism, German weapons are in combat with the Russian planes. To assure that France can become a true national and socialist community we are engaged in this battle against Bolshevism."[31] The intellectuals at *Nuevo Orden* were taking a position not only at the local level but in the worldwide ideological conflict. The ideological acceptance and appreciation of the economic terms that were to direct the new world gave theoretical support to the Argentine nationalists:

> War will give National-Socialist Germany the political power to create an economic system based on private property, with the restrictions demanded by the general welfare, which will replace the capitalist or Marxist ideas of Judaism with a true socialism. The foundation of this European socialism will be a new measurement of value based more on labor than on gold. . . . This system based on labor is reminiscent of that of Marx but without destroying private property. . . . German socialism will make it possible to achieve a rational division of labor in accordance with the characteristics and needs of the European continent.[32]

According to this analysis, the new antiliberal order led by a new sort of fascist or Nazi imperialism would be beneficial for the emancipated economies of Latin America.

> The high living standard of Germany will be possible in all of Europe, when the different economic and cultural possibilities of the countries would be developed. . . . The political and military power of Europe would be strengthened by this policy of order and social justice, applied to the most cultural region on earth. America and Asia would evolve in the same way and would constitute new corporativist and autarkic economic unit.[33]

Not all of the *Nuevo Orden* intellectuals agreed. Rodolfo Irazusta was more reserved in his analysis of the results of a future new world order led by Germany. Nevertheless, it was clear for all of them that the real danger would come more from the imperialism of the democratic nations than from fascism. "They assure us that if Italy and Germany struggle against England it will not take them long to develop actions against us, as if the reasons that the totalitarian nations had in struggling against the British empire are similar reasons for being aggressive against us."[34] To the *Nuevo Orden* nationalists it seemed clear that economic emancipation for Argentina would be de facto anti-British and anti-American. Hence there were grounds for the denunciation by the democratic parties of the "anti-Argentine" and pro-Axis activities of the nationalists, even if that criticism was sometimes exaggerated. No proof of espionage for the Third Reich was found, but in ideological terms the Argentine nationalists had taken a clear position.

Consider Ramón Doll's defense of the nationalist position. In responding to the accusations of the democratic senators of the "Investigating Commission," Doll affirmed that there was no danger of Nazi infiltration in Argentina. "No honest Argentine would be able to defend the Nazis," he said.[35] At the same time he maintained that Judaism, British imperialism, and the oligarchy in combination were the real dangers to Argentina. "For Argentina," according to Doll, "Germany is the guarantee, while Britain represents serfdom."[36] That sort of argument pointed to the connection between the new order and the politics of neutrality. Despite the intellectual effort to differentiate this argument from the one developed in *Nueva Política*, both intellectual centers pointed to the fascist success in the war as a sign of a new order that would replace the old liberal order, considered as responsible for setting the stage for Argentina's political and economic subjugation. Therefore, claimed Sánchez Sorondo of *Nueva Política*, liberalism is an ideology that England identifies with the concept of civilization in order to exploit other peoples. Indeed, what benefits Great Britain is to the detriment of countries like Argentina, for whom the idea of liberal civilization implies the "resignation of our frontiers." The response to Great Britain is fascism. However, this does not imply, as noted by Doll, that the Nazis are infiltrating Argentina.

Bruno Jacovella of *Nuevo Orden* explained this point quite clearly:

The persecution unleashed against persons and organizations advocating a fascist type of ideology (to use the conventional term, which includes all national revolutionary movements emerging and triumphing in the world today) does not have its origins . . . in the fear that Germany will send its troops across the sea to invade us. . . . [The fear is] that a revolution like that carried out by Hitler could take place here.[37]

A "Hitler-style" revolution, thus, means national liberation against liberal imperialism. This type of revolution coincides with neutralism.

The defense of neutrality was not based on political convenience, nor did the *Nueva Política* intellectuals stand to profit financially from it. Similarly, for *Nuevo Orden* this stance of neutrality was ideological rather than pragmatic. Elements of economic nationalism, anti-Semitism, and of praise for a new world order guided by the fascist states could be found in both strains of thought.

A different but complementary position toward neutrality was promoted by FORJA intellectuals. They developed their own campaign in
defense of neutrality and defined nationalism in their own way. The ideological endorsement of neutrality, along with their direct hostility to the
liberal order, did not mean that there was an ideological identification
between right- and left-wing nationalism. Nevertheless there was a clear
attempt to advance a common political attitude and synthesis at the ideological level, which, even without being formalized, became the basis for
the subsequent development of populist and integralist nationalism.[38]

FORJA and *Nuevo Orden* intellectuals maintained intense communi-
cation. Arturo Jauretche's works were published in *Nuevo Orden* under
a pseudonym. He outlined his approval of the new attitude of the nationalists toward the Yrigoyenist phenomenon, while continuing to maintain
that nationalists must be guided by a pure nationalism, free of any foreign
philosophical conceptualization.

On those grounds, the FORJA position on neutrality was clearly
expressed in Jauretche's analysis of imperialism and World War II.
FORJA was rooted in the ideological values of Yrigoyenism and its tra-
ditional policy of neutrality, denying support to either side in the conflict.
In pamphlets distributed around Buenos Aires, FORJA maintained that
Argentines should not be confused by the notion that they would be
going to war in order to defend "democracy and freedom in the world."
Instead they would go to Europe to die in defense of Great Britain, "the
owner of our railways, a great part of our lands, and almost the whole of
Patagonia."[39] FORJA's directorate, in considering these facts, declared its
position:

> In view of the European crisis—a conflict between imperialists, some
> of them organized under liberal democratic guises, others under to-
> talitarian principles—Argentina is relegated to the status of a colony
> of British and international plutocracy. As such, it must activate a con-
> sciousness of emancipation and organize the forces that will liberate it
> from any foreign dominion.[40]

No matter what the result of the war, FORJA continued, the Europeans
intend to keep Latin America under their imperial control.

The question was summed up by Jauretche in a slogan that became
part of the mythology of Argentine popular nationalism: "The issue is
not changing the collar but refusing to be the dog."[41] This slogan combined the differing perspectives of the right-wing nationalists and young
FORJA Yrigoyenists on the neutrality question. Despite the two groups'

ideological differences, they had certain similarities and, in some cases, made attempts at political collaboration. The most significant took place in 1939 when Raúl Scalabrini Ortiz was editing *Reconquista*, the result of which was an internal split in FORJA. Some of its members, notably its president Luis Dellepiane, defined the Scalabrini enterprise as a "pro-Axis" neutrality. Suspicions were raised about German financial support for the newspaper, and several of its contributors were criticized (Manuel Gálvez, Rodolfo Irazusta, and Ernesto Palacio, the *Nuevo Orden* nationalists). The paper's position was to defend neutrality, while expressing very clearly its preferences: "What is the danger facing Italy? Italy is threatened on its own national and imperial land by other hegemonic and imperial powers."[42] Its ideological line was plainly guided by the attempt to prove that the British and plutocratic imperialist designs in Latin America were similar to their designs in Europe. Italy fulfilled the role of a nation culturally "colonized" and subjugated by the plutocratic nations. *Nuevo Orden* and FORJA were in agreement that they were involved in the same struggle for neutrality, although, in contrast with the integralists, no one in FORJA openly advocated a new fascist order. Nonetheless, all nationalists, whether of right or left, shared the idea that a new world fascist order would be best for Argentina's political and economic emancipation from liberal imperialism.

Thus, the populist left did not address the issue of neutrality in World War II exactly as the right did, but it did accept one of its assumptions, namely, that in an era characterized by a clash between two concepts of civilization—liberalism and Marxist socialism on one side and fascism and national socialism on the other—the fascist formula, which represented a total cultural revolt against the liberal world, was helpful to peripheral countries in their quest for political and economic emancipation. In other words, while anti-imperialism led the populist left to reject any collaboration with the democratic powers and drove it to a strategic collaboration with the right, the fascist orientation of the integralist right led it to a position of pro-Axis neutrality. By the late 1930s, both sides came to see economic autarky and modern industrialization as a vital nationalist goal, and they came to share a belief that social justice emanated from authentic popular sources rather than from any theory of universal human rights. This meant that the concept of "the people"—understood as a mythical entity created during a historical confrontation against liberal modernizers—was the source of a concept of social justice that stood in stark contrast to liberal or socialist ideas of welfare. In this sense they helped to elaborate a key idea in Argentine politics, namely, that social justice and social modernization are associated, as affirmed by

Ramón Doll with a type of fascist-populist "nationalism itself which is anti-imperialism,"[43] while liberal rule is associated with oligarchic rule and foreign interests.

As I have already pointed out, the modernist sectors of *Nuevo Orden* found a common language with populists rather than with the reactionaries of *Nueva Política*. However, what deserves emphasis is that this ideological evolution was prompted not by abandonment of the modernists' nationalist authoritarian ideology, but by new theoretical convictions portraying liberalism as imperialist and fascism as an ideology of cultural and political emancipation.

Doubts notwithstanding, there was no liberal infiltration in the political thought of the *Nuevo Orden* intellectuals. But although the Maurrasian concepts of hierarchy and corporativist society were shared by both *Nuevo Orden* and *Nueva Política* intellectuals, the accent on national liberation and on a populist but hierarchical democracy was especially developed by the *Nuevo Orden* group.

Nothing better summed up this new integralist-populist ideology, which expressed the reactionary, the modernist, and the populist faces of *Nuevo Orden* and *Nueva Política* combined with a spirit of fascist-style outreach to the masses, than the Alianza Nacionalista, the most radical of the nationalist groups.

Alianza Nacionalista: Plebeian Integralism and the Struggle for Neutrality

Starting in the 1930s, the Alianza Nacionalista combined the elitist and populist ideological tendencies of Argentine nationalism. No movement was more representative of the struggle for a pro-Axis neutrality than the Alianza.

All nationalists, in one way or another, sympathized with and supported Alianza activities, which were publicized in all the nationalist periodicals. Intellectuals from different nationalist factions participated in and supported the *Alianza's* political meetings and the social gatherings that formed an integral part of its political life. Some of these meetings were attended by fascist-influenced "putschist" generals like Juan Bautista Molina and by intellectuals like Juan Queralto, Carlos Ibarguren, Rodolfo Irazusta, and Ernesto Palacio, who were impressed by the Alianza's activism.[44] The Alianza was a nationalist group that combined elitism with a new populist and pro-worker approach, aimed at conquering the masses, and it succeeded in organizing mass rallies every May 1 until 1943. By using the symbols of the national-socialist tradition, the Alianza conveyed the primary ideological message that nationalism, not international socialism, was really on the side of the Argentine worker. The rally of May 1, 1942, had a larger turnout than the one organized by the socialists. This success reflected the new popular appeal of nationalism, which the Alianza Nacionalista had been defending from the outset. Its populist bias was reflected in its slogans: "Against capitalism that has imposed its . . . tyranny over the working masses! Against super-capitalism and Marxism! For the moral and material significance of the Argentine proletariat! For the economic freedom of the nation! We demand social justice!"[45] Emphasizing the movement's anti-conservative and multiclass characteristics, the organization's paper, *Alianza*, declared: "Here at the Alianza, united in a common effort of liberation . . . and social solidarity, the worker in sandals, the young student, the rural laborer, the native-born landlord, and the honest industrialist feel like comrades."[46]

Although in terms of its constituency the Alianza became a mass movement only in the late 1940s and early 1950s, its populist, anti-imperialist rhetoric and mobilizing efforts had characterized its activities from the start.[47] A young member remembers the Alianza as a national syndicalist movement that represented "the meeting of people and army, the seminal use of violence . . . of self sacrifice," and recalls the feeling "of belonging to a movement that was . . . above our individual wills."[48]

This feeling was the reason for the Alianza's creation in 1937, when Juan Queraltó, who had been president of the Nationalist Union of Secondary School Students (the youth branch of the Legión Cívica Argentina), created a new organization, the Alliance of Nationalist Youth. Queraltó was disappointed by what he considered the lack of revolutionary spirit in the Legión Cívica. Considering the revolutionary potential of the younger members of the Legión, Queraltó believed that a new nationalist framework might provide an outlet for a more youthful and active spirit. This new spirit helped win the support of important nationalist figures like Alfredo Turella (a contributor to *Bandera Argentina*), Ramón Doll, Jordan Bruno Genta, and General Juan Bautista Molina, who became one of the movement's principal leaders.

In 1941 the Alianza changed its name to Alianza Libertadora Nacionalista, although its basic ideology remained the same. Its fundamental principles were the protection of capital where it fulfilled a social function, the protection of labor, and worker participation in the revenues of companies, through official "bourses" that would deliver dividends destined for social services. It also advocated an elaborate program to nationalize the most important public services, and intensive industrialization. Indeed, the Alianza described its complete philosophy as a new social order. Until that time, "every social policy concerning worker rights has been based on winning improvements within the liberal capitalist organization, while the organization itself stayed intact. Our national revolution will transform the concept of labor itself. [Labor] is not only a subordinate factor, but it is associated with the production of wealth."[49]

Within this framework, the businessman would be the organizer and the state his controller. The Alianza was convinced that in this way it could defend the worker's share of the national wealth, the businessman's private initiative, the economic function of capital, and discipline in production. "The workers should organize their own offensive: unite within each labor union . . . appoint their own leaders, and defend the natural and legitimate aspirations of Argentine labor—national economic recovery and an equitable distribution of the wealth produced by our land."[50]

This theory led to the logical, political, and ideological conclusion that divided the opposing fronts in Argentina and around the world: on one hand, the nationalist forces that represented the real interests of the workers, and on the other, "communism and the reactionary forces [that] had united in a common front" against the worker and against national liberation. In fact, Alianza held that communism actually aided foreign capitalism, creating ideal conditions for it, insofar as communism's weak sense of nationalism and its idea of class struggle were determined by pure reformism, while "the idea of a revolution that would restore and reorder the national economy, confronting its severe problems, is being killed."[51]

This ideological line in fact reflected all the developments of Argentine nationalism. The Alianza attacked the problems of dependent and nonindustrialized countries. The national syndicalist state, which offered a new morality and a different form of social relations, was the only revolutionary organization that could oppose the financial imperialist powers and their associates in the national oligarchy. In the words of the Alianza's founder, Juan Queraltó,

> our struggle against the oligarchy goes hand in hand with our struggle against Marxism. We repudiate the landlords' oligarchy, since its existence delays national progress; [we repudiate] the capitalist oligarchy, because it is the bulwark of reaction, and [we repudiate] the political oligarchy . . . because it lacks patriotism.[52]

These positions signified not only a theoretical critique of liberal democracy and Marxist socialism but a direct attack on the Argentine economic and political establishment. The Alianza accepted the economic analysis already developed by nationalists like the Irazustas and the FORJA group, who saw unbridled capitalism as a cause of economic stagnation and social disintegration in dependent societies. That was why the nationalization of oil and public services was the key to economic independence, which in turn was a prerequisite for social justice.[53]

The Alianza's plan included proposals for agrarian reform, with an emphasis on the problem of land distribution—a subject few nationalists had considered before. Enrique Osés, who cooperated with the Alianza through his weekly paper, *Crisol*, supported the Alianza argument for agrarian land redistribution as a key to industrial production. Redistributing the land in rural workers' favor was a moral goal, but, more significantly, it was also the basis for modernizing agricultural production:

> We do not want the future of our homeland to be an agrarian future. . . . Our Argentina must become the center of world . . . industrial production. But we must realize that we can reach that point only if we know how to resolve the agrarian problem. . . . We can insure that all agrarian production is not monopolized by foreign trusts doing business at the expense of the Argentine people.[54]

The nationalists accordingly demanded more extensive state intervention in the economic process in order to control the basic sources of production. They called for the nationalization of the frozen-meat industry, regulation of credit, and government price controls.

Nevertheless, most of the nationalists rejected the idea of handing direction over to the state bureaucracy. Neither those focused on production like Lugones nor the Catholic corporativists advocated increasing state bureaucracy. Their ideal was that a harmonious society would respond to the demands for economic production while also reducing the inefficient, politicized state bureaucracy. The hierarchical, corporativist system would be truly democratized, or "popularized," while Yrigoyenist economic nationalism would be stripped of the paternalistic populism that had expanded the state bureaucracy and weakened the productive capacity of the state. In this new conception, increased production and social justice went hand in hand.

Like all the other nationalist groups, the Alianza believed that the new nationalist order in Argentina would eventually be part of a new world order. In the meantime it awaited the military leader that would guide it, a leader such as General Juan Bautista Molina. General Molina disappointed his nationalist followers in 1941, causing a split in the movement and giving rise to the Unión Cívica Nacionalista. Nevertheless, there were no basic ideological differences among the members and ex-members of the movement. The Unión Cívica Nacionalista became a political party whose slogan reflected the new ideological developments in nationalism: "Sovereignty, economic recovery, and social justice." These were the principles that would be advocated by most of the different strains of nationalism prior to the military revolution in 1943 and Peronism. It was also the slogan that would guide the nationalist coalition that supported Argentine neutrality during World War II.

CHAPTER 7

The Military in Power and Early Peronism
The Consolidation of the Integralist-Populist Formula

"The Military in Power: Revolution, Counterrevolution . . .
What Kind of Revolution?"

In the late 1930s public debate on the issue of neutrality became intense, and the correlation between the question of neutrality and the future of Argentina's democracy became stronger than ever before. The streets of Buenos Aires were filled with demonstrations both for the Allies and for neutrality. Pro-Allied movements such as Acción Argentina were created not so much to advocate that Argentina support the Allies as to show support for the democratic political system. The liberal democratic camp, organized in associations such as Acción Argentina, supported President Roberto Ortiz and manifested their fear of fascism both in domestic affairs and abroad. In early 1940 the nationalists, for their part, managed to reach the masses for the first time by means of political demonstrations organized by the Alianza de la Juventud Nacionalista, using "neutrality" and "sovereignty" as their key ideas. Over time, neutrality became a principal theme around which the nationalists organized. These domestic attacks against President Ortiz reflected the ideological radicalization that came to a head when the Commission to Investigate Activities against Argentina was created on June 19, 1941. The socialist representative, Antonio Solari, denounced the activities of the German Embassy in

Buenos Aires in the Chamber of Deputies, pointing to the German financial aid received by newspapers like *Bandera Argentina, Crisol,* and *El
Pampero,* which had published German-backed propaganda. The crux of
the problem was the spying activities for Germany allegedly carried out
by major Argentine nationalist intellectuals such as Enrique Osés, director of *El Pampero,* the journalist Juan Carlos Goyeneche, and the nationalist leader Manuel Fresco.

The possibilities for action by a Nazi fifth column in Argentina were
greatly exaggerated. Nevertheless the connections between some Argen-
tine nationalists and Germany were not merely ideological. For example,
Juan Carlos Goyeneche's trip to Germany as a reporter for *Nueva
Política* and *Sol y Luna* was much more than a work assignment.[1] The
Intelligence Service of the Federal Police had also recorded meetings at
General Juan Bautista Molina's home in which the German ambassador
Edmundo Von Thermann and the German general Gunther Niedenführ
met with important figures in the Argentine army, such as Generals Juan
Pestarini, Rodolfo Marquez, and Francisco Reynolds.[2] The meetings were
by no means unusual events, although they were not widely publicized.
More important than these meetings between nationalists and German
embassy officials and the alleged financial support from Germany for
nationalist newspapers like *El Pampero,* however, was the fact that in the
early 1940s pressure for neutrality became part of a larger effort to over-
turn the liberal order.

With the sudden death of Roberto Ortiz and his replacement by
Ramón Castillo, there was a new political option. Like Ortiz, Castillo was
a representative of the conservative Concordancia and could not be
defined as a corporativist nationalist.[3] However, in sympathizing with the
Axis in the world conflict, he differed from Justo and Ortiz, who had
favored the Allies. Whereas Ramón Ortiz showed hostility to the nationalists, Castillo had a clear affinity with the nationalist intellectuals and
nationalist army officers. Castillo's political actions were based on two
convictions. Domestically, he refused to allow the Radical Party to return
to the political process in any manner; in foreign policy, he was convinced
that the Axis powers were going to win the world conflict. With the support of Foreign Minister Enrique Ruiz Guiñazu, who admitted his support for the nationalists, Castillo was openly hostile to the United States.
In the assessment of the German Embassy in Buenos Aires, Castillo
would guide his political actions toward "tolerant solutions for both parts"
(Argentina and Germany), that is, toward neutrality.[4]

This open defiance of American interests earned Castillo widespread
admiration among the nationalists, especially the Alianzistas. After the

Pan-American conference in Rio (1942), Alianza enthusiastically endorsed the anti-war policies, claiming that the country "had not only reaffirmed its sovereignty and defended its most legitimate interests but had also interpreted the authentic feeling of the people south of the Rio Grande."[5]

In September 1942 the nationalists handed President Castillo a petition with a million signatures declaring support for his international policies. Castillo recognized that at some point the nationalists would share governmental power.[6] The neutrality thesis of the nationalist right was gaining momentum and making its influence felt in politics. This was well understood by the U.S. officials in Argentina. As Cordell Hull recalled, the United States was convinced that there were "ever-increasing pro-Axis elements based in . . . Argentina . . . steadily moving up the continent with the idea of overthrowing other governments and setting up pro-Axis regimes, like in Bolivia."[7] It was an exaggerated conclusion, but it summed up how the United States viewed Argentina at the time.

The crisis that triggered the military upheaval came in 1941 as a result of the ambiguity shown by President Castillo toward both the issue of neutrality and the new political order advocated by the nationalists and broad sectors of the army. President Castillo, with the army's approval, declared a state of siege in order to prevent demonstrations for or against neutrality. At the same time, however, he was reluctant to agree to the military's request to dissolve the Congress, although he did dissolve the city council, another symbol of the "decadent democracy" attacked by the nationalists.

Despite Castillo's attempt to comply with some of the army's demands, there was a growing consensus among army leaders that Castillo, a representative of the old conservative order, was personally incompetent and could not successfully meet the challenges of a new era. Moreover, army leaders doubted the government's ability to defend the country's sovereignty in the face of Brazil's growing strength.[8] On the domestic front there was increasing dissatisfaction with the government's economic strategy, which, together with certain malpractices, provoked moral outrage among army leaders.[9] Castillo's support for the candidacy of Robustiano Patrón Costa, an aristocratic conservative, was the last straw, and triggered general hostility at army headquarters.

By the late 1930s the old conservative formula had become ineffective. The future looked bleak to the army. A fraudulent election would probably bring into office a weak candidate likely to lead Argentina away from neutrality. The other possibility was the rise of the Unión Democrática, a popular front that advocated a leftist, pro-Allied position. Neither options were acceptable to army officers who aspired to bring Argentina into the camp of nationalist states struggling against liberalism. In short, this was a turbulent period of emerging nationalist options—tinder that could reignite the flame quenched with the defeat of Uriburu's September 1930 revolution.

On June 4, 1943, the armed forces under General Rawson took power. The coup surprised not only the Argentine public but also the nationalist intellectuals—even though they could be presumed to support it ideologically. In the words of Marcelo Sánchez Sorondo, it was the "revolution we announced,"[10] but in fact no one was expecting it.

There was good reason for Sánchez Sorondo's claim. Although this time the military upheaval was carried out by officers of various political persuasions, it was held together by a group of soldiers of the GOU (Grupo de Oficiales Unidos—Group of United Officers) who were deeply influenced by nationalist preaching.[11] Among them were General Pedro P. Ramírez, Colonel Emilio Ramírez, and Colonel Juan Perón, who together with Colonels Eduardo Avalos and Enrique Gonzáles were the most influential officers.

In spite of Sánchez Sorondo's confidence in the character of the "revolution," however, the early political decisions of the military regime did not clearly reveal the basic ideological direction of the regime. General confusion characterized the first stages of the revolution. General Rawson, who had defeated General Molina in the elections for the presidency of the Círculo Militar, was considered a democratic nationalist, and hence the liberal press initially reacted favorably to the revolution. At the same time, right-wing nationalists were impressed by his first public speech, in which he attacked the corruption of the political system while refraining from criticizing the role of financial capital in Argentina.

Further confusion about the goals of the revolution was caused by Rawson's resignation on June 7. He was replaced by General Pedro Pablo Ramírez, a former war minister under President Castillo. Ramírez declared that the military government's goal was to "renew the national spirit" of the country by giving an "Argentine ideological content to the whole country."[12] The moral and nationalistic tenor of his speech raised the expectations of the nationalists. Sánchez Sorondo addressed these words to the military:

> Since June 4th there has been a break in continuity, but it seems as though a sort of apolitical oasis has been reached. . . . What is missing is an intelligent interpretation of events, what is properly called a doctrine. Today revolution consists of deeds and of the motivation for our

action. . . . You, the military, who make your lives a profession of honor, on June 4 made a profession of faith.[13]

Sánchez Sorondo's "doctrine" was not evident in the words and deeds of the military leaders of the revolution. Still, nationalists hoped that the Uriburu experience would not be repeated.[14] Twelve years of ideological development had transformed the political understanding of both the Argentine nationalists and the new cadre of army officials, who had shifted their support from traditional authoritarianism to national authoritarianism and fascism. A clear result of this development was that the new nationalism, which appeared to be expressed in the military regime, was pitted against liberal democratic parties and organizations as well as against the old conservative authoritarianism that marked Uriburu's short military regime. Under the lead of Ramírez it seemed that the principles of the new order would be consolidated. Yet the evidence of this happening was contradictory.

The anticommunist and antisocialist agenda of the regime was apparent immediately. Leaders and militants of the Communist Party were arrested. The CGT 2—the majority sector of the CGT (Confederación General del Trabajo)—was banned outright because it comprised the most important Socialist and Communist unions. Other unions, such as the Unión Ferroviaria, were harassed. Initially it seemed that the government's anticommunist convictions and economic program would favor the economic interests of the oligarchy.

Jorge Santamarina, the minister of economy, met with the capitalists' approval because of his policy of austerity and budget balancing. The same was true of the minister of agriculture, Diego I. Mason, who promised the landholders that the restrictive practices applied in the 1930s would be eliminated. At the same time, there were clear indications that the government would not support a policy that resulted in economic hardship for the poor. The nationalists were not displeased with this line. The new nationalist government's aim was to develop an autonomous state that was not dependent on the economically dominant classes. This convinced the nationalists that their ideology had penetrated the army. The nationalist press understood the social character of this de facto nationalist government: "One of the [military] movement's basic points, set out in the revolutionary proclamation, was to outlaw foreign capital maneuvers [in the country]."[15] *Crisol* published President Ramírez's views on the social question: "The army has moved . . . to provide a solution to the problems of the people, especially the problems of the working masses."[16]

Such views of GOU army leaders, distinct from the ideology of *uriburismo*, also produced a positive reaction among the left-wing Yrigoyenists of FORJA. A declaration by FORJA's national executive on June 4, 1943, stated:

1) The overthrow of the [old] "regime" constitutes the first stage of any politics of rebuilding nationality and authentic expression of sovereignty.
2) Setting up a moral system that will govern the country's institutional development . . . is an essential principle on which any possibility of national creation must rest.
3) The gradual and harmonious imposition of a program of economic, political, and cultural emancipation of a country is what the people are demanding.[17]

The statement concluded with the observation that FORJA would follow political developments with restrained optimism.

The integralist and populist nationalists were convinced that the coup d'état would evolve into a moral shift, from liberal corruption to a revolutionary government that would provide answers to the social problems and economic emancipation. Moreover, it appeared to be the real expression of Argentine national identity: "If the liberal democracy that we have suffered [until now] had been originally Argentine, nationalism would not have produced the fruits that it has."[18] Once again, the nationalists fostered a dichotomy: liberalism was antinational and therefore could not take root, while the army portrayed the spirit of the true nation.

Thus, the Argentine army met the expectations of both left-wing and right-wing nationalists. By maintaining Argentina's neutrality in the world conflict, by threatening the liberal democratic order, and by presenting an alternative social and political plan to the one defended by democratic socialism, the nationalist army embodied the ideological evolution of Argentine nationalism from military *uriburismo* to a different integralist-populist formula that combined the aspirations of the nationalist right and left.

This new ideology was to be a synthesis of reactionary politics (focused on a total rejection of liberal democratic or socialist values) and technological modernity, based on the ideology of nationalist productionism and industrial autarky. Under the influence of modernity as conceived by Lugones, Argentina was envisioned as a potential regional power, autarkic, independent, and nationalist. Yet this modernizing thrust was to be tempered by the spiritual qualities of Catholicism, which became the reverse side of this "third way" to modernity. As noted earlier, there were inherent tensions between the Catholic and the integralist-populist faces of the nationalist formula vis-à-vis questions of modern social mobilization, industrial autarky, and populism. However, the general perception based on the early performance of the military regime was that a synthesis had been established between these reactionary and modern populist motives.

Reactionary Catholicism and Industrial Modernization

National development and industrialization were not of interest to right-wing Catholics. However, they understood that the kind of state under church and army control that they wanted to bring about could not be sustained without technological modernization.

Politically, they sought to bring religion to bear on the army and the state. Between 1932 and 1934, an intense link was developed between the army and Acción Católica Argentina. An important figure on the army side was Lieutenant Victor E. Montes, who in one of his conferences "drew a parallel between the constitutions of the army and Acción Católica."[19] Most important was Monsignor Antonio Caggiano, the general chaplain of the army, an advisor to Acción Católica, and the major proponent of linkages between the church and the army. One of the important activities through which Acción Católica priests stressed their links with the army was the "Soldier's Mass." Army chaplains traveled to distant army positions to conduct the mass and meet the soldiers. A new activism was likewise evident in the conferences and lectures held by army chaplains, which had increased in number compared to the Uriburu period.

Army chaplains became central to the enterprise of joining "church and sword."[20] Patriotic-religious ceremonies, accompanied by a wave of diocesan congresses, constituted the preparatory stage for the new links between the church and the army. National identity was redefined by the formula "God, Fatherland, and Family." Non-national doctrines, primarily liberalism and Marxist socialism, were considered betrayals of the nation.

Monsignor Caggiano helped introduce clergy into the army, including Amancio González Paz, a hard-core nationalist, and Fathers José F. Bozzo and Roberto Wilkinson, both graduates of the Gregorian University in Rome and respected as intellectuals. One of Caggiano's main problems was how to assure that military priests would remain primarily loyal to the church rather than to the army. In other words, Caggiano had to control the spiritual role of the army without, however, losing the spiritual and organizational autonomy of the church. The army chaplains stressed their common interest in opposing communism. One of the most popular books among the army officers was Monsignor D. Nepal's *El imperio soviético*, published in 1934. More than 110,000 copies were sold, and the *Revista del Suboficial* recommended it for all army officers, especially those of lower rank, who were thought to be targeted by communist propaganda.

These linkages between the army and ecclesiastical figures produced immediate political results when right-wing Catholics were appointed to key educational and ideological posts. This trend became especially clear when the conflict with the United States over the question of neutrality intensified. The nationalist, anti-Semitic writer Gustavo Martínez Zuviría (Hugo Wast) was named minister of justice. Alberto Baldrich and Federico Ibarguren were appointed provincial governor and municipal commissioner in Tucumán, respectively. General Luis Perlinger, one of the most radical members of the GOU, was made minister of the interior. Still more important, however, was the ideological function played by right-wing Catholics in the universities and other intellectual institutions. Bruno Genta was named director of the Litoral University; Hector Llambías became director of the philosophy department in Mendoza; Tomás Casares, the originator of the Cursos de Cultura Católica, was appointed rector of the University of Buenos Aires; and José Ignacio Olmedo was named president of the National Education Council. Moreover, Atilio Dell'Oro Maini was appointed dean of the law faculty, while Alfredo Villegas Oromi, Máximo Etchecopar, Hector Bernardo, and Ramón Doll, all of them militant nationalists, occupied minor but influential educational and political positions scattered throughout several provinces. Most of them were Catholics of the right who were in tune with the ideology of the regime and were convinced, moreover, that the military revolution should take an ideologically unambiguous stance toward the nation viewed as "a military reality," in the sense of Bruno Genta. Indeed, they saw no contradiction between real freedom and military rule.[21]

Political parties were banned, freedom of the press was extraordinarily limited, the autonomy of higher education was abolished, and finally on December 31 a governmental decree imposed religious education in all public schools. Martínez Zuviría's message was very clear: "We must Christianize the country . . . we must encourage the birth rate instead of immigration, we must insure the benefits of work . . . we must extirpate those hateful and atheist [liberal] doctrines."[22]

The army, however, was influenced not only by ideas from Catholic integralism but also by proposals for nationalist mobilization. In other words, the military revolution of 1943 was more than simply an authoritarian, conservative, anticommunist government. It endeavored to launch a nationalist revolution that would preserve the institutional and moral status of the church and would also aspire to modern industrialization. The notion of making Argentina a "productionist regional power" became an essential part of its ideology. The army leaders, influenced by the Lugonean concept of national strength and sovereignty, rejected any theory of "false pacifism" that would have identified peace with the option of disarmament and dependence on liberal Western powers.

The prevailing conviction within the army was that with the world at war, neutrality would strengthen Argentina materially and spiritually. The army's neutralism thus was accompanied by a push toward industrialization and economic autarky. This move led to a confrontation with the hegemonic interests of the United States, which was pressuring Argentina to abandon its neutrality.[23]

It should be kept in mind, as noted earlier, that Independent Socialists, such as Federico Pinedo, had also promoted the politics of industrialization and import-substitution in Argentina associated to American interests. Pinedo and Justo represented the interests of the growing national bourgeoisie, whose ambition was to be partners of foreign capitalism. Their model of political development was democratic, and their vision of economic development was inspired by Western democracies. In contrast, the autarkic approach, emphasizing self-sufficiency, advocated an authoritarian state and the idea of mobilizing the nation.

One question is why the Argentine army shifted its economic thinking from the liberal production-centered approach of Pinedo to autarky and hence confrontation with American interests. What did that shift mean? Some of the reasons were directly related to the hostile stance of the United States toward Argentine industrialists. Other reasons, as I have argued, were related to the development of a nationalist productionist ideology whose proponents believed in ideological confrontation with the "plutocratic" nations.

There is no question that the business dealings between the local industrial class and foreign (especially American) capital did not work easily for Argentina. Indeed, American interests were divided over Argentina's path to industrialization.[24] The Coordination Office of Inter-American Affairs, headed by Nelson Rockefeller, supported Latin American industrialization. The American secretary of state, Cordell Hull, who represented farmers who competed with Argentine products, opposed it. Cordell Hull and subsequently James Byrnes led the anti-Argentine policies that prevailed after Roosevelt's death. Nonetheless, until the Chapultepec conference in 1945, the United States encouraged industrial development in Latin America. Between 1940 and 1945, Argentina could have begun a period of collaboration with Western democracies as Brazil did. It is well known that one of the main preoccupations in military circles was the boycott by the United States of arms to Argentina, which stood in stark contrast to American assistance to Brazil.

Yet the new industrial policies of the military ran contrary to those of Pinedo, as well as to the pro-American tendency that had characterized the policies of Alvear, Justo, and Ortiz. The path to industrialization that began with the military revolution of 1943 was accompanied by an ideological preference for the Axis powers.

It was a propitious time for industrialists, inasmuch as the military government's short-term industrial and production policies were intended to strengthen national industry. However, while both the fascist autarkic and the democratic path to industrialization favored industrial interests, the differences must be noted. The democratic approach emphasized economic rationality, while the fascists placed the Maurrasian idea of "politique d'abord" or national political goals over pure economic rationality.

Argentina's process of technical modernization, therefore, responded to a geopolitical criterion, based on the conviction that the Axis powers were superior to the liberal democratic powers. For the military leaders and for most of the nationalist intellectuals, the Axis symbolized the type of nondependent, proud, industrial development that suited countries at a disadvantage in the world capitalist competition. That explains why most industrial policies advanced by the government were criticized by the nostalgic old liberal regime and by economic technocrats. All of them believed that autarkic industrialization was expensive and artificial.

The *Revista Militar* published several articles whose central thesis was that the country had to take an autarkic road to development. Protesting against pacifist currents in public opinion, these articles focused on "strategic dependencies": autonomy of equipment and communications.[25] Although the authors of some of the articles were not enthusiastic about fascism and Nazism, they praised the authoritarian corporativist system of those regimes for reestablishing the equilibrium of all productive forces of the nation.[26]

The most prominent nationalist intellectuals were aware of the problem of the role of the state in economic organization during times of world conflict. According to Julio and Rodolfo Irazusta, a liberal or a moderate socialist was incapable of understanding what "raison d'état" meant, nor could a liberal ever understand that foreign capital played a negative role in a dependent society like Argentina. More than any other nationalist intellectuals, the Irazustas expounded the relationship between economic dependency, underdevelopment, and political enslavement, and he insisted that the basis for national emancipation had to be a national-istic industrial program.

Among the proposals presented by the *Nuevo Orden* intellectuals were ones prohibiting foreign capital from operating public services and promoting the industries needed for economic autonomy, primarily the industries of national defense.[27] The key concept was preparation for a war economy, and the conclusion was that only an organized, mobilized, and organic society in which political liberalism was suppressed could under-take the massive industrialization necessary for survival in a Darwinian world.

When these ideas were adopted by leaders of the military regime they took on a momentum of their own. The question is, to what extent did ideology rather than pragmatic interests guide the political actions of the military regime? To what extent did this ideological buildup become a cognitive framework that distorted the view of the political reality in Argentina?

As the studies of Carlos Waisman have suggested, this ideological elaboration, which conceived the idea of political sovereignty based on an authoritarian regime, autarkic industrialization, anti-imperialism, and neutralism in the war, was hardly rational or pragmatic. As we have seen, other voices advocating import-substitution, democratic politics, and alignment with the American-led democratic coalition in the war were also heard.

Elite responses to critical changes in the domestic or external envi-ronment are mediated by their existing patterns of thought. Argentina's military leaders confronted political challenges armed with very strong theoretical convictions. Despite structural changes in the world system, including economic depression, and despite political problems in the domestic arena, such as the growing political unrest of the working class—all of which produced economic and political threats to various groups in Argentine society—different political attitudes could have been adopted to confront these problems. However, the military elites were convinced that the fascist solution was the right one. As noted by Carlos Escudé, the role of an antiliberal nationalist gestalt in Argentina's offi-cial culture, which resembled fascist dictatorships more than Western democracies, had a special significance because of the characteristics of Argentine society. After 1943, Argentine governmental elites were no longer cosmopolitan in outlook and skeptical of local myths, but quite the opposite.[28]

Pragmatic factors were also of vital importance in compelling political actions. Some authors have emphasized the role played by industrialists in promoting industrial policies. Juan C. Portantiero and Miguel Murmis speak of the hegemonic plan of a sector of the propertied classes—principally that sector comprised of the less powerful industrialists—and of the political and military bureaucracy that represented them.[29] However, that relationship is not clear, and it is hardly proof that the new industrialist class was decisive in providing the impulse for the industrialist policies of the army leaders.

The sociologist Torcuatto di Tella has stated that the newly emergent marginal industrialists were among the groups comprising the new elite who had reached power, and who opposed the status quo.[30] Although these observations are relevant, I claim that the new cultural and ideological framework brought about by the revolution of the right and adopted by the most important leaders of the GOU is the most important factor in explaining the elites' conviction that only the Axis war against the Allies could set Argentina on the path toward a nondependent form of modern industrialization.

The results of these strategies were expressed by Winston Churchill with a dose of sarcasm: "Argentina his chosen to dally with the evil, and not only with the evil, but with the losing side."[31] The long-term results were even worse.

The Rise of Peronism and the Dismantling of Liberal Argentina

The end of the military regime was directly related to its neutralist policies. From 1943 onward, Argentina, in the person of Foreign Minister Segundo Storni, attempted to develop a rational and comprehensible framework for its neutrality. Those governing Argentina tried to convince the United States that a future rupture of diplomatic relations with Germany was possible, using that as a bargaining chip in negotiations for American military support. Not only did Cordell Hull reject the Argentine request, but the Americans attempted to publicize alleged Argentine collaboration with the military fascist revolution led by the Movimiento Nacionalista Revolucionario in Bolivia, and threatened to freeze Argentine bank deposits in the United States. Capitulating to American pressure, President Ramírez finally agreed to break diplomatic ties with the Axis. This step precipitated his own fall from power, since nationalist ministers like Martínez Zuviría and Colonel Enrique P. González defined this governmental act as a betrayal of the nation and pressed for Ramírez's resignation.[32]

The presidency was then occupied by another hard-line nationalist, General Edelmiro J. Farrell, who reinstated the intransigent nationalist line in the government. A new set of radical nationalists filled key governmental posts, joining those who had served under Ramírez, such as Interior Minister General Luis Perlinger and General Juan Pistarini of the Ministry of Public Works. General Edelmiro Farrell's administration was characterized by a renewal of the nationalist and militarist spirit. Old myths were revived: the vigor and heroism of the army, which preserved the country's traditional Hispanic character; the worship of God; and the emphasis on the nation's sovereignty and combative morality. In every Argentine school classroom, the blackboard displayed slogans such as "Another son is a new guardian of sovereignty" and "The new Argentina seeks healthy, strong, and heroic women."[33] Despite ideological radicalization, even Farrell could not withstand the American offensive against Argentina. The Allied victories strengthened the determination of the United States to make Argentina toe the line, and Cordell Hull did not hesitate to define Argentina as the Nazi headquarters on the American continent.

In February 1945, when the defeat of the Third Reich was all but final, Argentina was invited to sign the Chapultepec Treaty in Mexico, at the Conference on Problems of War and Peace. Argentina's participation in the conference, which would signal its return to the Western liberal fold, was contingent upon certain conditions. Argentina had to declare war on Germany, an ultimatum that again pitted the moral doctrinaires against the pragmatists—although in fact both sides supported neutrality as a matter of national sovereignty. Nonetheless, Argentina's attempts to defend its position were doomed to failure—something that Perón, already the strongman in the government, understood very clearly. He knew that his sympathy for the Axis would not help him in his quest for political power. Accordingly, he cast his lot with those advocating a break between the military government and the nationalists (*rupturistas*), thereby helping to tip the balance in favor of the only step Argentina could afford to take at that point, and Argentina declared war on the Axis.[34]

The nationalists were faced with a dilemma. They could not accept the abandonment of neutrality even for tactical reasons, and yet they could not withdraw their support from a government that represented the kind of political authoritarianism they had been struggling to achieve for more than a decade. Their direct influence on the military government can be said to have come to an end when Perón was named vice president of the nation and began to consolidate the political power he had built up during his term as secretary of labor. Perón understood that the new rules of the game demanded the sacrifice of certain principles of Argentina's foreign affairs policy in order to proceed with internal reforms.

Did Perón make substantial changes to the military revolution of 1943, or did he merely add a reformist face to the national corporativist system installed with the revolution of 1943, of which he had been one of the main ideologues? Although Perón's personal style enabled him to approach the working-class masses in a way that his fellow officers could only dream of, and although his policies for working-class welfare generally proved to be effective, his welfare policies made the creation of a modern universal social welfare state in Argentina more unlikely. Indeed, Perón's politics of inclusion of the working class represented an original Argentine experience, a particular response to Argentina's democratic shortcomings. At the same time, they resembled Italian fascism rather than the British welfare state. Perón's successful political and social reformism, characterized by the association of political authoritarianism and social justice for the working class, did not improve but rather reduced Argentina's chances of becoming an industrial democracy. Namely, Perón's reformism hampered rather than improved the conditions for developing an industrial society relying on political democracy and an autonomous working class. Like his army GOU colleagues, Perón believed that the economy must be at the service of the nation. The nation was composed of its "living forces," namely, its productive classes, which were brought under a state corporativist structure. Perón aspired to develop production along the lines of what Lugones had said of national strength, albeit accompanied by social policies. Hence, for Perón, the economic equilibrium that blended productionist policies based on "national interests" with populist social justice and expansion of the internal consumer market was certainly biased toward the latter. Ultimately, however, the idea of social justice did not entail any type of political autonomy for workers. The "living forces" of the nation were those that were identified with the Peronist syndicalist state.

Perón's labor policies continued the line promoted by his self-designed Syndical Statute, promulgated by the military government in 1943, which reflected the attempt to achieve corporativist authoritarian control over labor organizations. Housing rents were reduced and higher salaries were established for the most poorly paid government workers. This reform thrust gained momentum in November 1943, when the Departamento Nacional del Trabajo, until then a minor branch of the interior ministry, became the Secretaría de Trabajo y Previsión, an autonomous department headed by Perón. Decree 156,074 (November 27, 1943) made Perón responsible for taking the steps necessary make the country's productive forces more harmonious,[35] thereby initiating Perón's meteoric rise to power. The nationalist press reacted with enthusiasm to his appointment and to what was considered an attempt to establish a productive economic system with clear implications for social justice.

> Perón's declarations to the press . . . conformed to what we have been maintaining in these pages for ten years. The problems of labor and its relations with capital have defeated the provisions of legislators and statesmen of the beginning of the century. . . . [Now] the state will abandon its passivity . . . and the cold repressive attitude of early times, which just favored . . . those who abuse the weaknesses of others.[36]

Perón had also grasped the importance of the new working class, which was made up of immigrant workers living in the industrialized cities. Since the mid-1930s the nationalists themselves had been proclaiming that a nationalist revolution could not forego the support of "nationalist" masses. They considered the "new working classes" to be part of the Argentine nation, while the organized workers and the revolutionary working-class leadership were seen as foreign-oriented and antinationalist. Perón was very clear on this point:

> I am personally a syndicalist . . . and as such I am anticommunist, but I believe that labor must be organized on a syndicalist basis, so that workers, rather than the leaders and agitators, would be the ones to reap the benefits of their sacrifice. . . . I have advised the Department [of Labor], an organization that works toward the goal . . . of improving the living conditions of the workers, though without tolerating any social conflict. . . . I won't tolerate the action of agitators . . . most of whom are not even Argentines but foreigners who have not known how to respect the nationality of my homeland. . . . [37]

Perón came into contact with the union leaders through the good offices of Lieutenant-Colonel Domingo Mercante, the son of a railway worker. He met with syndicalists from the dissolved CGT, and in 1943 he stepped in on the side of the workers in the Berisso "Frigoríficos" strike in La Plata. With his support, the first collective agreement was reached between labor and government. However, the negotiations were carried out not with the representatives of the strong communist leadership of the union but with a new rank-and-file leader, Cipriano Reyes. Reyes would became the most important figure of the Partido Laborista, which later supported Perón's rise to power (even though Reyes became an enemy of Perón and was subsequently jailed). Perón plainly sought to co-opt the labor movement, either through support of nonorganized sectors of the working class or through infiltration of the existing organized labor movement. In 1943, for example, he placed his associate Mercante as government overseer in the Union Ferrroviaria. With Mercante's help, Perón reversed previous divisive measures taken by the military against the leadership of the union. However, the new measures taken by Peron amounted to little more than promises of social justice and extended material concessions, which were conditioned on personal loyalty. Moreover, as Perón warned union leaders, foreign ideologies of socialism and communism would no longer be tolerated.

Perón's visit to Italy between 1939 and 1941 stimulated his admiration of Italian fascism, especially the way it offered a solution to problems of the working class.[38] Perón's approach to industrial relations clearly resembled Mussolini's. As labor secretary in the military junta, he brought most of the unions under his control through the 1945 Law of Professional Associations, whose provisions were almost identical with Mussolini's labor code. Bargaining between the government and the growing unions culminated in decree 23,852 (October 2, 1945). The decree gave unions full legal rights while eliminating parallel unions. It provided the architecture for elections of delegates and stewards and a model for bargaining with employers, with vague allusions to co-participation in management decisions. It also gave unions legal rights to participate in politics, giving workers the green light to form the political party that would eventually win the elections of February 1946. However, legal status required recognition from the Labor Secretariat (Article 43). Under this law, only government-recognized unions and employers' associations could sign labor contracts, and only one employer association and one labor union were to be allowed in each economic field. Strikes and lockouts were forbidden.

Were the workers the direct beneficiaries of the Peronist order? Did they support it? Much has been written since Gino Germani's theory of modernization, which portrayed the workers as irrational for backing Perón's policies. Critics of modernization theories, such as Murmis and Portantiero, have argued that it was rational for workers to support a multiclass movement ruled by an authoritarian regime. Other scholars, including Juan Carlos Torre, Daniel James, and Jeremy Adelman, have been critical of both the developmental and revisionist theses. They point to the opportunities for and constraints on workers within different political situations.[39] The net result, however, was that the workers negotiated a "new order" with Perón that was beneficial for them.

The trade-off of concessions to labor in return for conditional support eventually paid off for both the working class and Perón. The decree of October 2, 1945, enabled the two largest unions, the commercial and the rail unions, to become the first two labor associations certified in Argentine history. The commercial union became the vanguard of the working-class resistance that was to stand behind Perón when he was dismissed and then jailed by his army colleagues on October 9, 1945. A whole network of labor organizers was at work throughout the working-class neighborhoods of Buenos Aires. Recently organized workers, Argentina's *descamisados*, were joined by previously organized workers who provided a firm organizational basis.

The myth of October 17 was in reality a mass mobilization that permanently linked the fate of labor to that of the "worker colonel." On that day, which was to become an integral part of Peronist mythology, workers in the capital, organized by Eva Duarte, Cipriano Reyes, and Colonel Mercante, poured into the streets. The Peronist masses, workers from the poor neighborhoods of Avellaneda, converged on the streets under the passive gaze of the police forces. They demanded Perón's release from jail, where he had been incarcerated since October 9 as a result of the military coup attempted by General Eduardo Avalos in order to block Perón's rise to power. Perón was soon released, and on the same day, while speaking to the people from the balcony of Casa Rosada, he called for "creation of an indestructible bond of brotherhood between the people and the army."[40]

The military commanders realized they had to yield to the pressure for elections. Perón ran for the presidency in 1946, endorsed by two parties, the Labour Party of Cipriano Reyes and the Unión Cívica Radical (Junta Renovadora). They were opposed by a coalition of parties (Socialist, Communist, "Alvearist" Radicals, and Conservatives) representing the parties of a modern secular liberal democracy. Socialists like Nicolás Repetto, the Communist Rodolfo Ghioldi, and liberal oligarchs, such as Joaquín S. de Anchorena, marched together in the famous March of the Constitution and Liberty. They were defending liberal institutions and the constitution, and advocated a return to secular education in schools. On January 1, most newspapers published the education policy of the Unión Democrática, defining very clearly what could be regarded as liberal Argentina. From that point onward, church authorities could not be totally indifferent to the elections. Even though they were suspicious of Perón, and in some cases directly hostile toward him (especially the influential priest Miguel de Andrea), church authorities were even harsher toward the democratic coalition which openly supported secular education. *El Pueblo* said, "It is impossible to be Catholic and support secular education."[41]

In the 1946 election, Perón and those who represented the integralist-populist formula ran against the liberal-democratic candidates who had the endorsement of the American ambassador, Spruille Braden. That American intervention in Argentine politics directly contributed to Perón's victory. Perón himself reduced the political confrontation to a slogan: "Braden or Perón." This formula transformed the confrontation between two different political conceptions into a confrontation between the nation and U.S. imperialism. The determination of the Americans to prove Perón's complicity with the Nazis guaranteed Perón's success. Such complicity could never be proven, despite the "Blue Book" published by the Americans in an attempt to provide evidence. Perón, like the nationalists before him, represented an alternative view of national populism frequently identified with fascism. At the same time, that ideological bond did not necessarily entail membership in a fascist international. Moreover, by the time he took office the war was over, and it would have been absurd for a pragmatist like Perón to identify himself as a fascist.

Despite his attempt to distance himself from fascism, Perón's corporativist intentions were well known from his tenure as secretary of labor during the military regime. Some Perón supporters nonetheless expected that his type of political corporativism would develop into a new type of social democratic movement. One of the figures influencing him was the general secretary of the Commercial Workers Union, Angel Borlenghi, a long-time admirer of the British industrial relations system. He envisioned industrial, not craft, trade unions, strong enough to bargain independently with employers, and loosely affiliated to a political party so as to ensure the political defense of the system. Similar ideas were held by Cipriano Reyes, Luis Gay, and Luis Monzalvo, the leaders of the Partido Laborista. They were soon disappointed with Perón. Interviewed many years later in Quilmes, Cipriano Reyes said,

> Negotiations with Perón were a nightmare. We were thinking of a democratically-controlled Labor Party. . . . I soon realized that Perón wanted total control. . . . The worst moments were our contact with Evita. She pointed to me and ordered me . . . "Ciprianito, radicalize the workers for me. . . . You know, I'm very *radicala*. . . ." "Madam," I responded, "I am a democrat, I cannot radicalize the workers." Soon

I understood that Evita wanted to radicalize the workers in order to have them in her hands. I could not accept radicalization nor be like putty in Perón's hands.[42]

What Cipriano Reyes could hardly have understood was that both trends, radicalization and corporatization, were two faces of the same policy.

In the wake of the presidential election of 1946, one of Perón's first actions was to dissolve the Partido Laborista and form his own Peronist party. Monzalvo accepted Perón's decision, while Reyes maintained an intransigent position toward the confirmation of an autonomous, non-corporativized social democracy. The rational attitude of most workers was to accept Perón's reformist policies, paying for them with the loss of their political liberties and their right to autonomous collective action.

Argentina's long-term industrial policy and the fundamental principles of the Peronist *justicialista* doctrine were mapped out in a decree issued by the military government on August 25, 1944 (Ordenamiento Económico y Social). Through this decree, developed and implemented by the Consejo Nacional de Postguerra, Perón shaped the country's economic and social organization. The plan spoke of economic emancipation, stimulation of production, creation of heavy industry, full employment, and social justice. The government announced its intention to achieve a "just equilibrium among all the factors that take part in production, . . . collaboration between labor and employer organizations, humanization of the function of capital, . . . and improvement in workers' living conditions."[43]

This program was based on the conviction that although Argentina did not have territorial ambitions, world politics demanded the development of a strong, autarkic nation. Perón wanted to develop heavy industry while promoting social justice.[44] Public-private industrial complexes were created to exploit national resources, and long-term loans were offered to national industry.

All the instruments created by the state during the Perón administration were intended to further these ends. The symbol of the state regulatory economic power was the IAPI (Argentine Institute of Production and Trade), created to promote the Five-Year Plan for industrialization initiated in October 1946. Perón forced farmers to sell to the IAPI at low, fixed prices and then made profits for the government by selling those goods on the free market. The law that most frightened the rural oligarchy, however, was the Estatuto del Peón, which recognized agricultural laborers as workers with labor rights. Although this law was promoted by

Enrique Osés in the pages of the right-wing paper *Crisol*, left-wing nationalists like Jauretche had also pressed Perón to pass it. On the surface, industrialists might welcome legislation that would give rural workers more buying power for their products; however, industrialists still feared the regulatory power of the state and the labor legislation that accompanied the IAPI's industrial policies. The first Five-Year Plan (1947–1951) was devised to transform a "civic and peaceful country into a country in arms,"[45] and the second Five-Year Plan confirmed the tendency to "strengthen the armed forces in order to support the . . . decision to be a sovereign, just and free nation."[46] In other words, the basic conviction was that the new economic efforts to be carried out by the military establishment would not be in opposition to the social and economic interests of the people, but rather totally in their favor. This meant that the military factories would search for the necessary raw materials in order to deepen industrial development.[47]

The armed forces were charged with launching a plan to develop the infrastructure for heavy industry (mainly steel) and advanced technology. The factories created between 1946 and 1955 under the guidance of the General Bureau of Military Manufacture served military as well as civilian purposes. On June 12, 1947, the Argentine Congress passed law 12,987, which authorized construction of chemical plants and the creation of the steel company SOMISA (Sociedad Mixta Siderurgica Argentina) as planned by military authorities. The army was also charged with creating an aeronautical industry and an automotive industry, both of which later became part of the state-owned IAME (Industrias Aeronauticas y Mecánicas del Estado). A revision of the 1853 federal constitution in 1949 provided a constitutional framework for implementation of the new ideology. Perón's close collaborators, the Spaniard José Figuerola (a Catalan syndicalist during the dictatorship of Miguel Primo de Rivera, who had immigrated to Argentina in 1930), the law professor Arturo Sampay, and Domingo Mercante, had proposed the amendments that established the new basis for social reform. The revised chapter III listed a series of rights inspired by Catholic encyclicals that had spoken out against abuses in the capitalist system and in favor of state intervention in the economic sector. Under this formula, wages were allowed to rise by as much as 40 percent from 1946 to 1949.

The combination of nationalist industrialization with social welfare goals, which faithfully reflected the integralist-populist formula, functioned only until 1949, the watershed year for labor in Argentina. From 1949 on, Perón's policies were guided by productivity rather than social justice. Wages declined by over 20 percent, while greater discipline was imposed on the unions.[48] In fact, from 1949 until 1955, Perón's populist policies resembled fascist corporativist practices more than they did under his pre-1949 social reformism. Perón encouraged the organization of the working class, although only under state control, because "it suits the state to have organic forces it can control and lead rather than inorganic forces that escape its leadership. . . . We do not want unions divided into political factions, because it is precisely political unions that are dangerous."[49] In other words, worker welfare could be guaranteed only under the tutelage of the hierarchical state.

From an ideological standpoint, welfare politics was clearly an issue that most Argentine nationalists of both the right and the left believed could be resolved only in a national-syndicalist state. The entire Peronist ideology was built around the doctrine of *justicialismo*. Differing slightly from fascism, but radically opposed to the pure materialism of liberal and Marxist ideologies, the "third way" of *justicialismo* sought a unifying point between idealism, materialism, collectivism, and individualism.[50] In its rhetoric, however, *justicialismo* was reminiscent of Italian fascism in that it emphasized nationalism, authoritarianism, and leadership. Ultimately, the rights of citizens were ranked lower than their national responsibilities. The basic idea was that of an organized community in which the individual would reach personal happiness, but the concept of personal happiness was disassociated from bourgeois egoism.

A community [is one] where the individual really has something to offer to the common good, something to contribute and not only his mute and fearful presence. . . . Society will have to be a harmony in which no dissonance is produced, matter does not have the upper hand, and there is no state of fantasy. . . . In such a regime, freedom is not an empty word because it is always determined . . . by the sum of freedoms and by the general ethical and moral condition.[51]

The Peronist ethical state, like the fascist state, excluded bourgeois egoism and the expression of independent ideas. "Some say that we must capture the independent opinion [holders]. Great mistake. . . . We must marginalize them. . . ."[52] In other words, the concept of community was opposed to that of civil society. While the latter invites pluralism, the idea of community in Ferdinand Tönnies's sense is like the idea of a movement, which basically rejects differences of opinion and rejects the concept of party politics.

The fourth section of the first Five-Year Plan dealt with cultural matters and considered ways that cultural uniformity might be created. It noted that Argentina's various cultural institutions lacked spirituality and a unifying framework, as well as the appropriate orientation needed to guide national culture. The program published in 1947 expressed the early intention of Peronism to shape and mold a new national consciousness, particularly through the education system. The second Five-Year Plan, published in 1951, sought to impose the *justicialista* doctrine on the entire nation as an official way of thinking.[53]

Indeed, in 1952 *justicialismo* was legally defined as the "National Doctrine." It expressed the spirit of the Organic Statute of the Peronist Party. Article 2 emphasized that the Peronist party is unified around its doctrine and that any position conspiring against that unity would be rejected. Article 74 stated that the best way to learn to command is to learn to obey, and article 77 stated that there are two highest figures in Peronism, Juan Perón and Eva Perón.

Another issue of importance is the relationship between Peronism and the Catholic Church. Despite the break between Peronism and the church during the 1950s, Perón's *justicialista* program and especially the new constitution of 1949 included clear motifs and thus were to the liking of ecclesiastical authorities. As already noted, the church had indirectly supported Perón's election in 1946 because Perón was associated with the religious educational policy adopted by the 1943 military revolution. Further, Perón ordered the party congressmen of the new congress in 1946 to vote for passage of decree 18,411, which favored religious education and had already been promoted by the former regime.

The fervent debate on this decree in the Chamber of Deputies, in June 1946, lasted for a week and was heavily covered by the press, which had grasped the long-term importance of the decisions to be taken. The Peronist position was defended by two Catholic nationalists, Justo Díaz de Vivar and Raúl Bustos Fierro. Practically the only opposition among the Peronists in the legislature was led by Cipriano Reyes, who had reached the point of breaking with Perón. (Reyes, representing the secular social democratic side of Peronism, could no longer endure the fascist turn in the movement.)

In Perón's view, a shift in social and economic policies had to be accompanied by a radical change in education policies. This position was made clear in the congressional debate.[54] Argentine education before Peronism, his supporters argued, had led the people to such a pluralism of ideas that "Argentines nowadays, reflect on these basic issues in a diverse and contradictory way. In this country there is no conceptual unity on fundamental state principles."[55] Peronism represented the truly national heritage rooted in the spiritual Spanish and Catholic tradition, and the role of religion was to consolidate a national morality. All of Argentina's national heroes, it was argued, even the most liberal among them, had been deeply Catholic and had defended religion; this was evidenced in the constitutional dispositions favoring the Catholic religion, which reflected three hundred years of Catholic school teaching, from the Spanish conquest to 1884.

During the debate an attempt was made to draw a line between the 1880s generation, a "liberal minority" that attacked religion, and the people, who had defeated that minority in the 1946 election. Accordingly, Peronism represented the "real" Argentina, the Catholic Argentina now reemerging as a confirmation of the national soul. An authentic nationalism should be based on the cultural role of Catholicism, which was to provide cohesion in a country of immigrants. A return to the Catholic "essence" of Argentina meant a return to the values voted for by the people. The conclusion of the debate was that "we, Peronists, are spiritual and serious about doctrine while 'liberals' are pragmatic and rationalistic. They deny the national spirit, and have surrendered to foreign ideas."[56]

Despite its affirmation of the spiritual, Peronism went far beyond what the church could have expected of a conservative regime under pressure from the spiritual surveillance of the church. The spiritual option raised by *justicialismo* may have adapted Christian motifs to its own purposes, but it remained autonomous and later turned against the Catholic Church.

This is probably one of the main reasons why some of the most prominent right-wing nationalists had reservations about Perón's regime. However, there were far more controversial points in Peronist political praxis that raised suspicions among the rank and file of the nationalist right. The most reactionary of these, for example, suspected that Perón's style of government would be more democratic that they had originally hoped. Moreover, some of them launched harsh criticism at his foreign policy. One of the first initiatives taken by Perón was the approval of the Chapultepec Act and the United Nations Charter. As noted by Marcelo Sánchez Sorondo, the nationalists hoped to create a civilian GOU, that is, an ideological apparatus to support and legitimize Perón, but "the idea did not prosper because Perón supported the break with the Axis."[57]

The speed with which Perón shifted his international political allegiance strengthened the conviction of many right-wing nationalists that Perón was basically an opportunist.[58] To this conviction was added the growing distrust among the nationalist Catholics—Meinvielle, Sánchez Sorondo, Etchecopar, and Amadeo from *Nuevo Tiempo* and *Balcón*—who soon realized that Perón was not the elitist, autocratic general they had expected. At an early stage of Perón's government, one of the editorials of *Balcón* professed satisfaction with the fervent nationalist message delivered by Perón.[59] Later, they understood that the only alternative espoused by Perón "to democracy was demagogy."[60]

Criticism of Perón was not restricted to the more reactionary sectors of the nationalist right. Right-wing nationalists with anti-imperialist and populist tendencies were also suspicious of Perón's policies. For example, the brothers Irazusta broke with Perón because they felt that his anti-imperialism was less radical than his rhetoric had led them to believe. In fact, the Irazustas, along with their colleagues at *Nuevo Orden* and *La Voz del Plata*, distrusted Perón's statements on economic nationalism. They were convinced that Perón and the military government would perpetuate the liberal economic model that had allowed the British to dominate Argentine interests. Although the Irazustas believed that a nationalist popular movement was necessary, they could not accept the Peronists, whom they regarded as unprincipled. *La Voz del Plata*, a publication that followed the ideological line of *Nuevo Orden*, became the voice of the new Partido Libertador founded by the Irazustas. It criticized the military government's policies rather than its ideology; the Partido Libertador's goals were actually much the same as Perón's.

Even the Alianza Nacionalista, the political group that transmitted Perón's social message most clearly, had certain reservations about the Peronist regime. When Peronism developed into a huge popular force, the Alianza paper described with emotion those "people without shirts, but genuine people,"[61] who gathered in the Plaza de Mayo to listen to the leader's speech; yet despite this picture, the nationalists of the Alianza hoped that "time will put in the clean hands of nationalism the [task of] leading that proletarian mass."[62] Leonardo Castellani, an ardent supporter of the Alianza, argued against what he saw as the Peronist tendency to nurture mass populism without authoritarian guidance. He defined national syndicalism as aristocratic and antipopulist. Combining nationalism with syndicalism demanded flexibility from both sides: nationalism had to abandon its bourgeois roots, while syndicalism must "refrain from being . . . populist" and not transform the defense of labor into a pretext "to destroy anything that has some hierarchy . . . and represents the aristocracy."[63] Castellani was clearly referring to the possibility that the Alianza would be absorbed by Perón, a leader who, although authoritarian, apparently inspired the masses to mobilize spontaneously. Castellani's strictures notwithstanding, however, the Alianza was probably the most important group to support the military revolution of 1943. In spite of Perón's individual political style and the fact that, due to American pressure, he had severed diplomatic relations with Germany in 1945, the Alianza supported Perón in his election campaign. In other words, right-wing nationalists saw Peronism as a very two-sided phenomenon; they wanted to make it fit within a preconceived ideological model, but clearly it did not.

Having said this, there is no doubt that the nationalists of the right felt more affinities with Peronism than with the old liberal and conservative political establishment, despite their harsh criticism of what may be termed the pragmatic, non-doctrinaire side of Peronism. As Hector Bernardo observed, Perón's themes were "our themes. . . . The Revolution was nourished by the actions and thought of the generation called nationalist."[64] In *El Pueblo*, Manuel Gálvez exalted Perón. "I see Perón as a providential man. . . . Here in a place characterized by the absence of [leaders] . . . the emergence of this soldier, endowed with a marvelous intuition, is a most important event."[65] Several nationalists even saw in the popular "uprising" a political act related to Hispanic traditions: "Real politics is what we saw on the day of the popular declaration. . . . The first right of a people is to have a caudillo, which is an old Hispanic institution of personal government rather than by contract."[66]

Among the nationalist populist intellectuals of FORJA, support for Perón was forthright. In his book *El 45*, Félix Luna has confirmed, based on the testimony of Guillermo Borda, that FORJA members were the first in civil society to recognize Perón's leadership potential well before he became president. Early on, FORJA members gave Jauretche the mission of initiating a dialogue between FORJA and Perón. Jauretche described his first meeting with Perón effusively: "For me he is the ideal man to lead."[67] Jauretche became a personal advisor to Perón during Perón's term in the department of labor, and he sought to establish close contacts between Perón and the "intransigent" wings of the Radical Party, which was also one of Perón's goals.[68] Later, when Perón became president, Jauretche advised him to pay special attention to the government of the province of Buenos Aires, which Perón and Jauretche agreed should be run only by people associated with FORJA. There is no doubt that Perón ranked FORJA intellectuals higher than their counterparts of the revolution of the right.

Perón, however, was by no means a tool of the nationalist intellectuals. In that respect he was no different from Mussolini, Hitler, and other fascist leaders. Perón understood that those intellectuals were of little use politically, vis-à-vis the masses. Even so, despite their limited political and electoral importance—revealed in Perón's famous phrase defining them as *"piantavotos"* (scaring away the votes)—Perón acknowledged the important role they could play as the ideologues for a movement that lacked intellectual legitimacy, especially those who espoused anti-imperialism.

Perón was aware that alongside the political struggle was a metapolitical struggle, in which new concepts and new ideological elites should be promoted. This was an important issue to take into account for a revolution that sought to stay in power. For that reason, major FORJA figures were given important political and economic positions. Arturo Jauretche was nominated as president of the Banco de la Provincia de Buenos Aires, and other *"forjistas"* occupied central posts in Argentina's most important province. At the national level, the *forjista* Hipólito J. Paz was appointed foreign minister, Adolfo Savino, under-secretary of industry and commerce, and Carlos Maya, director of the Central Bank of the Republic.

Peronism was embedded within the intellectual and ideological framework that preceded it; it defined itself as the beginning of a new era and not simply as another example of social-democratic reformism. The tragedy, from the point of view of those who strove to create a movement that blended social justice with democratic practice in Argentina, was that Peronism integrated politically the ideological synthesis of the revolution of the right. Perón gave it political content and transformed it into a political culture. As noted by Daniel James, social justice and national sovereignty became credibly interrelated themes within Peronist rhetoric, rather than remaining abstract slogans.[69] Perón spoke the language of the people and understood the real political value of popular culture. He himself, and Evita Perón to an even greater extent, expressed the "feeling" of the simple worker better than any of the Argentine nationalists. While other movements addressed the same needs and offered similar solutions for the working class, Perón's success was related to his political rhetoric and based on his ability to recast the whole issue of citizenship within a new social context.[70]

The resemblance between Peronism and fascism is clear. Yet analysts like Tulio Halperín Donghi have held that Peronism could not repeat the fascist enterprise because fascism was devised to strengthen the instruments of existing political domination,[71] whereas Peronism represented a social revolution in which new classes rose to political predominance. This is probably one of the more important differences between Perón and the fascists. At the same time, Peronist social policies cannot be compared to the New Deal policies of Roosevelt and the development of welfare capitalism in Western Europe after 1945.[72] As Peter Ross has noted, there are sharp differences between the British welfare state, for example, and

Peronist welfare. By 1955 state welfare provisions in Argentina remained largely residual, and state control over welfare was tenuous. Far from being a monolith using welfare to bind workers to itself, the Peronist state looked more like a sponge that soaked up the demands of various interest groups. Welfare was thus dissipated rather than made universal.[73]

Hence, Perón's welfare policies, although not identical to the fascist corporatization of labor and capital, still owed much more to that model than to the modern democratic welfare state.[74] Ideologically, both Peronism and fascism elaborated a discourse that relied not on a particular social class but rather on the mass, the people, the nation. Both likewise developed an antiliberal concept of democracy summarized in the notion of the organized community. For both, the "movement" was representative of the nation and of a natural order that had been undone by liberalism. Perón and the nationalists who preceded him both in Argentina and in Europe saw liberalism as a foreign tool in the hands of the enemies of the country. For Perón they were traitors (*"cipayos"* and *"vendepatrias"*). In short, Perón could not be classified merely as a populist through his presidential periods, nor could fascism be considered an anti-worker or anti-welfare movement.[75]

Perón's authoritarianism, which responded to a "democratic clamor," was also of a new type, yet it leaned more toward the fascist model than old-style authoritarianism. This new form of authoritarianism was made clear when Perón declared a state of internal war rather than a curfew, thereby breaking with the custom of previous authoritarian governments (which demanded a problematic judicial elaboration).[76]

In more ways than one, Peronism constituted a link between the "third way" notion of fascism and the new "third way" of non-aligned countries after World War II. Perón himself said that since 1938 the third position had had a clear precedent in fascism and national socialism, and was the best way to tackle the problems of the postwar era.[77] He was convinced that fascism was the only revolutionary movement that could blend a left-wing social approach with a right-wing form of political organization. As Gálvez said in 1936, "Fascism . . . is a doctrine of the right in the sense that it opposes democracy and socialism, but from the social and economic point of view, it is a doctrine of the left."[78]

For the Argentine people, Peronism is associated with a new political style and with social justice. However, the Peronist message was far more than that, and it was reconstructed in different ways. As noted by Guillermo O'Donnell, during the 1960s and 1970s this message captured the imagination of young people who came from far-right nationalist Catholic circles. Hostility toward foreign influences, nationalist chauvinism, the exaltation of the chief or the caudillo, the idealization of violence not only as a means to an end but as a purifying catharsis, the radical rejection of liberalism and Marxism—these were the themes of most of the Peronist guerrilla groups that multiplied during those years. Such groups resembled the radical wings of European fascism, including those that never reached power and those that attained it, as in Mussolini's short-lived Republica de Salò. That, rather than Cuba, was the model. Peronism in power was a new type of revolution, namely, a national revolution,[79] which transcended Perón's rule.

Conclusion

In this study I have examined the emergence of a new form of nationalism and a reactionary path to modernity that have challenged the liberal version of democracy in Argentina since the 1930s. My primary contention has been that during the 1930s, despite differences, both right-wing and left-wing forms of nationalism came to share a vision of a new antiliberal, economically self-sufficient, and anti-imperialist Argentina. Liberal rights and democratic institutions—the symbols of democratic modernity—were not part of this view of an "emancipated Argentina." The hallmarks of this "new Argentina" would be popular mobilization, modern industrialization, and social justice.

I have suggested that this set of ideas was adopted by the military regime of 1943 and was further developed and popularized by Juan Domingo Perón, particularly during his first term as president. From that point onward, this new constellation of political ideas became part of Argentina's political culture.

Contrary to most analyses of Argentine nationalism, I have claimed that Argentina's right-wing nationalists were not simply reactionary, just as left-wing nationalists were not simply anti-imperialist populists or modernizers.[1] In fact, the right wing was modernizing and anti-imperialist, and it supported industrialization and social justice even before the left did so. The special brand of right-wing nationalism discussed in this book was not loyal to the old, conservative oligarchy, and indeed stopped supporting authoritarian protection of liberal economic rights. In the words of Carlos Ibarguren, the new ideological framework was not the "fruit of liberal democracy which is repudiated . . . and it is neither bourgeois, reactionary, nor capitalist."[2]

During the 1930s this line of thinking was complemented by another that had evolved from the populist tradition of the Radical party, thereby producing an integralist-populist synthesis which was pitted against liberal democracy. My thesis is that this ideological synthesis of the integralist right and populist left was the outcome of the conjunction of domestic and foreign ideological processes.

In domestic politics, starting in the 1930s, right-wing nationalists no longer struggled against populism, but instead turned against conservatives, liberals, and socialists—the political heirs of the nineteenth-century liberal oligarchic elites. In broad ideological terms, this shift coincided with an awareness by most nationalist right-wing intellectuals that fascism was not equivalent to authoritarian demobilization. The new understanding of fascism as an ideology that encouraged political mobilization under authoritarian control paradoxically enabled the Argentine rightists to reexamine the Yrigoyenist phenomenon and Argentina's populist tradition. Prior to 1930, they joined forces with the conservatives in order to overthrow the populist Yrigoyen regime. However, a new process began to take shape when prominent right-wing nationalists recognized that the populist Yrigoyen regime constituted the first modern challenge to the liberal conservative political and cultural order. Moreover, for some right-wing integralists, Yrigoyenism exemplified a type of local fascism rather than a democratic movement. More importantly, that type of mobilization provided them with the populist component they had previously lacked.

As Manuel Gálvez claimed, "Yrigoyenist" Radicalism, with its popular appeal, its vigor, and its heroic and rebel tradition, expressed an authentic Argentine fascism. However, Yrigoyen had never succeeded in becoming or achieving what the nationalists wanted; integralists like Ernesto Palacio and Ramón Doll, for example, criticized Yrigoyenism for not carrying through with its totalitarian tendencies. In other words, Yrigoyen's political rule never met the expectations that Yrigoyen himself had promoted. Nonetheless, despite Yrigoyen's shortcomings, the theoretical reflection on populism and fascism by the integralist right enabled it to envision a possible ideological collaboration with the populist left, rooted in the tradition of Yrigoyenist populism.

With regard to the ideological evolution in the Radical Party, I have pointed to the ideological and political split caused by the appearance of the rebel group of intellectuals, FORJA, who challenged the liberal establishment of the party. However, FORJA did not limit itself to a critique of the conservative Alvearist faction of the Radical party. In terms similar to those coming from the modernist sectors of the right, it also attacked Yrigoyen for not daring to go beyond the limits of Argentina's "liberal constitutionalism." Although Yrigoyen's policies at times bordered on illegality, he did not attempt to violate the constitutional order established by the oligarchic elites. FORJA concluded that Yrigoyen's type of populist rule did not meet the necessities of modernity, which demanded the abandonment of the liberal order. FORJA understood that the national revolution that it sought must be completely opposed to the idea of liberal democracy. Only by abandoning liberal democracy could Argentina become authentically sovereign and economically developed. Therefore, although FORJA spokesmen did not advance a modern industrialist ideology as did Lugones and Bunge, they thought that a modern autarkic Argentina could be created by enhancing the mobilizing, anti-imperialist, and antiliberal elements of nationalism.

Both the antiliberal integralist right and the populist left invoked the same national myths represented by the figure of Juan Manuel de Rosas, the symbol of *caudillismo* and of the antiliberal tradition in Argentine history. Both advocated the same principle of "national" social justice, differing from the rationalist and materialist basis of social democracy and reformist liberalism, and both supported a "pro-Axis" neutrality during World War II. Although their support for Argentine neutrality in World War II had distinct origins (the integralist right was fascist while the populist left defended a tradition of neutrality), both sides came to a shared understanding of their opposition to liberal democracy and rejected the imperialist designs of what they called the liberal "plutocratic" nations. For all of them, liberalism was equivalent to imperialism. More importantly, the nationalists regarded the liberal elites as responsible for undermining the productive capacities of the country and leading it to underdevelopment. By different routes, they thus helped link the idea of economic and cultural anti-imperialism to the struggle of fascism against the liberalism represented by British and American imperialism in league with local unpatriotic liberals. They saw in fascism a new type of political and cultural revolution, and they believed that the old liberal order responsible for Argentine political and economic dependency would collapse with the defeat of the Western democracies in World War II.

The main idea developed in this book in contrast to most previous analyses is that the Argentine antiliberal right, far from opposing the views of the populist left, actually endorsed them. Only a combination of both lines of thought can explain the broad ideological front against liberal democracy that developed in Argentina in the 1930s, the cultural impact of which lasted until the early 1980s.

A central conclusion of this book is that one of the political accomplishments of Argentina's "revolution of the right" was to introduce this set of beliefs, which distorted Argentina's political reality, to the minds of the military leaders who took power in 1943. Hence, despite their political weakness as an organized and unified political movement, the ideologues of the "revolution of the right" succeeded in promoting the idea that Argentina's peripheral status kept it from achieving modern development and humiliated it. They succeeded in linking social justice with authoritarian politics rather than with liberal rights. In short, they made anti-imperialism, social justice, and autarkic industrialization all part of a single ideological package, long before the left-wing revolutionaries of the 1970s adopted most of these issues. Argentina would not modernize unless it was liberated from "political and economic liberalism."

A question is whether there was a necessary correlation between the quest for industrialization on the one hand and autarkic policies and authoritarian rule on the other. Socialists like Alfredo Palacios and Juan B. Justo as well as conservatives like Federico Pinedo had also advanced industrialist tendencies by promoting import-substitution, although at the same time they promoted political democracy. The nationalists of the right and left, however, believed that Argentina's problem was not primarily economic, but was rather a cultural and political problem related to the country's national identity. The nationalists did not accept the type of import-substitution promoted by Pinedo. According to them, the type of industrialization promoted by socialists or conservatives would not emancipate Argentina from its condition of dependent development, which for most nationalists led to economic misery and political subjugation. For most nationalists, only an independent and autarkic type of industrialization would permit economic development and political independence.

I have attempted to demonstrate in this book that although the liberal democratic world powers were portrayed as contributing to Argentina's uneven and dependent development, the fascists' political success was perceived as contributing to the opposite. Therefore, most nationalists believed that Argentina, while remaining politically and ideologically independent of the Axis powers, should cast its lot with them against the world's democratic forces. In other words, fascism appeared to be the most radical attack on the liberal imperialist foundations of the plutocratic nations and their local associates. These convictions developed by Argentina's nationalists and accepted by the military rulers in 1943 led Argentina to deep internal and foreign political crises. Indeed, the Argentine military rulers who took power in 1943 believed that Argentina was on the brink of social unrest and that the enemies of the country were both the "plutocratic" nations abroad and the internal democratic front within Argentina, made up of liberals, communists, socialists, and antipersonalist

Radicals. Furthermore, they insisted on maintaining a "dignified" policy of neutrality during the war as a precondition for the development of an industrialized, economically independent country.

I do not deny the pragmatic factors behind Argentine support for neutrality, namely, that in the early stages of the war Argentine and British economic interests converged in favor of Argentina's policy of neutrality. From the moment the United States entered the war, however, the difficulty of maintaining neutrality was clear to the British as well as to Argentine liberals. Yet for the nationalist military rulers and for most nationalist intellectuals, the debate on neutrality involved much more than Argentina's strategic position in the world conflict. It was part of a larger and more extensive debate on Argentina's path of development and on a contested collective identity. In this confrontation, they argued, a dependent country such as Argentina, in disarray because of what was assumed to be social turmoil and cultural decadency, should not support the struggle of Western democracies against the Axis.

Argentina paid a high economic and political price for defending these convictions that led it to remain neutral in World War II and to shift its political and economic path of development. Internationally, the military rulers were humiliated by the United States, and during the final days of the war they were forced to declare war on Germany. Despite that declaration of war, however, the United States remained suspicious of Argentina's military leadership, and hence Argentina's reliability remained in question.

The most important price, however, was paid domestically. From a narrow perspective, the crisis with the United States finally led to the end of the military regime and to its replacement by Perón. In essence, Argentina's military rulers suffered the consequences of their own policies of "dignity" toward the world conflict.

In broad socioeconomic and political terms, the question is whether the end of military rule and Perón's rise to power brought a new democracy to Argentina. Several studies have focused on the question of whether Peronism represented a reversal of the policies of the military regime of 1943 and therefore represented the advancement of a kind of social democracy, or whether Perón continued the basic principles established by the GOU. Indeed, the debate on Peronist social strategies continues to this day. In this study I have dealt only with the first Peronist presidency, and I have maintained that this first Peronist regime continued the ideological synthesis elaborated by the nationalist right and left while adding a populist slant to it. Perón celebrated the role of the working class as the most important productive sector in Argentine society, and his direct links with the workers represented an approach that most

of the nationalist intellectuals and military leaders had no hope of achieving. This approach has led some analysts to label Perón's social policies as
progressive. Others, such as Carlos Waisman, have noted that despite its
short-term effectiveness, which generated enthusiastic support for the
regime among "old" syndicalists as well as among "new" members of the
working class, in the long run Peronism diminished rather than increased
Argentina's potential for becoming an industrial democracy.[3] Perón's
policies of populist mobilization under authoritarian control, social justice backed by the "organized community" rather than universal rights,
and autarkic industrialization as the basis for political sovereignty did not
contribute to Argentina's economic development and in the long run did
not contribute to the well-being of the working class.

Obviously Peronism represented much more than an ideology, and the
complexity of the Peronist phenomenon cannot be explained on ideological grounds alone. There is a wide range of explanations of the Peronist
phenomenon. I agree with those analysts who have defined the Peronist
appeal as a "community of feeling" or as a "structure of feeling" in order
to take into account those stresses and displacements which escape formal
ideological expression, yet define a particular quality of social experience
and relationship.[4] As Daniel James has observed, one of the characteristics
defining this structure of feeling was a deeply ingrained *obrerismo*, an
exaltation of what could be called "pro-labor populism." Normally pejo-
rative terms—"*la chusma*," "*los grasas*," "*los descamisados*"—took on a
positive meaning in the Peronist organized community. Conversely, the
nonworker was viewed with bitterness and contempt.[5] The nonworker was
representative of the non-national, the "*cipayo*," "*vendepatria*," and so
forth. All of these nonproductive elements were part of the cosmopolitan
liberal state.

At the same time, I contend that this structure or community of feelings
was part of the ideological corpus of the new nationalism, which combined
a shared hatred of formal democracy, as expressed in parliamentary politics
and professional politicians, with complete servility to the national leader.

I have argued that the distinction between the two communities—the
national and the liberal—was advanced and popularized by the right-wing
and populist nationalist intellectuals of the revolution of the right. The
patria real, for its interpreters of the right or of the left, meant redefining
the national collective identity and the path of socioeconomic development, which stood in complete opposition to the *patria liberal*. In this
sense, the most important result from my analysis in this book is that both
right and left contributed to ending the chances for the creation of a liberal
democratic discourse in Argentina for a long period of its political history.

Perón did not contribute much to this development ideologically, but he transformed the integralist populist formula into a social and political reality and he widened the gap in more ways than one, by placing the organized community, the national syndicalist state, in full opposition to the idea of a liberal Argentina.

A question that remains to be considered is whether the ideological analysis in this book aids in the understanding of the political and economic projects of the military regimes of the 1960s and 1970s and the political violence triggered by them. David Rock's *Authoritarian Argentina* provides evidence of the continuity of the political values of right-wing authoritarianism during the military regime of the 1970s. This book does not extend to these political developments.

It is striking, however, that the authoritarian regime of the 1960s made Peronist-style populist authoritarianism its primary target. It can be argued in more ways than one that the bureaucratic-authoritarian regimes of the 1960s and the Process of National Organization of the 1970s contradicted some of the central positions of the integralist-populist ideology advanced by the revolutionary right and later by Peronism. Indeed, although a great deal of the authoritarian, antiliberal discourse of the "revolution of the right" was adopted by the military regimes, the emphases of the revolutionary right on anti-imperialism, "nationalist" social justice and the integration of the workers into the nation were left aside. The paradox is that after 1955 this same integralist-populist formula, which in this book I have related to fascism and later to Peronism, was attributed to left-wing subversion by the new military regimes. The task for the new military regimes was to sever the link between the social, mobilizing side of the nationalist formula and the authoritarian, anticommunist, and antisocialist side.

After 1955 the Argentine military pledged that it would prevent the Peronists from regaining power and halt the spread of "subversion" from abroad. The military's basic assumption was that the world was already involved in a Third World War against communist subversion. Anticommunist writings by Argentine right-wing nationalists were combined with other prominent sources, this time coming from the United States and France. The corporativist and technocratic plans of Lugones for development and his faith in the military as the only organism capable of providing order and meaning to Argentine society contributed to the doctrine of national security. Bruno Genta and Julio Meinvielle's convictions that Argentina was a bastion of Western values confronting "barbarian" Soviet subversion were also an integral part of the ideology of the military regimes.

This legacy was complemented by political philosophers, such as James Burnham, who elaborated a theoretical formulation for success in the Cold War. His books *The Managerial Revolution* (1941) and *The Struggle for the World* (1947) and his column "The Third World War," published in the *National Review*, influenced conservatism in the United States and reached as far as the armed forces of Argentina.

As a result, fundamental individual freedoms were curtailed and subversion was attacked wherever it could be found. However, the model of national organization based on authoritarian rule and the attempt to reintegrate Argentina within the international financial system were at odds with the beliefs held by most of the intellectuals of the revolutionary right of the 1930s. The pure "authoritarian" regime discouraged political mobilization in the name of technocratic values. In contrast, the nationalists of the right who preceded Peronism embraced national mobilization and pro-labor social justice. In other words, the military regimes took up only one part of the political legacy of the revolution of the right, namely, authoritarian rule, while leaving aside the social and populist aspect of that nationalist legacy.

Juan Corradi has correctly depicted what he defines as the reduction by the military rulers of the 1970s of the complex problems of Argentina into a simple dichotomy: friend and foe, closely resembling Carl Schmitt's dichotomy of friend and enemy.[6] My contention is that the revolution of the right set this dichotomy within a different framework. The military regimes in the 1960s and 1970s included as foes the communists as well as the Peronists, and as friends the military forces and their economic or financial technocratic allies. The revolution of the right in the 1930s defined its friends as nationalists of both right and left, and its foes as the Marxist left, liberals, and the conservative right. The ideological dichotomy set up by the revolution of the right, similar to that of fascism, can be summed up as the conflict between the productive sectors of the nation and "parasitical" foreign capitalism in partnership with the local bourgeoisie.

This dichotomy was adopted by Peronists of both the right and the left. The radical groups of the right and left, such as the Tacuara, the Montoneros, and the "Triple A," their differences notwithstanding, were all in agreement in their total rejection of the old liberal-conservative establishment. These groups were the conservative and revolutionary faces of the same ideological construct, best represented by the idea of the "third path" that Perón defined in *La hora de los pueblos* and which I claim was elaborated during the 1930s.

The Allied defeat of Germany and Italy, Perón argued, eliminated all possibilities of a "*socialismo nacional*."[7] However, in Perón's view the struggle of the Third World was a postwar continuation of the struggle of fascism against the "plutocratic" bourgeois nations. The Peronist right and left were the revolutionary and conservative sides of the "national socialist" path, and they aspired to assault the liberal state, bourgeois society, and financial capitalism. Both defended some type of national syndicalism, praised violence, and espoused a mythical notion of the "people."

It is thus not surprising that the Montoneros recruited their rank and file particularly from sectors defined as nationalist Catholics, thereby indicating a movement from Catholic right to nationalist left. Even though right- and left-wing Peronists waged bitter war, especially in the 1970s, both scorned liberal democracy and strove to bring about a Peronist "national socialist" Argentina.

Another question this study has sought to consider is whether this revolution of the right in Argentina was a unique phenomenon, namely, whether this ideological phenomenon reflects only the conditions of ideologues and intellectuals in a dependent or peripheral society. I have attempted to show that the peripheral modernizing mentality, or the idea that modern development in terms of social mobilization and industrialization requires that liberal institutions be dismantled, was one of the central ideas of the conservative revolution, of which fascism was the most extreme embodiment. Various European intellectuals promoted the idea of national socialism not only as a political alternative to liberal democracy and Marxist socialism but as an alternative for a civilization totally at odds with the ideas of enlightened modernity. These intellectuals intended to achieve modern social mobilization and technological superiority by rejecting the moral values of liberal and socialist modernity. For most of these ideologues the ideas of liberal rights and democracy belonged to the "plutocratic" nations, for whom the concept of "humanism" was merely an imperialist tool.

Fascism was the most radical offshoot of this ideological trend. However, although fascism was proper to a particular time and place, this type of ideology is not limited by borders and time periods. The conservative revolution does not belong to the past. It remains a tempting solution that appears under various ideological guises. Under different names and with new social and economic bases, new forms of regional populism, radical ethno-nationalism, illiberal democracies, right-wing movements, and so on remind us that the old ideological formulas are far from gone. The contemporary reaction to the globalization of liberal ideas and liberal rights may serve as a precondition for the emergence of a new "national organic" path to modernity along the lines of the conservative revolution. As in the past, this formula attracts radical ideologues of right and left. By the same token, the revolution of the right, whose final results were expressed in the 1943 revolution and Peronism, did not produce a drastically different message from other forms of populism in Latin America; yet because of its intellectual and urban content it was more akin to European fascism than to Latin American populism.

Hence, a final question that may be raised is to what extent the integralist-populist model, which brought together the antiliberal right and left, has disappeared, especially when democracy seems to be the only legitimate "game in town" in Western societies. It must be borne in mind that a deep antiliberal counterculture, which is expressed in varying forms and degrees, is still a living part of Argentina's politics. Different types of military uprisings and new types of regional populism, such as that of General Antonio Bussi and his Fuerza Republicana, or Aldo Rico's MODIN in the province of Buenos Aires (which became a "third political force" during the parliamentary elections of 1993), are manifestations of the latent appeal of resurrected "old" formulas. Although the popular appeal of Aldo Rico's MODIN has been damaged and democracy seems to have been consolidated in Argentina, new types of "military-populist" rebellions should not be ruled out in any political analysis, especially in times of economic and political crisis.[8] I suggest that particular attention should be paid to the ideological message contained in the synthesis of antiliberal values with political and economic anti-imperialism and themes of social justice.

The rejection of liberal values, cosmopolitan society, and globalization, accompanied by a quest for cultural and economical "emancipation," may still be a temptation during periods of political crisis. This may happen again in societies such as that of Argentina, which was and continues to be a peripheral capitalist society and whose entry into the world market has been made contingent on a reduction of the sovereign role of the state, with the resulting high social costs.

The temptation to embrace updated versions of nationalist populism as an alternative to the failures of democratic modernity is always a latent one. As I suggest here, this formula is not limited to Argentina. It is a political formula rooted in historical and philosophical tradition throughout the world. It has its ideological forerunners and its embodiments under particular regimes which, even if unsuccessful, may be revisited if political liberalism in a globalized world fails to provide broad social and political solutions.

Notes

Introduction: The Right and the Idea of Reactionary Modernism

1. Zeev Sternhell, *La droite révolutionnaire, 1885–1914: Les origines fran-
çaises du fascisme* (Paris: Seuil, 1978), and *Neither Right nor Left: Fascist Ideology in France*, trans. David Maisel (Berkeley: University of California Press,
1986).

2. Gordon A. Craig, *Germany, 1866–1945* (New York: Oxford University
Press, 1978), pp. 486–487.

3. Jeffrey Herf in his book *Reactionary Modernism: Technology, Culture,
and Politics in Weimar and the Third Reich* (New York: Cambridge University
Press, 1984) has labeled reactionary modernism a particular current within the
groups of Weimar conservative revolutionaries. They converted technology from
a component of alien Western *Zivilisation* into an integral part of German
Kultur. In fact, however, although German intellectuals had radicalized that
trend, it characterized a wide variety of radical-right European intellectuals and
movements of the time.

4. This view contrasts with Nicolas Shumway's assertion that what was
apparently new in the 1930s was often a repetition or reworking of Argentine
thought of earlier times or at least was in dialogue with it. See Nicolas Shumway,
The Invention of Argentina (Berkeley: University of California Press, 1991), p. ix.

5. Shumway assumes that the military junta's argument against populism
was made in great part in the name of "armed civilization," the tradition which
had its antecedents in the writings and actions of leading nineteenth-century "liberal" figures such as Bartolomé Mitre and Domingo Sarmiento.

6. The most recent and important books written about Argentine nationalism
are David Rock's *Authoritarian Argentina: The Nationalist Movement, Its History
and Its Impact* (Berkeley: University of California Press, 1993), and Sandra McGee
Deutsch and R. H. Dolkart, eds., *The Argentine Right: Its History and Intellectual
Origins, 1910 to the Present* (Wilmington, Del.: Scholarly Resources, 1993). These

books are analytically more sophisticated than Marysa Navarro Gerassi's precursor book on Argentine nationalism, *Los nacionalistas* (Buenos Aires: Jorge Alvarez, 1964). Rock's analysis, as well as the various articles composing the McGee-Dolkart book, deal almost entirely with right-wing nationalism. They do not challenge the "consensual" thesis emphasizing the limited relationship between right-wing nationalism and Peronism. Although these books have contributed to clarifying the right-wing content of Argentine nationalism, they have passed over the contribution of the "Yrigoyenist populist" tradition to antiliberal nationalism. I believe that this "amnesia" results from the legitimate role historically and currently played by the Radical party in Argentine politics. In Argentina, two relevant books were written during the 1970s and 1980s: Cristián Buchrucker, *Nacionalismo y peronismo: La Argentina en la crisis ideólogica mundial (1927–1955)* (Buenos Aires: Ed. Sudamericana, 1987), and Enrique Zuleta Alvarez, *El nacionalismo argentino*, 2 vols. (Buenos Aires: La Bastilla, 1975). Both books are well documented, especially the latter, which is written by a former nationalist intellectual. In his book, Zuleta Alvarez attempts to differentiate, unsuccessfully in my opinion, between a republican non-fascist nationalist wing (the one to which he belonged) and a fascist reactionary one. Both ideological lines complemented each other and were complemented by the populist wing of the Radical Party of Hipólito Yrigoyen. The former book, written by one of Ernst Nolte's students, uses a phenomenological approach emphasizing particular differences among the components of the nationalist movement. Although Buchrucker conducts a serious analysis, his overemphasis of differences sometimes blurs the substance and the common ground between the various nationalist groups, which belonged to a single nationalist family. In fact, Buchrucker's book, like the others, fails to see the line of continuity between the cultural and ideological rebellion of nationalism and the Peronist movement.

Furthermore, although the above-mentioned books provide extensive treatment of Argentine nationalism, they do not radically challenge the common view, which sees rightist nationalism as a nostalgic movement associated with the liberal oligarchy. This thesis was especially sustained by authors who attempted to reexamine the "North-American imperialist" view of Peronism as fascism. See Juan José Hernández Arregui, *La formación de la conciencia nacional (1930–1960)* (Buenos Aires: Hachea, 1960), and Jorge Abelardo Ramos, *Revolución y contrarrevolución en la Argentina: Las masas en nuestra historia* (Buenos Aires: Amerindia, 1957). Based on the desire to free Peronism from its fascist connotations, these authors accentuated the emancipatory, populist, and authentic roots of Peronism, rooted in the left anti-imperialistic wing (FORJA) of the Radical Party. On the other hand, the liberal oligarchy was associated with Uriburu's 1930 revolution and the authoritarian nationalist movement. These works attempt to rehabilitate Peronism as an authentic revolutionary, anti-imperialist movement and as a precursor to the left-wing anti-imperialist struggle in Latin America. As noted, they attempt to respond to American works which, under the influence of the theories of modernization of the 1950s, have defined Peronism as a reactionary movement. Among these studies is John Johnson, *Political Change in Latin America: The Emergence of the Middle*

Sectors (Stanford, Calif.: Stanford University Press, 1958). A slightly more sophisticated analysis is that of Kalman Silvert's *The Conflict Society: Reaction and Revolution in Latin America* (New Orleans: Hauser Press, 1961). A more important study which reflects the distinction between populist nationalism and a nostalgic, traditionalist nationalism is Arthur P. Whitaker's "Argentina, Nostalgic and Dynamic Nationalism," in a book published with David C. Jordan, *Nationalism in Contemporary Latin America* (New York: Free Press, 1966).

7. Sandra McGee Deutsch, *Las Derechas: The Extreme Right in Argentina, Brazil, and Chile (1890–1939)* (Stanford, Calif.: Stanford University Press, 1999).

8. Rock, *Authoritarian Argentina*, p. 20.

9. See Sandra McGee Deutsch, *Counterrevolution in Argentina, 1900–1932: The Argentine Patriotic League* (Lincoln: University of Nebraska Press, 1986).

10. See Carlos H. Waisman, *Reversal of Development in Argentina: Postwar Counterrevolutionary Policies and Their Structural Consequences* (Princeton, N.J.: Princeton University Press, 1987).

11. Cited in Miguel Angel Scenna, *FORJA, una aventura argentina* (Buenos Aires: Ed. Belgrano, 1983), p. 240.

12. Archivio del Ministero degli Esteri Italiano, Buenos Aires, August 1, 1942. Cited in Loris Zanatta, *Del estado liberal a la nación católica: Iglesia y ejército en los orígenes del peronismo, 1930–1943* (Quilmes: Universidad Nacional de Quilmes, 1996), p. 272.

13. The issue of fascism in Argentina bore little relation to German or Italian immigrants or to a geopolitical decision coming from Germany to use Argentina's territories. The geopolitical decision may have had consequences, but it is not the core of the "fascist political culture" in Argentina. As asserted by Ronald C. Newton, *The "Nazi Menace" in Argentina, 1931–1947* (Stanford, Calif.: Stanford University Press, 1992), there was no real threat from Germany to Argentina. Indeed, direct Nazi influences were less than had formerly been believed. The emphasis in the present book is on how Argentina developed its own type of national socialism, which had little need to draw on the Nazi model.

14. For one of the latest views, among others, at odds with mine, see Austeen Ivereigh, *Catholicism and Politics in Argentina, 1810–1960* (New York: St. Martin's Press, 1995).

15. See Mark Falcoff, "Orange Juice with General Perón: A Memoir," *The American Scholar* 62 (Summer 1993): 392–393.

Chapter One. Reactionary Modernism, Fascism,
and the Language of Cultural Emancipation

1. A very important and enlightening discussion on fascism and the "modernization" of consciousness appeared in *Comparative Political Studies* 10, no. 2 (July 1977). There, James Gregor responds to Arthur L. Greil's claim that the content and style of fascism were based on romantic epistemology, faith, and sentiment, while modern consciousness was related to rational liberal consciousness.

Henry A. Turner likewise held that no matter what kind of modernizing policies were implemented during the fascist and Nazi regimes, their aims were basically antimodernizing. (See Henry A. Turner, Jr., "Fascism and Modernization," in Henry A. Turner, Jr., ed., *Reappraisals of Fascism* [New York: New Viewpoints, 1975], p. 131.) Gregor answers most of Greil's assumptions, trying to prove that what seemed like "traditional attitudes" were proper characteristics of the Soviet regime as well as of radical guerrilla movements like those of Che Guevara or Mao. See James Gregor, "Fascism and the Countermodernization of Consciousness," *Comparative Political Studies* 10, no. 2 (July 1977): 239. Similarly, see Anthony James Joes in the same issue, "On the Modernity of Fascism: Notes from Two Worlds," p. 259. However viewed, it was not the comparative approach in Leninism that made fascism a modern political movement. The ideological synthesis of a new organic nationalism with a moral and antimaterialist socialism was itself the result of a modernizing intellectual revolution, albeit not utopian, liberal, or socialist in character. In fact, "radical nationalism was a vision of the future, not of the past. In this sense it harnesses the cultural aspirations of many who were comfortably placed in the emerging bourgeois society . . . [and] whose political sensibilities were offended by the seeming incapacity of the establishment to respond to the left-wing challenge" (Geoff Eley, "What Produces Fascism: Preindustrial Traditions or a Crisis of a Capitalist State," *Politics and Society* 12, no. 1 [1983]: 71). This assertion in fact challenges the view that connects the concept of revolution only to rational "utopian" ideologies.

    2. See Leopoldo Zea, "Fascismo dependiente en América Latina," *Nueva Política* (Mexico Enero-Marzo, 1976), pp. 149–151. See also Agustín Cueva, "La fascistización de América Latina," ibid., pp. 156–157; Theotonio Dos Santos, *Socialismo o fascismo: Dilema latinoamericano,* 2d ed. (Prensa Latinoamericana, 1972).

    3. Eugen Weber has raised the question of whether fascism could be included in this current of thought: Is it a revolution or a counterrevolution? See Eugen Weber, "Revolution? Counter-Revolution? What Revolution?" in Walter Laqueur, ed., *Fascism, a Reader's Guide: Analyses, Interpretations, Bibliography* (New York: Pelican Books, 1976), p. 488.

    4. See Herf, *Reactionary Modernism.*

    5. Cited in Stanley Payne, "The Falange," in Nathanael Greene, ed., *Fascism: An Anthology* (New York: Crowell, 1968), p. 273.

    6. See Juan Linz, "Comparative Study of Fascism," in Laqueur, *Fascism, a Reader's Guide,* pp. 14–20. See also Juan Linz, "Political Space and Fascism as a Late-Comer: Conditions Conducive to the Success or Failure of Fascism as a Mass Movement in Inter-War Europe," in Stein Ugelvik Larsen, Bernt Hagtvet, and Jan Petter Myklebust, eds., *Who Were the Fascists? Social Roots of European Fascism* (Bergen: Universitetsförlaget; New York: Columbia University Press, 1980). The best book for a typology of fascism is Stanley Payne, *Fascism, Comparison and Definition* (Madison: University of Wisconsin Press, 1980).

    7. See Stanley Payne, *A History of Fascism, 1914–1945* (Madison: University of Wisconsin Press, 1995), p. 7.

8. Roger Griffin, *The Nature of Fascism* (New Brunswick, N.J.: Routledge, 1995), p. 4.

9. Roger Eatwell, "On Defining the Fascist Minimum," *Journal of Political Ideologies* 1, no. 3 (1996): 313.

10. This thesis is developed by Zeev Sternhell in *Neither Right nor Left* and "Fascist Ideology," in Laqueur, *Fascism, a Reader's Guide*, as well as in Zeev Sternhell, with Mario Sznajder and Maia Asheri, *The Birth of Fascist Ideology: From Cultural Rebellion to Political Revolution*, trans. David Maisel (Princeton, N.J.: Princeton University Press, 1994). Sternhell sees fascism as the ideological synthesis of a new radical nationalism and a new anti-Marxist socialism, based on Sorel's moral revision of Marxism and the Italian national revolutionary syndicalists' revision of Marx's theory of value. The first meetings of Sorelian syndicalists with the integral nationalist followers of Charles Maurras at *Les cahiers du Cercle Proudhon* in 1910 and *La Lupa* in Italy in 1911 represented the first ideological synthesis of fascist ideology, long before it was translated into political practice.

The quest to merge the ideal with the physical, the cultural with the material, the spiritual realm with biology, and nature with society in order to reveal the ultimate unity and hidden essence of "nature" is the key to understanding the new radical nationalism. This new concept of nation was based not on natural law and respect for constitutional rights, but on an organic personality flowing from the historical, cultural, and blood rights of the "*Volk*." At the same time, the focus on psychological and moral revolutionary aspects was to produce Sorel's revision of Marxism, which removed the latter's rational and Hegelian foundation. On the particular importance of Georges Sorel's revision of Marxism as the ideological cornerstone of fascist ideology, see Sternhell, with Sznajder and Asheri, *The Birth of Fascist Ideology*. Sternhell, *La droite révolutionnaire*, pp. 341–347, attempts to demonstrate the particular leftist and revolutionary roots of fascism.

The evolution from left-wing Marxism to a new moral revolutionary position in Sorel's political thought marked the beginning of an interesting ideological trend that led avowed Marxist intellectuals like Doriot, Déat, de Man, and Mosley to a new revolutionary conception. This conception allowed some of them to combine a new ideological synthesis with radical nationalism. On Sorel's political thought, see Michael Curtis, *Three against the Third Republic: Sorel, Barrès, and Maurras* (Princeton, N.J.: Princeton University Press, 1959); Jack J. Roth, *The Cult of Violence: Sorel and the Sorelians* (Berkeley: University of California Press, 1980); and John L. Stanley, *The Sociology of Virtue: The Political and Social Theories of Georges Sorel* (Berkeley: University of California Press, 1981). Sternhell does not delve into the causes of fascist success or failure in different places, but maintains that when structural crises appeared, fascism as an ideology had already matured and presented a real ideological alternative. Although integral nationalism represents a rejection of the political values and revolutionary violence of the French Revolution, it is one of the ideological pillars of fascism. In "Fascism and the French Revolution," *Journal of Contemporary History* 24, no. 1 (January 1989), George Mosse suggests a different interpretation. Mosse claims that although fascism arose as a protest against the liberal and materialist symbolism of the French Revolution, that revolution provided fascism with some of its political ideas. The concept of nationalism and politics as a civil religion is part of the legacy of the French Revolution. A new nationalism was based upon a new "religious" concept, "the general will of the people." According to Mosse, this "nationalism provides the link between the French Revolution and Fascism; the nationalization of the masses was a common bond between the French and the Fascist revolutions" (p. 7).

11. For an opposing view, see Kenneth Tucker, Jr., *French Revolutionary Syndicalism and the Public Sphere* (Cambridge: Cambridge University Press, 1996).

12. E. Rossoni, "Direttive fasciste all'agricoltura" (Rome: La Stirpe, 1939). Cited in Roger Griffin, ed., *Fascism* (Oxford: Oxford University Press, 1995), p. 77.

13. See Alan S. Milward, "Fascism and Economy," in Laqueur, *Fascism, a Reader's Guide*, p. 448. José Antonio, the founder of the Spanish Falange, emphasized the pro-labor tendency of the fascist state to such a degree that a conservative journalist, on hearing José Antonio's speech on the day the Falange was founded, assured him that many socialists would support the Falange's program. "In the end the liberal state comes to offer us economic slavery. . . . Therefore socialism had to appear, and its coming was just. The workers had to defend themselves against a system that only promised them political rights but did not strive to give them a just life" (José Antonio at the foundation of the Falange, Teatro Comedia, Madrid, October 3, 1933). See Stanley Payne, *Falange: A History of Spanish Fascism* (Stanford, Calif.: Stanford University Press, 1961), p. 38. In a similar spirit, Oswald Mosley wrote, "Finally the home market was to be sustained by a high wage system intended to produce an equilibrium between production and consumption." Oswald Mosley, *My Life* (London: Thomas Nelson and Sons, 1968), p. 90.

14. Enrico Corradini, "Nationalism and the Syndicates." Speech at Nationalist Congress, Rome, March 16, 1919, in George Steiner and Adrian Lyttelton, eds., *Roots of the Right: Italian Fascism from Pareto to Gentile* (London: Jonathan Cape, 1973), p. 163.

15. Mario Sznajder, "Economic Marginalism and Socialism: Italian Revolutionary Syndicalism and the Revision of Marx," *Praxis International* 11, no. 1 (April 1991): 114–127.

16. Robert Brasillach, *Notre avant-guerre* (Paris, 1981), pp. 290–291.

17. Giovanni Gentile, "Che cosa e il fascismo," lecture delivered in Florence on March 25, 1925 (Vallecchi, Florence, 1925).

18. Benito Mussolini, "Political and Social Doctrine," in *Fascism: Doctrine and Institutions* (Rome, 1935) p. 26. Cited in Sternhell, "Fascist Ideology," in Laqueur, *Fascism, a Reader's Guide*, p. 331.

19. Herf, *Reactionary Modernism*, p. 1.

20. In Germany, as noted by Gordon Craig, conservative revolutionaries, although they were contemptuous of Hitler, constituted the intellectual avant-garde of the right-wing revolution that took place in 1933. Ernst Jünger refused a seat in

the parliament for the National Socialist German Workers Party (NSDAP)—mainly because he despised parliamentary politics even as a tactic—but he acknowledged and praised National Socialism as the clearest expression of the national will and wished it to succeed. Edgar Jung, a Catholic thinker, whose position was far from the Nazis, advocated a coalition with them. A similar position was taken by Stapel, who saw the Nazi movement as a "breakthrough force" and advocated a coalition of the NSDAP and the Catholic Center Party.

21. See Stefan Breuer, *Anatomie der Konservativen Revolution* (Darmstadt, 1993).

22. See Oswald Spengler, *Der Untergang des Abendlandes*, vol. 2, p. 1002. Cited in Herf, *Reactionary Modernism*, p. 57.

23. Fritz Stern, *The Politics of Cultural Despair: A Study in the Rise of Germanic Ideology* (Berkeley: University of California Press, 1974), p. xvii.

24. Edgar Jung, cited in Buchrucker, *Nacionalismo y peronismo*, p. 163.

25. See Rock, *Authoritarian Argentina*, p. 10.

26. Carl Schmitt, *The Concept of the Political* (New Brunswick, N.J.: Rutgers University Press, 1976), p. 54.

27. See Ernst Gellner, *Nations and Nationalism* (Oxford: Basil Blackwell, 1983); Eric Hobsbawm, *Nations and Nationalism since 1780* (New York: Cambridge University Press, 1990); Liah Greenfeld, *Nationalism: Five Roads to Modernity* (Cambridge: Harvard University Press, 1992).

28. John Breuilly, *Nationalism and the State* (New York: St. Martin's Press, 1982).

29. Hobsbawm, *Nations and Nationalism since 1780*, p. 10.

30. Benedict Anderson, *Imagined Communities* (New York: Verso, 1982).

31. Greenfeld, *Nationalism: Five Roads*, p. 6.

32. Ibid., p. 10.

33. Fichte summoned German youth to initiate the grand task of creating a new, more vital culture, through education, urbanization, and prosperity. He claimed that because German was the only truly living language in Europe, Germany was destined to become the regenerator of the world. Ernst Renan asserted that a nation is a living soul, a moral consciousness defined by a shared rich heritage of memories, animated by the demand of daily common consent. See J. G. Fichte, *Addresses to the German Nation* (Chicago, 1922), pp. 68–69.

34. Julio Irazusta, lecture delivered at the church "Nuestra Senora del Socorro," Buenos Aires, during the Semana Maurrasiana, November 16, 1972. Cited in Julio Irazusta, *Estudios históricos politicos*, Biblioteca del Pensamiento Nacionalista Argentino (Buenos Aires: Ed. Dictio, 1973), p. 191.

35. Charles Maurras, *Enquête sur la monarquie*, 6th ed. (Paris, 1914), p. 421.

36. Ernst Nolte, *Three Faces of Fascism: Action Française, Italian Fascism, National Socialism* (New York: New American Library, 1965), p. 137.

37. Ibid., p. 128.

38. Ivereigh, *Catholicism and Politics in Argentina*, p. 27.

39. Zeev Sternhell, *Maurice Barrès et le Nationalisme Française* (Paris: Ed. Complexe, 1985), p. 353.

40. Maurice Barrès, *Scènes et doctrines du nationalisme* (Paris: Plon, 1925), vol. 1, p. 222.

41. A wide variety of theories have been written on corporativist politics. Scholars like Philippe Schmitter have emphasized that the corporativist tendency was an authentic and ideologically independent phenomenon and have defined it as a system of interest representation in which the constituent units are organized into a limited number of singular, compulsory, noncompetitive, hierarchically ordered, functionally differentiated categories, recognized or licensed by the state (Philippe Schmitter, "Still the Century of Corporativism," in Fredrick B. Pike and Thomas Stritch, eds., *The New Corporativism* (Notre Dame, Ind.: University of Notre Dame Press, 1974), pp. 84–131. Regarding the fascist concept of corporativism, see Alan Cassels, "Janus: The Two Faces of Fascism," in Turner, Jr., *Reappraisals of Fascism*. Cassels claims that corporativism is an innate impulse of Italian fascism. Corporativism offers us a guide to the fascist movement's real nature, inasmuch as it is a system that confronts the problems of the modern industrial age in an eminently rational manner. It does not propose a retreat to a preindustrial, rural paradise, but instead, somewhat eclectically, it tries to adapt ideas from the recent past. For a comprehensive theory of corporativism, such as the sociopolitical system of the twentieth century, see Mikhail Monoilesco, *Le siècle du corporativisme* (Paris: Felix Alcan, 1938), who has demonstrated that fascism, national socialism, and Stalin's Soviet Union share similar corporativist trends. Another current, namely, Ibero-Spanish social corporativism, has been defined as a patrimonial political style that prevented the development of a modern democratic system of government, as well as of a fascist reaction. This type of traditional corporativism, as represented by Salazar in Portugal, sought to reconcile liberal economic interests and a controlled semi-authoritarian political system by introducing both a corporative chamber for the representation of social and economic interests and a directly elected national assembly. The goal was to preserve not only economic liberalism but also the cultural and political hegemony of the conservative elites. See Howard Wiarda, "Towards a Framework for the Study of Political Change in the Ibero-Latin Tradition"; Ronald Newton, "On Functional Groups," "Fragmentation," and "Pluralism in Spanish American Society"; and Richard M. Morse, "The Heritage of Latin America," all in Louis Hartz, ed., *The Founding of New Societies* (New York: Harcourt, Brace and World, 1964).

42. Associazione Nazionalista Italiana, in *Il Nazionalismo* (Rome: ANI, 1920), pp. 14–15.

43. For Lenin, the bourgeois democratic revolution entailed a dissolution of pre-capitalist structures in the social formation. Using this concept, Lenin extrapolated his analysis of the development of capitalism in Russia to colonial societies. In the colonies, however, unlike Russia, it was the bourgeoisie that was in the vanguard of the struggle for the bourgeois-democratic revolution. This was the basis of those national movements in which the bourgeoisie needed the nation-state to meet the needs of capitalist development.

The central theoretical question of the Comintern in 1920 was where to focus the struggle against imperialism: on the war against capitalism as a whole, or in helping the national bourgeoisie to establish a modern capitalist system after the feudal structures were dissolved, as Lenin advocated. In fact, this was a theme in Lenin's draft theses on the national and colonial questions, in which he maintained that the communist movement should "support" but not necessarily lead the national liberation movements. In 1928, after a policy of outright collaboration with the Kuomintang in China that led to the counterrevolution of 1926–27, the Sixth Congress of the Comintern declared that the national bourgeoisie no longer represented the national democratic revolution.

In 1935 the Comintern returned to the tactical position of the popular front for the "colonized world." Faith in the national bourgeoisie was reestablished, and in subsequent years the Communist Party accepted the statist conception of engineering a revolution from the top in the underdeveloped world. Lenin's long-established two-state theory of revolution was accordingly replaced by a populist "non-capitalist path to development," which in certain ways accommodated the conception of "dependency" and the struggle against imperialism in a fascist and populist framework rather than in terms of a rational Marxist analysis. See Hamza Alavi, *Capitalism and Colonial Production* (London: Croom Helm, 1982).

The official doctrine of Latin American communist parties was long characterized by a primitive "stage-by-stage" view of development and socialism, originally formulated by the early Russian social democrats. This view produced a moderate political strategy which was accompanied by a servile relationship with Moscow. In general, of course, Communist Party moderation fit well with Moscow's aversion to Third World revolutions liable to escape Soviet control. As I have noted, the confluence of Marxism and nationalism known as dependency theory arose as a reaction against official Marxism and reformism. However, although the dependency theory was based on the confluence of Marxism and nationalism, it transcended the nationalist discourse based on cultural or national destiny. Dependency became a new kind of anti-imperialist doctrine during the 1960s and 1970s because it viewed the mechanisms of oppression analytically in the operation of a world economy rather than in the subjection of some nations by others—the focus of integral and populist nationalists in Argentina during the 1930s and 1940s. A different emphasis on national individuality and on the "special destiny" of the country was the common denominator between the nationalists' conception of anti-imperialist policies and populism and fascism during the 1930s and 1940s. This relationship between national liberation and fascism is also perceptible in analyses of other fields.

The way nationalists saw their relationship with fascism was well illustrated in the Lehi publication *Eretz Israel*, which appeared in France: "It seems paradoxical to say that fascism and the Hitlerian oppression contributed more to developing the national liberation spirit than liberal democracy, which was used by imperialism as the most perfect adaptable mask. . . ." See Jackes Zeitun, "Le role d'Israel dans la lutte anti-imperialiste," *Eretz Israel*, September 16, 1948.

44. Peter H. Smith, *Argentina and the Failure of Democracy: Conflict among Political Elites, 1904–1955* (Madison: University of Wisconsin Press, 1974), p. 31.

45. Steve Stein, "Populism and Social Control," in Eduardo P. Archetti, Paul Cammac, and Bryan Roberts, eds., *Sociology of Developing Societies: Latin America* (Hampshire, London, 1987), p. 133. On these particular interpretations of populism, see Ghita Ionesco and Ernst Gellner, eds., *Populism: Its Meaning and National Characteristics* (New York: Macmillan, 1969); and Ernesto Laclau, *Politics and Ideology in Marxist Theory* (London: N.L.B., 1977). It should be pointed out that Latin American populist movements were not uniform and monolithic. Some of them were closer to social democratic parties, while others resembled fascism—as in the case of Peronism. The differences among them are analyzed in Torcuato di Tella, "Populism and Reform in Latin America," in Claudio Veliz, ed., *Obstacles to Change in Latin America* (London: Oxford University Press, 1965), pp. 47–74. There is also another mode of cultural analysis, which stresses the distinction between the Ibero-American tradition and the fascist one. The Ibero-American tradition developed a concept of corporativism that should be distinguished from fascism and Nazism. See the essays by Wiarda, Newton, and Morse cited in note 43 above, in Hartz, *The Founding of New Societies*. This type of analysis relates the concept of corporativism to authentic cultural trends in the Hispanic American world. It does not explain, however, why so many grassroots nationalist intellectuals worldwide continued to find inspiration in the fascist revolution, seeing in it a path back to their essential being. For instance, explaining the English tradition's affinity with fascism, A. L. Gausfound wrote: "Like all political movements that have affected this country, Fascism . . . comes to Britain in a form adapted to the genius of our people. . . . British fascism may well draw much of its inspiration from a nearer source and seek to create a new and dynamic spirit of Elizabethan England" (*Fascist Quarterly* 18, no. 1 [1935]).

46. See the thesis presented by di Tella, "Populism and Reform in Latin America," in Veliz, *Obstacles to Change in Latin America*.

47. A. F. K. Organski, *The Stages of Political Development* (New York: Alfred A. Knopf, 1965), and Barrington Moore, *Social Origins of Dictatorship and Democracy* (Boston: Beacon, 1966).

48. James Gregor, *The Fascist Persuasion in Radical Politics* (Princeton, N.J.: Princeton University Press, 1974), p. 408.

49. Waisman, *Reversal of Development*, p. 33.

50. Juan Corradi, *The Fitful Republic: Economy, Society, and Politics in Argentina* (New York: Westview Press, 1985), p. 31.

51. Paul W. Drake, "Conclusions, Requiem for Populism," in Michael L. Conniff, ed., *Latin American Populism in Comparative Perspective* (Albuquerque: University of New Mexico Press, 1982), p. 218.

52. Eugen Weber, "The Men of the Archangel," *Journal of Contemporary History* 1 (1966): 105.

53. On the Chilean Nazi movement of González von Marées, see Mario Sznajder, "A Case of Non-European Fascism: Chilean National Socialism in the 1930s," *Journal of Contemporary History* 28, no. 2 (April 1993). On the integralistas in Brazil, see Helgio Trindade, *Integralismo, o fascismo brasileiro na*

decada de 30 (Rio de Janeiro: Difel, 1979). See Deutsch, *Las Derechas*, on Argentina's, Brazil's, and Chile's radical right in comparative perspective. On the Sinarquista movement in Mexico, see Jean Meyer, *El sinarquismo: ¿un fascismo mexicano? 1937–1947* (Mexico City: Joaquín Mortiz, 1979).

54. Eugen Weber, *Varieties of Fascism: Doctrines of Revolution in the Twentieth Century* (Malabar, Fla.: Robert E. Krieger Publishing, 1964), p. 47.

55. Isaiah Berlin, "Populism," *Government and Opposition* 3 (1968): 179.

56. Leopoldo Lugones, "Defensa del estado," *La Nación* 31 (October 1930).

57. Ronald H. Dolkart, "The Right in the Década Infame, 1930–1943," in Deutsch and Dolkart, *The Argentine Right*, p. 65.

58. Enrique Peruzzotti, "Constitucionalismo, populismo y sociedad civil: Lecciones del caso argentino," *Revista Mexicana de Sociología* 61, no. 4 (October–December 1999): 165.

Chapter Two. Nationalism and the Rebellion against Positivism

1. Shumway, *The Invention of Argentina*, p. 214.

2. Josefina Ludmer, *El género gauchesco: Un tratado sobre la patria* (Buenos Aires: Ed. Sudamericana, 1988), p. 22.

3. Jorge Luis Borges, "Prólogo," in *Facundo* (Buenos Aires: El Ateneo, 1974), p. vii.

4. Diana Sorensen Goodrich, *Facundo and the Construction of Argentine Culture* (Austin: University of Texas Press, 1996), p. 3.

5. See Leopoldo Zea, *The Latin-American Mind*, trans. James Abbot and Lowell Dunham (Norman: University of Oklahoma Press, 1963), pp. 20–26.

6. See Rodolfo Puiggrós, *El yrigoyenismo* (Buenos Aires: Jorge Alvarez, 1965), chap. 3.

7. Rodolfo Rivarola, "Filosofía de la elección reciente," *Revista Argentina de Ciencias Politicas* 8, cited in David Rock, *Politics in Argentina, 1890–1930: The Rise and Fall of Radicalism* (Cambridge: Cambridge University Press, 1975), p. 29.

8. See José Luis Romero, *El Desarrollo de las ideas en la sociedad argentina moderna del siglo XX* (Buenos Aires: Ed. Solar, 1983), p. 20.

9. Alejandro Korn, *Influencias filosóficas en la evolución nacional* (Buenos Aires: Ed. Solar, 1983), pp. 233–234. First published by Claridad, Buenos Aires, 1936.

10. Carlos Bunge, *Nuestra América, ensayo de psicología social*, 6th ed. (Buenos Aires: Ed. Vaccaro, 1918), p. 248, cited in Martin Stabb, *América Latina: En busqueda de una identidad* (Caracas: Monte Avila Editores, 1969) p. 32. First published as *In Quest of Identity: Patterns in the Spanish American Essay of Ideas, 1890–1960* (Chapel Hill: University of North Carolina Press, 1967).

11. Gino Germani, *Política y sociedad en una época de transición: De la sociedad tradicional a la sociedad de masas* (Buenos Aires: Paidos, 1963), pp. 180–181.

222   *Notes to Pages 40–47*

12. James Scobie, *Buenos Aires: Plaza to Suburb, 1870–1910* (New York: Oxford University Press, 1974), p. 273.

13. Hilda Sabato, "Citizenship, Political Participation, and the Formation of the Public Sphere in Buenos Aires, 1850s–1880s," *Past and Present*, no. 136 (August 1992): 160.

14. Carlos H. Waisman, "Argentina: Autarkic Industrialization and Illegitimacy," in J. Linz, Larry Diamond, and S. M. Lipset, *Democracy in Developing Countries: Latin America* (Boulder, Colo.: Lynne Rienner Publishers, 1989), p. 59.

15. Yaacov Oved, *El anarquismo y el movimiento obrero en Argentina* (Mexico: Siglo Veintiuno, 1978), p. 38.

16. Ronaldo Munck, with Ricardo Falcon and Bernardo Galitelli, *Argentina: From Anarchism to Peronism. Workers, Unions, and Politics, 1855–1985* (New York: Zed Books, 1987), p. 51.

17. On revolutionary syndicalism in Argentina, see Edgardo Bilsky, *La Semaine Tragique en 1919* (Paris: Memoire de Diplome EHESS, 1984).

18. See the full text in Jacinto Oddone, *Historia del socialismo*, vol. 2 (Buenos Aires: Talleres Graficos La Vanguardia, 1934), pp. 82–87.

19. Munck, with Falcon and Galitelli, *Argentina: From Anarchism to Peronism*, p. 68.

20. See Samuel Baily, *Labor, Nationalism, and Politics in Argentina* (New Brunswick, N.J.: Rutgers University Press, 1967), chap. 21.

21. Juan B. Justo, *Teoría y práctica de la historia* (Buenos Aires: La Vanguardia, 1931), vol. 4, p. 225.

22. The Socialist party benefited from the growing population in the urban areas. By 1914, over 50 percent of the Argentine population lived in urban areas. Between 1890 and 1914 the middle class, especially the urban middle class, increased rapidly, comprising 30 percent of Buenos Aires by 1914. Extensive immigration increased the population of Argentina from 3.9 million in 1895 to 11.2 million in 1930. See Ernest A. Duff, *Leader and Party in Latin America* (Boulder, Colo.: Westview Press, 1985), p. 81.

23. See Rock, *Politics in Argentina*, chap. 4.

24. See Puiggrós, *El yrigoyenismo*, chap. 4.

25. Peter Smith, *Argentina and the Failure of Democracy*, p. 31.

26. "VII Congreso del Partido Socialista," in *La Acción Socialista* [Buenos Aires] 17 (April 16, 1906).

27. Diego Abad de Santillán, *La FORA: Ideología y trayectoria del Movimiento Obrero Revolucionario en la Argentina*, 2d ed. (Buenos Aires: Proyección, 1971), p. 207.

28. Julio Arraga, in Rock, *Politics in Argentina*, p. 84.

29. Cited in Hebe Clementi, *El radicalismo: Trayectoria política*, 2d ed. (Buenos Aires: Ed. Siglo Veinte, 1983), p. 9.

30. Korn, *Influencias filosóficas en la evolución nacional*, p. 225.

31. See José Enrique Rodó, *Ariel* (1910; reprint, Buenos Aires: Ed. Sopena, 1948).

32. Diego Pro, *Coroliano Alberini* (Mendoza: Valle de los Huarpes, 1960), pp. 84–85.

33. Carlos Alberto Erro, *Tiempo lacerado* (Buenos Aires: Ed. Sur, 1936), p. 82, cited in Stabb, *América Latina: En búsqueda de una identidad*, p. 237.

34. Fredrick B. Pike, "Making the Hispanic World Safe from Democracy: Spanish Liberals and Hispanismo," *Review of Politics* 33, no. 3 (July 1971): 311.

35. On the influence of José Ortega y Gasset in Argentina, see Tzvi Medin, "Ortega y Gasset en la Argentina: La tercera es la vencida," *Estudios Interdisciplinarios de América Latina y el Caribe* 2, no. 2 (July–December 1991): 25–37. Medin analyzes Ortega's third visit to Argentina during the years 1939–1942. Unlike other visitors, Ortega was not welcomed by the Argentine intellectual milieu. According to Medin, Ortega's ideas had had a different impact on Argentine intellectuals during the Spanish Civil War. Although Ortega was an "exile" during the Civil War, his subsequent return to Spain and his silence, as well as his neutrality during World War II, provoked increasing unease.

36. Ricardo Rojas, *La restauración nacionalista* (Buenos Aires: Ed. Pena Lillo, S.R.L., 1971), p. 18.

37. Ibid., p. 19.

38. Ibid., p. 131.

39. Earl T. Glauert, "Ricardo Rojas and the Emergence of Argentine Cultural Nationalism," *Hispanic American Historical Review* 43 (February 1963): 3. On the Jewish colonization of Argentina, see Haim Avni, *Historia de la inmigración judia a la Argentina 1810–1948 (Jerusalem: Magnus Press, 1983)*. On the question of immigration and liberal cultural nationalism, see Leonardo Senkman, "Nacionalismo e inmigración: La cuestión étnica en las élites liberales e intelectuales argentinas, 1919–1949," *Estudios Interdisciplinarios de América Latina y el Caribe* [University of Tel Aviv] 1, no. 1 (January–June, 1990): 93.

40. Rojas, *La restauración nacionalista*, p. 124.

41. Ibid., p. 130.

42. Glauert, "Ricardo Rojas," p. 3.

43. Rojas, *La restauración nacionalista*, p. 128.

44. Manuel Gálvez, *El diario de Gabriel Quiroga: Opiniones sobre la vida argentina* (Buenos Aires: A. Moen, 1910), p. 55.

45. See Mónica Quijada, *Manuel Gálvez: 60 años de pensamiento nacionalista* (Buenos Aires: Biblioteca Política Argentina, 1985), p. 29.

46. Gálvez, *El diario de Gabriel Quiroga*, p. 153.

47. Manuel Gálvez, *El solar de la raza* (Buenos Aires: Ed. Dictio, 1980), p. 16.

48. See Manuel Gálvez, "Mal metafísico," in *Obras escogidas* (Madrid: Aguilar, 1949). On Gálvez and the Jews, see Leonardo Senkman, "El judío en la obra de Manuel Gálvez," in Leonardo Senkman, *La identidad Judía en la literatura argentina* (Buenos Aires: Ed. Pardes, 1983), pp. 415–430.

49. Bartolomé Mitre's newspaper *La Nación*, one of the leading influences in the "Europeanization" of Argentine society, praised Jewish accomplishments in the arts, sciences, and business. However, it opposed the plans for Jewish settlements in the interior. The editors predicted that the Jews would not adapt themselves to

Argentine conditions, but would form an isolated enclave. See Deutsch, *Counterrevolution in Argentina*, p. 45.

50. Gálvez, *El solar de la raza*, p. 45.

51. Peter Smith, *Argentina and the Failure of Democracy*, pp. 93–94.

52. Gabriel del Mazo, *El radicalismo: Ensayo sobre su historia y doctrina* (Buenos Aires: Ed. Gure S.R.L., 1957), vol. 1, p. 15.

53. Clementi, *El radicalismo: Trayectoria política*, p. 10.

54. José Luis Fernandez, "Yrigoyenismo: Una tradición popular en la historia argentina," in Luis A. Romero, J. J. Fernández, Lilia A. Bertoni, et al., *El radicalismo* (Buenos Aires: Ed. Carlos Perez, 1968), p. 55.

55. Félix Luna, *Yrigoyen* (Buenos Aires: Desarrollo, 1964), p. 161, and del Mazo, *El radicalismo*, p. 55.

56. This is the thesis defended by John J. Johnson in *Political Change in Latin America: The Emergence of the Middle Sectors*, 8th ed. (Stanford, Calif.: Stanford University Press, 1967), chap. 6. See also O. Cornblit, "La opción conservadora en la política argentina," *Desarrollo Económico* 14, no. 56 (1975): 627.

57. Carlos Ibarguren, *La historia que he vivido* (Buenos Aires: Ed. Universitaria, 1969), pp. 282–283.

58. Lisandro de la Torre, elected senator from the Santa Fe province, was a former member of the Unión Cívica Radical who had resigned from the party at the 1897 convention because of his personal conflict with Yrigoyen. De la Torre upheld the basic principles of the Radical Party because he was a morally guided politician and believed that the party was reformist and democratic. He also favored the ideas about modernization developed during the presidency of General Roca—the man who best represents the 1880s generation. After abandoning the Unión Cívica, de la Torre created a regional party, La Liga del Sur.

59. Joaquín Coca, *El contubernio* (Buenos Aires: Ed. Coyoacán, 1961), p. 9.

60. Puiggrós, *El yrigoyenismo*, p. 63.

61. Lilia Ana Bertoni, "Las transformaciones del partido y sus luchas políticas," in Romero, Fernández, Bertoni, et al., *El radicalismo*, p. 102.

62. Carlos Ibarguren, *La historia que he vivido*, p. 295.

63. Roberto Etchepareborda, ed., *Hipólito Yrigoyen: Pueblo y gobierno*, vol. 1 (Buenos Aires: Ed. Raigal, 1951), p. 313, cited in Rock, *Politics in Argentina*, p. 51.

64. Del Mazo, *El radicalismo*, p. 129.

65. "Manifiesto de la UCR," July 1915, in Etchepareborda, *Hipólito Yrigoyen: Pueblo y gobierno*, vol. 1, pp. 404–405.

66. Del Mazo, *El radicalismo*, p. 234.

67. Ibid., p. 235.

68. Ibid., p. 236.

69. The membership of FORA IX grew from 20,521 members in 1915 to 700,000 in 1920. See Alfredo Palacios, *El nuevo derecho*, 5th ed. (Buenos Aires: Ed. Claridad, 1920), p. 226. On the syndicalists' support for Yrigoyen's interventionism in labor matters, see Juan Carlos Grosso, "Los problemas económicos y sociales y la respuesta radical en el gobierno (1916–1919)," in Romero, Fernández, Bertoni, et al., *El radicalismo*, p. 125. On the abandonment of the general strike as

a revolutionary method, see also Julio Arraga, *El sindicato, los partidos políticos y las sectas* (Buenos Aires: Biblioteca de "La Acción Obrera," 1918), vol. 4, p. 17.

70. See Juan Carlos Torre, "Interpretando (una vez más) los orígenes del Peronismo," *Desarrollo Económico* [Buenos Aires] 28, no. 112 (January–March 1989).

71. Ricardo Caballero, *La reconstrucción de la U.C.R.* (Buenos Aires: 1930), p. 37, cited in del Mazo, *El radicalismo*, p. 60.

72. *Cámara de Diputados* 5 (1918–19): 293.

73. "Historia de la Fraternidad," in Puiggrós, *El yrigoyenismo*, p. 206.

74. Munck, with Falcon and Galitelli, *Argentina: From Anarchism to Peronism*, p. 82.

75. Miguel Angel Carcano, *Enfoque histórico sobre la Presidencia de Roque Sáenz Peña* (Buenos Aires: Balder Moen, 1924).

76. Ibid.

77. José Nicolas Matienzo, the minister of the interior, began the process of dismantling the paternalistic administration, but around February 1923, the government began to exercise caution. Rather than cut spending and isolate itself from its main source of popular support in the party, it adopted the alternative course of seeking additional revenue by increasing the customs valuations of imported goods by 60 percent. However, this elementary industrialist ploy was a short-term measure which did not resolve the basic ideological divisions in the Radical Party.

78. *La Nación*, February 14, 1928, cited in Alain Rouquié, *Poder militar y sociedad política en Argentina*, vol. 1 (Buenos Aires: Ed. Emece, 1983), p. 176.

79. Benjamin Villafañe, "Conferencia en el Parque Romano," January 19, 1928, p. 16. Cited in Rouquié, *Poder militar*, vol. 1, p. 176.

80. An interesting discussion on the reasons for the 1930 coup and the breakdown of democracy in Argentina is given by Peter H. Smith in "The Breakdown of Democracy in Argentina, 1916–1930," in Juan Linz and Alfred Stepan, eds. *The Breakdown of Democratic Regimes, Latin America* (Baltimore: Johns Hopkins University Press, 1978). Smith sees the process that led to the revolution of 1930 as basically a crisis in legitimacy. He uses Juan Linz's argument that the inefficiency and ineffectiveness of the democratic structure in upholding tacit political norms led to a legitimacy crisis which prevented any competent response to a destabilizing economic situation, and this paralysis further compounded the legitimacy crisis. See Peter Smith, ibid., p. 23. In fact, for the Argentine integral nationalists of *La Nueva República*, neither the conservative liberal-democratic political system nor the anarchic populism of the intransigent Yrigoyenist wing of the Radical Party could create a legitimate basis for coping with the new problems produced by social mobilization and economic modernization.

81. In spite of these unequivocal indications of crisis in the relations between Yrigoyen and the army, the process of alienation was rather gradual. This was reflected in the annual elections in the Círculo Militar, which were a clear barometer of the military attitude toward the government. In the elections of 1929, the list headed by General (Res.) Pablo Ricchieri, who supported the national

government, defeated the dissident generals whose candidates were Uriburu and Rodriguez. But tension had increased by the time of the elections of 1930, when only one anti-government list, led by General Francisco Velez, was presented. In his inaugural speech, Velez defined the army's attitude toward the government as one of "scrupulous consideration . . . but not obsession or servility." See Ronald A. Potash, *El ejército y la política en la Argentina, 1928–1945: De Yrigoyen a Perón* (Buenos Aires: Ed. Sudamericana, 1984), pp. 66–67.

82. See Juan V. Orana, *La logia militar que enfrento a Hipólito Yrigoyen* (Buenos Aires s/e., 1965), p. 107.

83. Uriburu's name was mentioned by Marshall Joffre in a personal conversation with Alvear. Joffre pointed out that the future minister of war was notoriously pro-German. See Félix Luna, *Alvear* (Buenos Aires: Libros Argentinos, 1956), pp. 58–59.

84. Archivo General de la Nación, Archivo General Uriburu, Legajo 1.320.

85. This is the name Yrigoyen gave his opponents. They were the "*acuerdistas,*" the term applied to those who agreed with the basic principles of the program of liberal modernization since the days of Bartolomé Mitre.

86. See José Maria Sarobe, *Memorias sobre la revolución del 6 de Setiembre de 1930* (Buenos Aires: Ed. Gure, 1934) p. 21.

87. See "Speech in the Colegio Militar, 1920," *Revista Universitaria* 6, no. 61 (1935), cited in Potash, *El ejército*, p. 48.

88. Carlos Ibarguren, Jr., *Respuestas a un cuestionario acerca del nacionalismo, 1930–1945*. Interview by José Luis Romero, 15 July 1971 (Buenos Aires: Talleres Gráficos Dorrego, 1971), p. 4.

89. Federico Ibarguren, *Orígenes del nacionalismo argentino, 1927–1937* (Buenos Aires: Ed. Celcius, 1967).

90. Ibid.

91. Mario Amadeo, *Ayer, hoy, mañana* (Buenos Aires: Ed. Gure, 1956), p. 109.

92. See Tomas Auza, *Católicos y liberales en la generación del 80* (Buenos Aires: Ed. Culturales Argentinas, 1975).

Chapter Three. The Origins of the Argentine National Right

1. Sternhell, "Fascist Ideology," in Laqueur, *Fascism, a Reader's Guide*, p. 353.

2. Leopoldo Lugones, "Nuestras ideas estéticas," *Philadelphia*, no. 6, December 7, 1901, p. 169.

3. Lugones, "Saludo a S.A.de Saboya," *El Tiempo*, June 11, 1896.

4. Lugones, "Socialismo y revolución," *La Montaña* 7, July 1, 1897, cited in Richard J. Walter, *The Socialist Party of Argentina, 1890–1930* (Austin: University of Texas Press, 1977), p. 34.

5. Alberto Conil Paz, *Leopoldo Lugones* (Buenos Aires: Ed. Huemul, 1985), p. 63.

6. *Cámara de Diputados*, January 14, 1919, p. 128.

7. "Forma vengativa del miedo a la Revolucion." See Leopoldo Lugones to León Kibrick, January 25, 1919, in "Encuesta de *Vida Nuestra*, sobre la situación de los judíos en la Argentina," *Vida Nuestra*, vol. 2, no. 17 (January 1919): 147, cited in Conil Paz, *Leopoldo Lugones*, p. 270.

8. *La Vanguardia*, July 21, 1931, cited in Conil Paz, *Leopoldo Lugones*, p. 383.

9. Lugones, "La ilusión constitucional," *La Nación*, October 17, 1923.

10. Lugones, *La patria fuerte* (Buenos Aires: Circulo Militar, Biblioteca del Oficial, 1930), p. 40. These principles were published in *La Nación* during the years 1913–1915, and were later compiled in two books: *Mi beligerancia* (1917) and *La Torre de Casandra* (1919).

11. Lugones, "La Francia heróica," *La Nación*, October 9, 1921.

12. Lugones, "El finalismo progresista," *La Nación*, January 6, 1924. See also Lugones, "Del Parlamento," *La Nación*, March 14, 1926.

13. Lugones, "Poesía obliga: De L. Lugones a Joaquin Castellanos," *La Nación*, August 18, 1923.

14. Lugones, "Democracia y tiranía," *La Nación*, February 21, 1927.

15. Lugones, *Didáctica* (Buenos Aires: Otero y Cia, 1910), p. 159.

16. Alfred Naquet, "Questions constitutionnelles," in Sternhell, *Maurice Barrès*, p. 83.

17. Lugones, "El deber de potencia," *La patria fuerte*, pp. 70–71.

18. Lugones, *La grande Argentina* (Buenos Aires: Ed. Babel, 1930), p. 113.

19. Lugones, "Fuerza y derecho," chap. 7 of *La organización de la paz*, which Lugones also refers to in "La hora de la espada," in *La patria fuerte*, pp. 35–37.

20. Lugones, *La patria fuerte*, p. 40.

21. Lugones, "Prefacio," in *La patria fuerte*, p. 9.

22. Lugones, *La patria fuerte*, p. 38.

23. Lugones, "El discurso de ayacucho," in *La patria fuerte*, p. 18.

24. Lugones, "Estética nihilista," *La Nación*, March 18, 1928.

25. The Irazusta brothers belonged to a wealthy family of the province of Entre Rios that supported the antipersonalist wing of the Radical Party. They began to study law in Buenos Aires in 1916 but did not pursue this career. In 1923 they both traveled to France, where they were influenced by their reading of Charles Maurras, published in the newspaper *L'Action Française*. Like the Irazustas, Juan Carulla was another prominent writer in *La Nueva República* and was also founder of the newspaper *Bandera Argentina*. He too went to Europe during World War I. His evolution toward the ideas of *L'Action Française* resulted from conversations with its principal members and from reading the works of Charles Maurras.

26. María Inés Barbero and Fernando Devoto, *Los nacionalistas* (Buenos Aires: Centro Editor de America Latina, 1983), p. 69.

27. Carlos Ibarguren, Jr., and Roberto de Laferrère, *Periodismo, política, historia* (Buenos Aires: Ed. Universitaria, 1970), p. 93.

28. See, for example, Mario Lassaga, "Crisis política," *La Nueva República*, January 17, 1931.

29. Charles Maurras, *L'Ordre et le desordre* (Paris, 1948), p. 14.

30. Juan Carulla, *Al filo del medio siglo*, 2d ed. (Buenos Aires: Ed. Huemul, 1964), p. 201.

31. Ibid., p. 229.

32. Ibid., pp. 97–98.

33. Ibid., pp. 100–101.

34. Julio Irazusta, lecture delivered in the Parroquia Nuestra Senora del Socorro, Buenos Aires, November 16, 1972, during the Semana Maurrasiana, cited in Julio Irazusta, *Estudios históricos políticos*, p. 184.

35. Ibid.

36. Rodolfo Irazusta, "Constitución y democracia," *La Nueva República*, April 28, 1928.

37. Ibid.

38. In the doctrine of the "land and the deceased," the nation is a territory where people share a memory, the deceased, and a heritage of ideals. Consequently, in order for France to be regenerated and for the nation and the state to be restored, individuals must be rooted in the earth and the deceased. (Maurice Barrès, *Scènes et doctrines du nationalisme*, vol. 1, p. 93. See also Barrès, *L'Appel au soldat* (Paris: E. Fasquale, 1900), p. 392, cited in Sternhell, *Maurice Barrès*, p. 385.

39. See Curtis, *Three against the Third Republic*, pp. 88–89.

40. Rodolfo Irazusta, "El precio del liberalismo," *El Baluarte*, December 25, 1929.

41. *La Nación*, June 28, 1936. This is an article about the translation into Spanish of *L'Enquête sur la monarchie*, in Julio Irazusta, *Estudios históricos políticos*, p. 170.

42. *La Nueva República*, January 31, 1928.

43. Rodolfo Irazusta, *La Nueva República*, December 13, 1930.

44. Julio Irazusta, "Las libertades del liberalismo," *La Nueva República*, January 10, 1931.

45. Rodolfo Irazusta, *La Nueva República*, March 2, 1929.

46. Ernesto Palacio, "Organicemos la contrarevolución," *La Nueva República*, May 5, 1928.

47. Ernesto Palacio, "Nacionalismo y democracia," *La Nueva República*, May 5, 1928.

48. Ernesto Palacio, "Nuevos Tiempos," *La Nueva República*, October 13, 1931.

49. Curtis, *Three against the Third Republic*, p. 227.

50. Carlos Ibarguren, *La historia que he vivido*, p. 366.

51. Ernesto Palacio, *La Nueva República*, July 5, 1930, cited in Federico Ibarguren, *Orígenes del nacionalismo*, p. 36.

52. On the Sarobe plan, see José Sarobe, *Memorias sobre la revolución*, pp. 60–78.

53. The voter participation in those elections was estimated at 75 percent of the Buenos Aires electorate; the Radicals won 218,830 votes against 187,340 for the conservatives and 41,730 for the Socialist Party.

54. The Radical Party was declared illegal and its political leaders exiled. Honorio Puyrredon and Mario Guido, the winners of the election in Buenos

Aires, together with Alvear, Pedro Tamborini, and Carlos M. Noel, the principal Radical leaders, were all exiled, thereby aiding the candidacy of General Justo.

55. The Klan Radical was a paramilitary shock troop organization of the Yrigoyenist wing of the Radical Party that appeared in July 1929 to combat party dissidents. These groups, composed of party committee members organized by Radical congressmen, clashed with the Liga Republicana in several street confrontations. However, in spite of the violent rhetoric during some organizational meetings and isolated propagandistic political acts—such as the one prepared to disrupt the speech of Agricultural Minister Juan B. Fleitas at the Sociedad Rural—no other violent acts by the Liga were cited.

56. Carlos Ibarguren, Jr., and Roberto de Laferrère, *Periodismo, política, historia*, p. 41.

57. Federico Ibarguren, *Orígenes del nacionalismo*, pp. 31–32.

58. Uriburu's address to officers at the banquet of the Armed Forces, July 7, 1931. See Rouquié, *Poder militar*, vol. 1, p. 245.

59. Lautaro Montenegro, *Origen de la Legión Cívica Argentina y la doctrina de su constitución* (Buenos Aires: n.p., 1931), p. 5.

60. As demonstrated in the study by Fernando Garcia Molina, Graciela Etchevest, Ana Maria Galibert, and Omar Cerdeira, "La Legión Cívica Argentina (1931–1932)," introductory lecture on the study of society by Prof. Rubén Berenblum, Universidad Nacional de Buenos Aires, 1985, p. 14.

61. Policía Federal, "Prontuario Carulla," Legajo 1, exp. 1, folio 52, Leg. Legión Cívica, June 15, 1931.

62. Policía Federal, "Prontuario Carulla," Legajo 1, exp. 1, folio 198, Leg. Legión Cívica, June 12, 1932.

63. *La Prensa*, September 30, 1931, p. 4.

64. Policía Federal, "Prontuario Carulla," Legajo 1, exp. 1, folio 239, Leg. Legión Cívica, June 1931.

65. Juan Orona, *La revolución del 6 de setiembre* (Buenos Aires, 1966), p. 236.

66. *La Vanguardia*, September 16, 1931, p. 1.

67. Federico Ibarguren, *Orígenes del nacionalismo*, pp. 86–87.

68. Policía Federal, "Prontuario Juan Carulla," exp. 10, folios 16, 17, Agrupaciones Nacionalistas.

69. Juan B. Molina, "Carta al Coronel D. Natalio Mascarello," Circular de la Legión Cívica Argentina, Buenos Aires, June 1941.

70. *Crisol*, September 12, 1936.

71. Deutsch, *Counterrevolution in Argentina*, p. 212.

Chapter Four. The Década Infame:
The Conservative Restoration and the Rise of Integral Nationalism

1. José Luis Romero, *Las ideas políticas en Argentina*, 3d ed. (Buenos Aires: Fondo de Cultura Económica, 1959), p. 237.

2. Peter H. Smith, *Politics and Beef in Argentina* (New York: Columbia University Press, 1969), pp. 134–135.

3. Guido di Tella and Manuel Zymelman, *Las etapas del desarrollo económico argentino* (Buenos Aires: Ed. Universidad de Buenos Aires, 1967), pp. 436–438.

4. David Tamarin, *The Argentine Labor Movement, 1930–1945: A Study in the Origins of Peronism* (Albuquerque: University of New Mexico Press, 1975) p. 26.

5. Di Tella and Zymelman, *Las etapas del desarrollo económico argentino*, pp. 452–455.

6. Carlos Ibarguren, *La Historia que he vivido*, p. 443.

7. David Rock, *Argentina: De la colonización a Alfonsín* (Madrid: Ed. Alianza America, 1988), p. 287. First published as *Argentina 1516–1982: From Spanish Colonization to the Falklands War* (Berkeley: University of California Press, 1985).

8. Alberto Ciria, *Parties and Power in Modern Argentina (1930–1946)*, trans. Carlos A. Astiz and Mary F. McCarthy (Albany: State University of New York Press, 1974), p. 25.

9. "What It Means for Both Nations: British Capital in Argentina," *Buenos Aires Herald*, July 9, 1933.

10. See Ysabel Rennie, *The Argentine Republic* (New York: Macmillan, 1945), pp. 235–239.

11. On the issue of internal migrations in Argentina, see Zulma L. Recchini de Lattes and Alfredo E. Lattes, *Migraciones en la Argentina: Estudio de las migraciones internas e internacionales, basado en datos censales, 1869–1960* (Buenos Aires, 1969).

12. See the statistics of the fiscal resources of the federal capital and the provinces. Alejandro Bunge, *La Nueva Argentina*, pp. 409–412, quoted in Ronald H. Dolkart, "The Provinces," in Mark Falcoff and R. H. Dolkart, eds., *Prologue to Perón: Argentina in Depression and War, 1930–1943* (Berkeley: University of California Press, 1975), p. 182.

13. José Luis Torres, *La patria y su destina* (Buenos Aires, 1947), pp. 172–174, cited in Ciria, *Political Parties*, p. 36.

14. Waisman, *Reversal of Development*, p. 109.

15. Diana Quattrocchi Woisson, *Un nationalisme de deracinés* (Paris: Editions du CNRS, 1992), p. 65.

16. Carl Schmitt, *Politische Romantik* (Munich, 1919) pp. 142–143, in Herf, *Reactionary Modernism*, p. 117.

17. Ibid.

18. George L. Mosse, *The Crisis of German Ideology: Intellectual Origins of the Third Reich* (New York: Schocken Books, 1981), pp. 4–5.

19. Julio Irazusta, *Ensayo sobre Rosas: En el centenario de la suma del poder, 1835–1935* (Buenos Aires: Colección Megáfono, 1935), pp. 28–29.

20. Amadeo, *Ayer, hoy, mañana*, p. 114. On the Argentine Catholic right wing, see John J. Kennedy, *Catholicism, Nationalism, and Democracy in Argentina*

(Notre Dame, Ind.: University of Notre Dame Press, 1958). Kennedy rejects the idea that the Argentine Catholics were fascists, or that they had any intentions of transforming the political order. Even though they did not struggle in the political arena, they were clearly antiliberal and played an important role ideologically and culturally in delegitimizing political democracy. See also Zanatta, *Del estado liberal a la nación católica.*

21. Arturo Jauretche, *FORJA y la década infame* (1962; reprint, Buenos Aires: Ed. Peña Lillio, 1984), pp. 57–58.

22. Julio Irazusta and Rodolfo Irazusta, "Historia de la oligarquía argentina," *Nuevo Orden,* August 1, 1940. This essay was included in Julio Irazusta and Rodolfo Irazusta, *La Argentina y el imperialismo británico: Los eslabones de una cadena, 1806–1833* (Buenos Aires: Ed. Condor, 1934). A contemporary book analyzing in a critical way the role of Argentine liberal elites is Shumway, *The Invention of Argentina.* This book in certain ways endorses in modern times the revisionist appeal of Argentine historiography.

23. Juan Pablo Oliver, "Los unitarios y el capital extranjero," *Revista del Instituto de Investigaciones Históricas Juan Manuel de Rosas,* vol. 2, no. 6 (Buenos Aires: December 1940).

24. Ernesto Palacio, "La historia oficial y la historia," *Revista del Instituto de Investigaciones Históricas Juan Manuel de Rosas,* vol. 1, no. 1 (January 1939): 9.

25. Ibid., p. 10.

26. Carlos Ibarguren, "La inquietud de esta hora," (series) Biblioteca del Pensamiento Nacionalista Argentino (Buenos Aires: Ed. Dictio, 1975), p. 35.

27. See Jorge Luis Borges, "Prólogo," in Arturo Jauretche, *El Paso de los Libres* (Buenos Aires, 1934).

28. Conil Paz, *Leopoldo Lugones,* p. 257.

29. Beatriz Sarlo, *Una modernidad periférica: Buenos Aires 1920–1930* (Buenos Aires, 1988), p. 212.

30. Sarlo, *Una modernidad,* p. 208.

31. Ibid., p. 217. See Eduardo Mallea's *Historia de una pasión argentina* (1937). The participation of Eduardo Mallea in *Sur* is analyzed by John King, *Sur: A Study of the Argentine Literary Journal and Its Role in the Development of a Culture, 1931–1970* (New York: Cambridge University Press, 1986), chaps. 3 and 4.

32. See Mark Falcoff, "Intellectual Currents," in Falcoff and Dolkart, *Prologue to Perón,* p. 112.

33. On the literary importance played by the magazine *Sur* and on the leadership of Victoria Ocampo, see King, *Sur: A Study.*

34. Leopoldo Lugones, "Rehallazgo del pais," *Revista Militar* (Buenos Aires), vol. 71, no. 447 (1938). The Revista Militar of the Círculo Militar published several articles by Lugones that emphasized the role of old myths of Argentine national culture for modern nationalism. Most of these articles appeared in the cultural supplements of *La Nación.*

35. Ramón Doll, "Rosas creador de un estado," *Acerca de una política nacional,* Biblioteca del Pensamiento Nacionalista Argentino (Buenos Aires: Ed. Dictio, 1939), p. 142.

232 Notes to Pages 106–113

36. Julio and Rodolfo Irazusta, *La Argentina y el imperialismo*, p. 198.

37. Doll, "Rosas creador de un estado," p. 144.

38. Federico Ibarguren, "Bibliografía, Vida de Don Juan Manuel de Rosas de M. Gálvez," *Revista del Instituto de Investigaciones Históricas Juan Manuel de Rosas*, vol. 2, no. 6 (Buenos Aires: December 1940): 127.

39. See "La Controversia sobre Rosas," *Bandera Argentina*, November 13, 1935.

40. Federico Ibarguren, "La misión histórica de España," *Criterio*, no. 459, December 17, 1936. The Bourbon program of enlightened modernization was characterized by the conviction that it was through an enlightened, dynamic, authoritarian state and through that alone, that the obscurantist, obedient society of Spain could be reinvigorated.

41. Richard Morse, "The Heritage of Latin America," in Hartz, *The Founding of New Societies*, p. 158.

42. "Democracia y liberalismo están indisolublemente unidos," *Crisol*, December 1, 1938.

43. Hector Sáenz y Quesada, "La Realidad Democrática en la Argentina," *Sol y Luna*, no. 6 (1941), p. 142.

44. Ibid., p. 141.

45. Julio Irazusta, *Ensayo sobre Rosas*, p. 29.

46. Rodolfo Irazusta, "La filiación histórica," *La Nueva República*, October 29, 1931.

47. Leopoldo Lugones, "La unidad romana," *La Nación*, March 23, 1929.

48. Juan Linz, "Religion and Politics," *Daedalus*, Summer 1991, p. 163, issued as vol. 120, no. 3 of the *Proceedings of the American Academy of Arts and Sciences*. Most of the nationalists interpreted the Catholic rebellion against the liberal state in defense of ecclesiastical prerogatives during the Roca government as the heart of the clerical challenge to the central function of the liberal state in Argentina. It was the struggle of the real nation against the artificial democratic liberal state. That struggle was prolonged in the *caudillista* traditional federalism of Juan Manuel de Rosas, which confronted the "modern centralism" of the centralizers and was another example of the development of an ideological common ground between authentic nationalism, the church, and traditional Catholicism.

49. Ivereigh, *Catholicism and Politics in Argentina*, p. 70.

50. One of the most important points of discord between the church establishment and President Roca was the replacement of a Catholic-oriented minister of justice and public instruction for Eduardo Wilde, a radical nonbeliever who was in the Roca coalition.

51. Ivereigh, *Catholicism and Politics in Argentina*, p. 31.

52. See "Una cuestión mal planteada," *Criterio*, no. 245 (November 10, 1932).

53. Zanatta, *Del estado liberal a la nación católica*, p. 118.

54. Ivereigh, *Catholicism and Politics in Argentina*, p. 115.

55. "De un tío estanciero a un sobrino diputado," *Criterio*, no. 675 (February 6, 1941).

56. "Declaración de Principios," *Restauración* (Buenos Aires, 1937), p. 3, quoted in Navarro Gerasssi, *Los nacionalistas*, p. 121. Acción Católica Argentina

was established through a collective pastoral letter by the ecclesiastical hierarchy on December 1, 1928, as a nonpolitical group, but it was inspired by the new Catholic social thought that had a clear political and ideological connotation as the social theory that offered an alternative to liberal democracy and socialist Marxism.

57. On the contradiction of a party like the Italian Partito Popolare, see "Los católicos y la política," *Criterio*, no. 189 (October 15, 1931).

58. As Anthony Leeden writes, "The emergence in Italy of the Comitati d'Azione per l'Universalita di Roma, created by Mussolini, confirmed that his famous claim that fascism is not merchandise for export had been proven wrong by the course of events." In the summer of 1933, *Critica Fascista* announced that "The motor of spiritual renovation, which we began in the Italian provinces a decade ago in the name of revolutionary fascism, only now begins to have repercussions." See Anthony Leeden, *Universal Fascism: The Theory and Practice of the Fascist International, 1928–1936* (New York: H. Fertig, 1972), pp. 104–105.

59. Alberto Filippi, *El libertador en la historia Italiana, Ilustración, "Risorgimiento," Fascismo* (Caracas: Biblioteca de la Academia Nacional de Historia, 1987), p. 150.

60. Carlos Ibarguren, "El cuadro político de mundo y la representación de los intereses sociales," lecture at the Law and Social Sciences Faculty in Buenos Aires, *Bandera Argentina*, August 12, 1932.

61. Juan Carulla, *La Nueva República*, September 22, 1928.

62. Ibid.

63. Amadeo, *Ayer, hoy, mañana*, p. 114.

64. Carlos Ibarguren, "La inquietud de esta hora," p. 56.

65. *Crisol*, September 12, 1936. On the impact of the Spanish Civil War in Argentine public opinion and its political establishment, see Mark Falcoff and Fredrick B. Pike, *The Spanish Civil War, 1936–39* (Lincoln: University of Nebraska Press, 1982). On Argentine Catholicism, which developed as an autonomous political force, see Ernesto Palacio, *Historia de la Argentina* (Buenos Aires: Ed. Alpe, 1954), p. 533.

66. The young Ramiro de Maeztu was a liberal and a great admirer of British civilization. His intellectual and ideological transformation began in 1919 at the end of World War I, when he published one of his most famous books, *La crisis del humanismo*, which expresses his new adherence to monarchical traditionalism.

67. Ramiro de Maeztu, *Defensa de la Hispanidad* (Madrid: Ed. Grafica Universal, 1934), p. 298.

68. *ABC*, Madrid, August 10, 1932.

69. César Pico, "Hacia la Hispanidad," *Sol y Luna*, vol. 9 (1942), p. 140.

70. Ibid., p. 138.

71. Gustavo Franceschi, "La Jerarquía y el orden temporal," *Criterio*, vol. 11, no. 560 (November 24, 1938), p. 315.

72. "Action Française, y fascismo ante la Santa Sede," *Criterio*, April 1929, p. 458.

73. Jacques Maritain, "Sobre la guerra santa," *Sur*, no. 35 (1937), p. 101, quoted by Mark Falcoff, "Argentina," in Falcoff and Dolkart, *Prologue to Perón*, p. 325.

74. César Pico, *Carta a Jacques Maritain sobre la colaboración de los católicos con los movimientos de tipo fascista* (Buenos Aires: Ed. Adsum, 1937), p. 13.

75. Julio Meinvielle, *Los tres pueblos bíblicos en la lucha por la dominación del mundo* (Buenos Aires: Ed Adsum, 1937), p. 54.

76. *Baluarte*, no. 20 (May–June 1934).

77. Leonardo Castellani, "Teoría y práctica," *Las canciones de militis* (Buenos Aires: Ed. de Formación Patria, 1945), p. 174.

78. Gustavo Franceschi, "Revolución y negativismo," *Criterio*, March 30, 1933, p. 295.

79. Ibid.

80. Ibid. In contrast to groups like La Liga Patriótica, which acted as civil guards during the workers' unrest in 1919, and contrary to the formula of international communism, Franceschi believed that Argentine nationalism had to produce an authentic political synthesis that could provide a solution to the social problem—a solution that would not favor the local bourgeoisie but that would respond to the needs of the lower classes. On the relationship between the Liga Patriótica and the Argentine nationalists, see Deutsch, *Counterrevolution in Argentina*.

81. Franceschi, "Revolución y negativismo," p. 294.

82. Jose María Estrada, "La recuperación de las cosas," *Sol y Luna*, vol. 7 (1942), p. 69.

83. Ibid., p. 74.

84. Ibid., p. 72.

85. Ibid.

86. See Julio Meinvielle, "De la guerra santa," *Criterio*, no. 494 (August 19, 1937).

87. Federico Ibarguren, "Charles Peguy y nuestro tiempo," *La Nación*, October 10, 1937. In Federico Ibarguren, *Avivando brasas* (Buenos Aires: Ed. Theoria, 1957), pp. 88–89.

88. Ibid., p. 91.

89. Ibid.

90. Federico Ibarguren, "Contrarreforma y capitalismo," *Dinámica Social*, no. 24 (August 1952): 157.

91. Eduardo M. Lustosa, "La idea corporativa," *Criterio*, March 31, 1938, p. 379.

92. The answer according to Lustosa is given by Pope Pius XI's distinction between socioeconomic corporativism and political corporativism. The latter could function without the former, "but political corporativism is ill-conceived without a social and economic base." See Lustosa, "La idea corporativa."

93. Ibid.

94. See Gino Arias, "El concepto de la riqueza y la propiedad," *Sol y Luna*, vol. 7 (1942), p. 101.

95. Julio Meinvielle, *Concepción católica de la política* (reprint, Buenos Aires: Ed. Theoria, 1961), p. 90.

96. See Julio Meinvielle, "Producción de la tierra," *Baluarte,* no. 22 (September–October 1934). On Meinvielle's economic conceptions, see Julio Meinvielle, *Concepción católica de la economía* (Buenos Aires: Cursos de Cultura Católica, 1936). A clear expositor of traditional antimodernist Catholicism and hard anti-Semitism, Father Meinvielle presented the Catholic dilemma in its most radical expression. Besides the numerous contributions to the Catholic press, Meinvielle wrote many books, some of which were very influential in many nationalist anti-Semitic movements like Tacuara that remained active into the 1960s. *Concepción católica de la politica* (1932), *Entre la Iglesia y el Reich* (1937), *Que saldra de la España que sangra* (1937), and *Los tres pueblos bíblicos en la lucha por la dominación del mundo* (1937) are some of the titles that projected Meinvielle's own extremist interpretation of the political philosophy of Thomas Aquinas.

97. Hector Bernardo, "Experiencias corporativas," *Nueva Política,* no. 2 (July 1940): 18–23, cited from Buchrucker, *Nacionalismo y peronismo,* p. 177. César Pico also attempted to close the gap between fascist modernism and traditional corporatism, asserting that the social corporativist organization would save the concept of private property from its bourgeois connotations or bourgeois interpretation. He thought that a non-bourgeois concept of private property was possible. César Pico noted that "The bourgeoisie . . . helped fascism at the beginning because of its fear of communism." However, the bourgeoisie was "disappointed when it found itself facing a corporativist economy that affected . . . its heavy earnings." See Pico, *Carta a Jacques Maritain,* p. 31.

98. Alberto Ezcurra Medrano, *Catolicismo y nacionalismo,* 2d ed. (Buenos Aires: Ed. Adsum, 1939), p. 32.

Chapter Five. The Integralist Right and the Populist Left:
Anti-Imperialism, Productionism, and Social Justice

1. Benito Mussolini, "The Doctrine of Fascism" (1933), in Steiner and Lyttelton, *Roots of the Right,* p. 56.

2. Enrique Osés, "Hacia una coordinación del fascismo universal?" *Crisol,* October 27, 1935.

3. Enrique Osés, "Reflector mundial," *Crisol,* December 12, 1935.

4. Julio and Rodolfo Irazusta, *La Argentina y el imperialismo,* p. 200.

5. Ramon Doll, "Del Servicio Secreto Inglés al Judio Dickman, 1939," Biblioteca del Pensamiento Nacionalista Argentino (Buenos Aires: Ed. Dictio, 1939), p. 209.

6. Julio and Rodolfo Irazusta, *La Argentina y el imperialismo,* p. 200.

7. Rodolfo Irazusta, "La Política," *Nueva República,* December 27, 1930.

8. Julio and Rodolfo Irazusta, *La Argentina y el imperialismo,* p. 80.

9. Ramón Doll, "Grandeza y miseria de la oligarquía argentina: La realidad nacional sin cartabones extranjeros," *Claridad* 13, no. 277 (1934). The article appeared in Doll, *Liberalismo en la literatura y la política* (Buenos Aires: Ed. Claridad, n.d), pp. 42–43.

10. Benjamin Villafañe, "Política económica suicida, país conquistado," in *La miseria de un país rico* (Jujuy: Tip. Lib. B. Buttazzoni, 1927), pp. 25–26. Benjamin Villafañe was a deputy from the province of Jujuy, governor from 1924 to 1927, and national senator from 1932 to 1941. He was active in the Radical Party until he left it around 1920, becoming a fervent enemy of Radicalism. His other works include *El atraso del interior: Cosas de nuestra tierra* (1939) and *El destino de Sudamérica* (1943). Also of fundamental importance in the development of an authentic economic nationalism were the works of Manuel Ortiz Pereyra, *Por nuestra redención cultural y economica: Apuntes de critica social Argentina* (1928) and *La tercera emancipación* (1926).

11. Villafañe, "Política económica suicida, país conquistado."

12. Federico Ibarguren, *Orígenes del nacionalismo*, pp. 160–161.

13. Leopoldo Lugones, "Propósitos," in ibid., p. 188.

14. *Revista económica Argentina* 32, no. 187 (1934): 13–15.

15. "Nuestro problema económico básico: El trigo," *Crisol*, December 13, 1938.

16. "La buena vecindad yanqui y la entrega de todo lo nuestro," *Crisol*, November 12, 1938.

17. For more than thirty years this daily paper was something akin to a fourth or fifth branch of the Argentine government, due to its rich sources of data and high-quality analysis.

18. See Mark Falcoff, "Economic Dependency," *Latin American Research Review* 25, no. 1 (1990): 62–63. In the same issue see also J. C. Korol and Hilda Sábato, "Incomplete Industrialization," p. 89.

19. Alejandro Bunge, *Una nueva Argentina* (Buenos Aires: Hyspanoamerica Ed. Argentina, 1987), p. 506.

20. Ibid., p. 507.

21. Ibid., p. 511.

22. Lugones, *La grande Argentina*, p. 117.

23. Ibid.

24. Ibid., p. 101.

25. Ibid., p. 98.

26. *Nuevo Orden*, vol. 2, no. 91 (April 22, 1942).

27. Lugones, "La América Latina," in *La patria fuerte*, p. 111.

28. Lugones, "El Estado de potencia," in *La patria fuerte*, p. 63.

29. Ibid.

30. Georges Sorel and the French and Italian syndicalists accepted private property and a laissez-faire economy more than any school of orthodox state socialism. On the basis of what they considered an orthodox interpretation of Marx, they saw any state intervention in the free economic process as dangerous for the future of socialism. Fascism was later to transform this basic stance into a

production-oriented national corporativism. The state would not intervene in the economic process as long as it served the interests of the state.

31. See the interesting remarks on the relation between agrarian wealth and the resulting degree of dependence on the industrial countries made by Colonel Luis Vicat during a lecture at the Círculo Militar. Luis Vicat, "Conference in the Círculo Militar," July 1926, in Jean Cazeneuve et al., *Ejército y revolución industrial*, trans. Carlos Aguirre and R. J. Walsh (Buenos Aires: Ed. Jorge Alvarez, 1964).

32. R. Marambio, "Hacia la autarquía militar," *Revista Militar* 71, no. 6 (1938): 867–868.

33. *Anales de la Unión Industrial Argentina*, May 1933.

34. Gustavo Martínez Zuviría, preface to Juan Lucio Cernadas, *Estrategia nacional y política de estado* (Buenos Aires: Ed. El Ateneo, 1938), p. 13.

35. Lugones, "Manifiesto," in Federico Ibarguren, *Orígenes del nacionalismo*, p. 75.

36. Ibid., p. 75.

37. See Lugones, "Propósitos," in ibid., p. 191.

38. Carlos Ibarguren, Jr., and Roberto de Laferrère, *Periodismo, política, historia*, pp. 100–101.

39. Leopoldo Lugones, *El estado equitativo* (Buenos Aires: La Editora, 1932), pp. 38–39.

40. Gregor, *The Fascist Persuasion in Radical Politics*, p. 178.

41. Carlos Sylvera, "Los enemigos del nacionalismo," *Clarinada*, August 1938, p. 4.

42. "Obra social del fascismo," *Clarinada*, March 1938.

43. See Falco Testena, *Il Giornale d'Italia* (Buenos Aires), July 5, 1933.

44. *Criterio* 278 (June–July 1933); Falco Testena, *Il Giornale d'Italia* (Buenos Aires), July 1, 1933.

45. Falco Testena, "Il fascismo e la classe lavoratrice," *Il Giornale d'Italia* (Buenos Aires), August 3, 1933.

46. Sternhell, "Fascist Ideology," in Laqueur, *Fascism, a Reader's Guide*, p. 371.

47. Julio Irazusta, "El obrerismo de Yrigoyen, respuesta a Manuel Gálvez," *La Nueva República* 19, June 23, 1928, in Julio Irazusta, *La política, cenicienta del espíritu* (Buenos Aires: Ed. Dictio, 1977).

48. Law 11,544 of 29 August 1929 instituted the eight-hour workday, provoking a strong reaction from industrialists. They considered it to be against the interests of national industry, given the rising costs of national production, worker benefits, and the commercialization of foreign products.

49. Julio Irazusta, "Las desventuras del oro," *La Nueva República*, November 4, 1931, in Julio Irazusta, *La política*, p. 308.

50. "'La Joven Argentina' y la 'Grande Argentina,'" *El Pampero*, October 14, 1943.

51. In the late 1930s and early 1940s, the labor movement grew in size and strength. From 1936 to 1940, the number of unionized workers grew by 28 percent. Most of them belonged to transportation unions rather than manufacturing and industrial unions. The active manufacturing population in the whole country

grew by 35 percent, an indication that labor was gravitating to industry. In the second half of the 1930s strikes rose by 50 percent over the first half. The years 1935–1937 saw a period of repeated strikes, reaching a peak in 1936, with construction strikes led by the Communists, who organized solidarity strikes and clashes in the streets. See Celia Durruti, *Clase obrera y peronismo* (Cordoba: Pasado y Presente, 1969), pp. 49–112. Most of the conflicts were actually concentrated in a few very militant unions led by Communists. In 1935–1937 the construction workers accounted for 55 percent of all the strikes in Buenos Aires, and in 1942 metal workers, also led by Communists, accounted for 63 percent (Departamento Nacional de Trabajo, División de Estadística, Investigaciones Sociales, 1942).

52. Ernesto Palacio, "Reacción y revolución. Quienes representan hoy progreso política?" *Nuevo Orden*, vol. 2, no. 61 (September 10, 1941).

53. "Nacionalismo y sindicalismo," *Bandera Argentina*, September 8, 1932.

54. "El Nacionalismo aspira a una mayor justicia social," *Combate*, May 15, 1935.

55. "La nueva Argentina aspira a la decisión franca del obrero," *Combate*, May 15, 1935.

56. "La explotación del trabajador sin defensa por parte del estado es causa de las huelgas," *Combate*, July 1937.

57. "El derecho a huelga," *Combate*, November 1937.

58. "Revolución política y económica," *Combate*, November 1936.

59. "Lo que queremos," *Combate*, November 1936.

60. "Estrangulamiento del trabajo nacional," *Bandera Argentina*, August 21, 1932.

61. Carlos Ibarguren, *La historia que he vivido*, p. 403.

62. Referring to a letter from the former national deputy Dr. Cafferata, reminding him that Dr. Cafferata himself had been accused in the chamber of deputies of being a Communist, Carlos Ibarguren remarked, "Just as Dr. Cafferata was accused of 'bolshevism,' they classified me as 'fascist.'" Cafferata's arguments were similar to Ibarguren's, but one was accused of communism, the other of fascism. Carlos Ibarguren, *La historia que he vivido*, p. 404.

63. See *La Razón*, May 12, 1967.

64. It should be noted that Fresco's personal economic interests were tied to the oligarchy, and hence suspicions were aroused about his real intentions. After the elections of 1940, President Ortiz, succeeding President Justo, decided to intervene in the province and removed Fresco from office. Fresco founded the Unión Nacional Argentina (Patria), which became a political party in 1941. Afterwards, through his newspaper *Cabildo*, he considered himself a leader of the nationalist movement, but other nationalists did not accept him.

65. Manuel Fresco, *Diario de Sesiones, Cámara de Diputados, Congreso Nacional*, June 15, 1932, p. 12.

66. Proof of such alarm was harassment by the Investigation Section of the Federal Police. Archivo Policial, "Informe confidencial y secreto, estadía de

Fresco en la ciudad de Azul" (Fresco's visit to Azul), Legajo DAP, no. 1347, July 1, 1946.

67. Archivo Policial, Memorandum, Manuel Fresco, April 8, 1942. The police description was very telling about the "grassroots" aspect of the participants, who were characterized as "de aspecto humilde usando como calzado zapatillas."

68. Roberto J. Noble, "La nueva ley orgánica del trabajo," speech pronounced in the Senate, Argentine Republic, Provinica de Buenos Aires, Departamento del Trabajo, Política obrera y legislación del gobierno de Buenos Aires, 1937, pp. 24–25. Cited in Waisman, *Reversal of Development*, p. 243.

69. *Crisol*, August 15, 1940, p. 3.

70. See Hernández Arregui, *La formación de la conciencia nacional*, p. 291.

71. Ibid.

72. Jauretche, *FORJA y la década infame*, p. 67.

73. Ibid., p. 68.

74. Hernández Arregui, *La formación de la conciencia nacional*, p. 291.

75. "Declaración Constitutiva de FORJA, 29 de junio 1935," in Scenna, *FORJA, una aventura argentina*, p. 71.

76. Pamphlet of the Grupo Universitario de FORJA, n.d. From the private archive of Darío Alessandro.

77. Jauretche, *FORJA y la década infame*, p. 136.

78. Arturo Jauretche, "Nacionalismo y democracia," *Forjando* (Buenos Aires), November 1941.

79. Raúl Scalabrini Ortiz, *Política Británica en el Rio de la Plata*, 9th ed. (Buenos Aires: Plus Ultra, 1986), p. 342.

80. Hernández Arregui, *La formacion de la conciencia nacional*, p. 305 n.

81. Ibid., p. 147.

82. Alberto Gutíerrez Ruiz, "La Coordinación de los Transportes," *Cuadernos de FORJA*, October 1936, p. 7. Private files of Darío Alessandro.

83. Arturo Jauretche, "Opinión pública y democracia," *Forjando*, November 1941.

84. Ibid.

85. Arturo Jauretche, *Los profetas del odio* (Buenos Aires: Ed. Trafac, 1957), p. 126.

86. Letter from Arturo Jauretche to José Benjamin Avalos. See Scenna, *FORJA, una aventura*, p. 312.

87. Scalabrini Ortiz, *Política Británica*, p. 350. By this criterion, Radicalism was a genuine nationalist movement rooted in the caudillo tradition. See also Ramón Doll's definition of Radicalism as "an authentic mass movement that was a reaction against the liberal system and not [an attempt to] improve and perfect it." Ramón Doll, *Acerca de una política nacional*, p. 115.

88. "A los pueblos de la República y de América," *Cuadernos de FORJA*, November 1939, p. 9.

89. It should be noted that the nationalist *uriburistas* considered themselves a barrier against foreign capital and its maneuvers in Argentina. See "Los capitales

extranjeros," *Crisol*, June 10, 1943. Their claim was rejected by the FORJA nationalists, however.

90. Julio and Rodolfo Irazusta, "La política británica en el Rio de la Plata por Rául Scalabrini Ortiz," in RIJHJMR, no. 5, 1940, pp. 155–159. Cited in Quattrocchi Woisson, *Un nationalisme de deracinés.*

91. FORJA, "Nacionalismo y radicalismo" ("Radicalizar la revolución y revolucionar al radicalismo"), July 1943.

92. Scalabrini Ortiz, *Política Británica*, p. 43. Cited in Buchrucker, *Nacionalismo y peronismo*, p. 268.

93. Tanque Oruga, "Frente Popular," *Clarinada*, August 1938, p. 14.

94. Ibid.

Chapter Six. The Integralist-Populist Synthesis and the New Order

1. On the campaign against communism, see Carlos M. Silveyra, *El Comunismo en Argentina: Orígen, desarrollo, organización actual* (Buenos Aires: n.p., 1936).

2. See Federico Ibarguren, *Orígenes del nacionalismo*, p. 352.

3. Ibid.

4. Ibid., p. 359.

5. "Nacionalistas y Conservadores," *El Fortín*, July 15, 1941.

6. Enrique Osés, "La lucha electoral del nacionalismo," in Osés, *Medios y fines del nacionalismo*, 2d ed. (Buenos Aires: Ed. Sudestada, 1968), p. 51.

7. "Doctrina y propósitos," *Bandera Argentina*, January 6, 1935.

8. Enrique Gwinplaine, "La corporación, la magistratura del trabajo y nuestros ideales de justicia social," *Crisol*, "Sección gremial," March 26, 1936.

9. Máximo Etchecopar, "Releyendo a Lugones," *Nueva Política*, September 4, 1940, p. 18.

10. Nimio de Anquim, "Liberalismo subrepticio y libertad cristiana," *Nueva Política*, no. 10 (March 1941), p. 10.

11. Rodolfo Irazusta, "Nacionalismo y totalitarismo," *Nuevo Orden*, April 8, 1942, p. 1.

12. "Permaneció fiel a su misión reparadora de los derechos del pueblo argentino, conculados por una oligarquía extranjerizante." Ernesto Palacio, "Repetto, Mario Guido y los partidos argentinos," *Nuevo Orden*, November 13, 1941, p. 2.

13. Ramón Doll, "El Dr. Culaciati le debe a todo el pais," *Nuevo Orden*, December 4, 1940, p. 3. In that definition, Radicalism appears as a proper nationalist movement that was rooted in the *caudillista* tradition. On the definition of Radicalism as "an authentic mass movement which was a reaction against the liberal system and not an [attempt to] surpass and improve it," see Doll, *Acerca de una política nacional*, p. 115.

14. Ibid.

15. Bruno Jacovella, "Defensa de la constitución, la democracia y la Ley Saenz Peña," *Nuevo Orden*, January 29, 1941, pp. 1–2.

16. Ernesto Palacio, "Definicion de nuestro movimiento," *Nuevo Orden*, November 6, 1940.

17. Ernesto Palacio, "Repetto, Mario Guido y los partidos argentinos," *Nuevo Orden*, November 13, 1941.

18. Manuel Gálvez, *Este pueblo necesita* (Buenos Aires: Libreria de A. García Santos, 1934), p. 127.

19. Ibid., p. 124.

20. Rodolfo Irazusta, "Una aclaración," *Nuevo Orden*, April 1, 1942, p. 3.

21. Ibid.

22. See "El monopolio oficial y el problema del combustible," *El Pampero*, October 15, 1943; "La ley 12.346 en el cuadro de la esclavitud económica," *El Pampero*, July 15, 1943; "La joven Argentina y la grande Argentina," *El Pampero*, October 14, 1943.

23. Interview with Bruno Jacovella held in Buenos Aires, August 1987.

24. Interview with Marcel Sánchez Sorondo at his home in Buenos Aires, August 1989.

25. Ernesto Palacio, "Los equivocos del nacionalismo," *Nuevo Orden*, July 9, 1941.

26. Ibid.

27. Rodolfo Irazusta, "Los filofascistas mal manejan la tópica creada por el nacionalismo," *Nuevo Orden*, August 20, 1941.

28. Ricardo Font Ezcurra, "Editorial," *Nueva Política*, October 1, 1941, p. 4.

29. Rodolfo Irazusta, "Organización y autonomía del nacionalismo," *Nuevo Orden*, April 2, 1938.

30. Ernesto Palacio, "Una explicación de nuestra farsa politica: El miedo al 'fascismo' como instrumento de gobierno," *Nuevo Orden*, October 8, 1941, p. 1.

31. Marcel Déat, "Bolshevismo y socialismo," *Nuevo Orden*, August 20, 1941.

32. Rodolfo Sotomayor, "La revolución mundial y la economía Argentina," *Nuevo Orden*, October 1, 1941, p. 7.

33. Ibid.

34. Rodolfo Irazusta, "Opiniones sobre la guerra y sus consecuencias," *Nuevo Orden*, November 6, 1940, p. 1.

35. Doll, "Del Servicio Secreto Inglés al Judio Dickman, 1939," p. 192.

36. Ramón Doll, "Quienes subestiman a Italia en esta guerra," *Nuevo Orden*, November 20, 1940, p. 5.

37. Marcelo Sánchez Sorondo, "La cerrazon del pasado inmediato," in *La revolución que anunciamos* (Buenos Aires: Ed. Nueva Política, 1945), p. 33; Bruno Jacovella, "Los acontecimientos de Europa y la conciencia Argentina," *Nuevo Orden*, August 22, 1941.

38. On the attempts at dialogue between the integralists and FORJA, see Serapio Lucero, "Los Nacionalistas y el liberalismo," *Nuevo Orden*, September 21, 1941, p. 3.

39. FORJA pamphlet, August 1930.

40. FORJA pamphlet, 1939. See Jauretche, *FORJA y la década infame*, p. 114.

41. See Scenna, *FORJA, una aventura argentina*, p. 204.

42. Orlando de Felsina, "La posición de Italia frente al conflicto en que se halla Europa," *Reconquista*, November 26, 1939.

43. Ramón Doll, "Del Servicio Secreto Inglés al Judío Dickman, 1939," p. 199.

44. Dinner in commemoration of Ireneo Branchs, secretary of the Alianza, Bar "Tres Ases," May 7, 1941, "Memorandum Sección Orden Político," División Investigaciones, Archivo Policial.

45. "Alianza de la Juventud Nacionalista," *Clarinada*, March 1938.

46. *Alianza*, November 8, 1945.

47. In 1953, Patricio Kelly assumed the leadership of the Alianza after a street fight with its founder, Juan Queraltó. From that day onward, the Alianza became a clearly proletarian movement whose basic activity was to combat opponents of Peronism.

48. José Luis De Imaz, *Promediando los cuarenta* (Buenos Aires: Ed. Sudamericana, 1977), pp. 34–35.

49. "Programa mínimo de gobierno de la Alianza Libertadora Nacionalista," *Tribuna*, December 20, 1945.

50. "El comunismo contra la causa del trabajo nacional," *Alianza*, October 2, 1945.

51. Ibid.

52. Speech by Juan Queraltó on May 1, 1939, *Combate*, June 1939.

53. "Alianza de la Juventud Nacionalista: Postulados de nuestra lucha," n.d., p. 5, cited in Navarro Gerassi, *Los nacionalistas*, p. 149.

54. See "La propiedad de la tierra para el trabajador rural, meta nacionalista," *Crisol*, December 9, 1938.

Chapter Seven. The Military in Power and Early Peronism: Consolidation of the Integralist-Populist Formula

1. See Buchrucker, *Nacionalismo y peronismo*, pp. 229–230.

2. Policia Federal "Sección Orden Politico"—Division Investigaciones, Memorandum Juan Bautista Molina (June 2, 1941). Other meetings were reported by the liberal as well as by the nationalist press, for example, the meeting at the Jockey Club on November 7, 1940, in which the German ambassador was hosted by the principal figures of the nationalist intellectuals and army officers. In that meeting the German ambassador talked about German immigration in Argentina, especially with regard to neutrality, a concept which did not necessarily mean indifference. Sympathy for an ideological cause was also evidence of approving neutrality. See "Agasajo al embajador de Alemania," *El Pampero*, November 7, 1940.

3. See Alberto Conil Paz and Gustavo Ferrari, *Política exterior Argentina, 1930–1962* (Buenos Aires: Huemul, 1964), p. 79.

4. Carlos Escudé, *Gran Bretaña, Estados Unidos, y la declinación Argentina* (Buenos Aires: Ed. Belgrano, 1988), p. 100.

5. *Bandera Argentina*, January 24, 1942, p. 3.

6. Buchrucker, *Nacionalismo y peronismo*, p. 226.

7. Cordell Hull, *The Memoirs of Cordell Hull*, 2 vols. (New York: Macmillan, 1948), in Ciria, *Parties and Power in Modern Argentina*, p. 99.

8. See Alain Rouquié, *Poder militar y sociedad política en Argentina*, vol. 2 (Buenos Aires: Hyspanoamerica Ed. Argentina, 1986), p. 14.

9. Juan José Real, *30 años de historia argentina* (Buenos Aires: Ed. Actualidad, 1962), p. 64.

10. Marcelo Sánchez Sorondo, "Discurso a los militares," *La revolución que anunciamos*, p. 251.

11. Authors such as Enrique Díaz Araujo, *La conspiración del 43* (Buenos Aires: Ed. La Bastilla, 1971), have downplayed the authoritarian and fascist orientation of the GOU. However, the documents published by Robert A. Potash, *Perón y el GOU: Los documentos de una logia secreta* (Buenos Aires: Ed. Sudamericana, 1984), confirm the basic thrust of our analysis. Moreover, it is clear that Perón, who was probably the most important member of the group, was in all likelihood the ideological author of the programmatic documents.

12. Speech of President Ramírez, *La Prensa*, June 16, 1943, in Rouquié, *Poder militar*, vol. 2, p. 13.

13. Sánchez Sorondo, *La revolución que anunciamos*, pp. 251, 258–259.

14. See Juan Perón, "Discurso a los estudiantes," December 21, 1945, in Juan Perón, *Tres revoluciones militares* (Buenos Aires: Ed. Escorpión 1963), p. 93.

15. "Los capitales extranjeros," *Crisol*, June 10, 1943.

16. *Crisol*, June 17, 1943.

17. Jauretche, *FORJA y la década infame*, pp. 149–150.

18. "Esto no lo borra nadie," *Crisol*, June 10, 1943.

19. "Dios y patria," *Semanario mercedario*, no. 287, October 8, 1933.

20. Zanatta, *Del estado liberal a la nación católica*, p. 149.

21. Bruno Genta, "La función militar en la existencia de la libertad," presented at a conference given at the Círculo Militar, June 23, 1943, *Revista Militar*, June 1943. Cited in Rouquié, *Poder militar*, vol. 2, p. 31. See also Bruno Genta, statement while assuming the function of *interventor* at the Universidad del Litoral, Paraná, August 17, 1943, in Buchrucker, *Nacionalismo y peronismo*, p. 82, and Bruno Genta, *Acerca de la libertad de enseñar y la enseñanza de la libertad* (Buenos Aires: Ed. Dictio, 1976).

22. *La Nación*, November 8, 1943, cited in Rouquié, *Poder militar*, vol. 2, pp. 36–37.

23. See Jorge Crespo, "Si vis pacem para bellum," *Revista Militar*, June 1939; Diego Perkins, "El horror de la guerra," *Revista Militar*, June 1940, and "Defensa nacional y pueblo," *Revista Militar*, February 1941.

24. For the United States, the world of 1942 differed dramatically from the world of 1938. President Roosevelt was convinced by 1942 of the real possibility of an attack by an extra-continental power on Latin America, and this led to a major shift in American foreign policy toward the region. (See Edmund Smith, Jr.,

Intervención yanqui en Argentina [Buenos Aires: Ed. Palestra, 1965], pp. 51–52.) Before the start of the hostilities in Europe, at the Pan-American Conference in Lima in 1938 and at the conference of ministers of foreign affairs in Panama in 1939, the United States urged Latin America to maintain a neutral position. This stance coincided with traditional Argentine foreign policy since Yrigoyen's times. It was also in keeping with the concept of neutrality sustained by President Ortiz, which was a clear representation of the political and ideological line of ex-president Agustín Justo. After Pearl Harbor, the United States demanded an end to neutrality in the continent, and at the Conference of Rio de Janeiro in 1942, great pressure was exerted against Argentina, which was the only country in Latin America that refused to break off relations with the Axis. President Castillo, who succeeded Ortiz as the representative of the Concordancia, decided to maintain the traditional concept of Argentine neutrality, albeit under a new international constellation and under different ideological influences. Foreign minister Enrique Ruiz Guiñazu, who had a clear pro-Axis tendency, succeeded in introducing the word "recommendation" into a U.S.-sponsored declaration on the breaking off of relations with the Axis, thereby eliminating the enforceability of the declaration. The United States harbored bad feelings toward the Argentine government and was not at all pleased with the action. American policymakers were determined not to break off relations with Argentina, in order to continue building U.S. trade in the region at the expense of the British. However, they punished Argentina by playing the card that could most hurt the nationalist-supported Castillo government, that is, altering the balance of power in the region by helping neighboring countries, especially Brazil, become militarily stronger. The Americans were determined to draw Argentina out of informal membership in the British Empire and bring the country into the orbit of the evolving "Pan-American" system. See Mario Rapoport, *Gran Bretaña, Estados Unidos y las clases dirigentes argentinas, 1940–1945* (Buenos Aires : Editorial Belgrano, 1981). As I have mentioned, there were also some democratic groups that favored neutrality and asked the United States for a pact of nonbelligerency that would not harm Argentine economic interests. On this point see Joseph S. Tulchin, "The Argentine Proposal for Non-Belligerency, April, 1940," *Journal of Inter-American Studies* 11, no. 4 (1969).

25. Assessment of the business attaché of the German Embassy, Dr. Otto Meynen, in Buenos Aires, July 20, 1942, Telegrama No. 2490, Roll 25/27, 140–142, in Potash, *El ejército y la política*, p. 258.

26. Oscar Saccheri, "El nuevo orden económico en Europa," *Revista Militar*, October 1942, pp. 727–773.

27. "Las bases de un programa nacionalista," *Nuevo Orden*, April 22, 1942, p. 5.

28. Carlos Escudé, "La irracionalidad Argentina Frente a la Segunda Guerra Mundial," *EIAL* (Estudios Interdisciplinarios de America Latina y el Caribe), Tel Aviv University, vol. 6, no. 2 (July–December 1995): 25.

29. Miguel Murmis and Juan C. Portantiero, *Crecimiento industrial y alianza de clases en la Argentina*, Documento de Trabajo 49 (Buenos Aires: Instituto Torcuatto di Tella, Centro de Investigaciones Sociales, 1968), p. 79.

30. Torcuatto di Tella, "Stalemate or Coexistence in Argentina," in James Petras and Maurice Zeitlin, eds., *Latin America: Reform or Revolution* (New York: Fawcett Publications, 1968), p. 255.

31. *The Times* (London), August 3, 1944. Cited in Waisman, *Reversal of Development*, p. 158.

32. For the political plot that brought about the resignation of Ramírez, see Rouquié, *Poder militar*, vol. 2, pp. 38–54.

33. "Homenaje a la revolución del 4 de Junio," *Revista Militar*, June 1944, pp. 1057–1114.

34. The fascist newspaper *El Pampero* was closed after its harsh criticism of the president. However, it reappeared later under the name of *El Federal*, and FORJA protested with a street demonstration in the city of Mar del Plata. The pamphlet edited by FORJA read: "Argentina, a republic of workers, soldiers and intellectuals, is attacked whenever it objects to pressures from imperialist capitalism." See Scenna, *FORJA, una aventura argentina*, p. 354.

35. See Rouquié, *Poder militar*, vol. 2, p. 32.

36. "El Estado regulará las fuerzas de la Producción," *Crisol*, October 30, 1943. See also "La Secretaría de Trabajo y Previsión," *El Pampero*, December 1, 1943.

37. Interview given by Perón to *El Mercurio* of Chile, republished in *La Prensa*, November 12, 1943. See Rouquié, *Poder militar*, vol. 2, pp. 39–40.

38. Evidence of Perón's admiration for fascism is easily found. In 1939 Perón was sent to Italy for a study mission by the Argentine army. At the Universities of Torino and Milan he studied political economy. He was impressed by the political and social practices of Italian fascism. Perón never denied it: "to guide people is a technique, the technique of leadership. A technique, an art of military precision. In 1940, I learned that in Italy . . . people really knew how to command." See the interview given by Perón to Eduardo Galeano, in Eduardo Galeano, *Reportajes* (Montevideo: Tauro, 1967), p. 74. During 1940 Perón visited Nazi Germany and countries it occupied. Upon returning to Argentina, he became the ideological mentor of the GOU.

39. For a debate on Argentine labor and Peronism, see Jeremy Adelman, "Reflections on Argentine Labor and the Rise of Peronism," *Bulletin of Latin American Research*, vol. 11, no. 3 (1992): 242–259.

40. Cited in Félix Luna, *El 45: Crónica de un año decisivo* (Buenos Aires: Ed. Sudamericana, 1975), p. 295.

41. *El Pueblo*, "Editorial," January 1, 1946.

42. Personal interview with Cipriano Reyes in Quilmes, Buenos Aires, June 1989.

43. Vicepresidencia de la Nación, Consejo Nacional de Postguerra, "Ordenamiento económico y social" (Buenos Aires: Kraft, 1944), pp. 55–56, 68.

44. See Presidencia de la Nación, "El sindicalismo justicialista a traves del pensamiento de Perón" (Buenos Aires: Subsecretaria de Informaciones, 1951), pp. 71–86.

45. Raúl Damonte Taborda, *Ayer fué San Perón (12 años de humillación argentina)* (Buenos Aires: Gure, 1955), p. 39.

46. Juan Perón, *20. Plan Quinquenal de la Nación Argentina* (Texto completo de la ley 14.184) (Buenos Aires: Hechos e Ideas, 1954), p. 441.

47. For a different view see Eldon Kenworthy, *The Formation of the Peronist Coalition*, Ph.D. thesis, Yale University, 1970, p. 265. See also Carlos Díaz Alejandro, *An Interpretation of Argentine Economic Growth since 1930* (New Haven, Conn.: Yale University, Economic Growth Center, 1967), p. 158. These authors claim that Perón's main concern was defending those industries that had arisen during the previous years to supply immediate consumer goods.

48. See Baily, *Labor Nationalism and Politics*, pp. 138, 142.

49. Juan Perón, *El pueblo quiere saber de que trata* (Buenos Aires, 1944), p. 161.

50. The *justicialista* doctrine formulated in 1949 combined most of the elements sustained by Perón himself since 1942, and by the nationalists during the 1930s. This new philosophy was formally announced by Perón in a congress of philosophy in Mendoza in 1949, and it became the official doctrine of Peronism. See Juan Perón's *El pueblo quiere saber de que se trata* (1944), *El pueblo ya sabe de que se trata* (1946), *Doctrina peronista* (1949), *La comunidad organizada* (1949), *Las veinte verdades del justicialismo* (1950), and so on. See also Eva Perón, *Historia del peronismo* (1951). One of the best commentators on Perón's *justicialista* doctrine is George Blanksten, *Peron's Argentina* (Chicago: University of Chicago Press, 1953).

51. Juan Perón, *La comunidad organizada* (Buenos Aires: Ed. Realidad Política, 1983), pp. 91–92.

52. Juan Perón, *Conducción política* (Buenos Aires: Ed. Mundo Peronista, 1952), p. 55.

53. For Perón's educational policies, see Monica Esti Rein, *Politics and Education in Argentina, 1946–1962* (New York: M. E. Sharpe, 1998).

54. The arguments expressed around the debate are summarized in Lila Caimari, *Perón y la Iglesia Católica: Religión, estado y sociedad en la Argentina (1943–1955)* (Buenos Aires: Ariel Historia, 1994), pp. 153–156.

55. *Boletín del Ministerio de Justicia e Instrucción Pública*, 1947, pp. 2059–2060.

56. Caimari, *Perón y la Iglesia Católica*, p. 154.

57. Marcelo Sánchez Sorondo, "Nacionalistas, la cuarta frustración," *Primera Plana*, Buenos Aires, year 5, no. 229, May 12–16, 1967, pp. 21–22.

58. Caimari, *Perón y la Iglesia Católica*, p. 74.

59. "Sumario," *Balcón*, June 28, 1946.

60. "Editorial," *Balcón*, August 30, 1946.

61. *Alianza*, November 8, 1945.

62. Ibid.

63. Leonardo Castellani, "Reflexión sobre las elecciones," conference organized by the Alianza in the Augusto Hall, *Tribuna*, April 13, 1946.

64. Hector Bernardo, *Para una economía humana* (Buenos Aires: n.p., 1949), pp. 18–21. Juan Perón and the rest of the GOU generals were clearly

influenced by the economic thought of Raúl Scalabrini Ortiz and José Luis Torres.

65. Manuel Gálvez, *El pueblo* (August 1944). Cited in Caimari, *Perón y la Iglesia Católica*, p. 75.

66. "Glosas del tiempo," *Tribuna*, November 2, 1945.

67. Scenna, *FORJA, una aventura argentina*, p. 349.

68. Ibid., pp. 355–359.

69. Daniel James, *Resistance and Integration: Peronism and the Argentine Working Class, 1946–1976* (Cambridge: Cambridge University Press, 1988), p. 21.

70. Ibid., p. 16.

71. Tulio Halperín Donghi, *La larga agonía de la Argentina peronista* (Buenos Aires: Ariel, 1994), p. 27.

72. James, *Resistance and Integration*, p. 21.

73. Peter Ross, *Policy Formation of Social Welfare in Peronist Argentina, 1943–1955*, Ph.D. thesis, School of Spanish and Latin American Studies of New South Wales, Sydney, 1988.

74. In terms of wage policies, for example, although wages dropped in Italy during the Great Depression, fringe benefits such as paid vacations, social insurance, family subsidies, and free medical care remained intact. However during the Ethiopian War, wages rose as a consequence of higher demand for labor.

75. See Paul Lewis, "Was Peron a Fascist?" *World Politics*, vol. 42, nos. 1–2 (1980).

76. Tulio Halperín Donghi, *La democracia de masas* (Buenos Aires: Paidos, 1972), p. 60.

77. See Juan Perón, *La hora de los pueblos* (Buenos Aires, 1973), p. 35.

78. Manuel Gálvez, "Posibilidades del Fascismo en la Argentina," in *Este pueblo necesita*, p. 119.

79. See Guillermo O'Donnell, *El estado burocrático-autoritario, 1966–1973* (Buenos Aires: Ed. Belgrano, 1982), p. 462.

Conclusion

1. The concept of reactionary restorationists has been developed by Buchrucker, *Nacionalismo y peronismo*.

2. Carlos Ibarguren, "La inquietud de esta hora," p. 56.

3. Carlos H. Waisman, *Modernization and the Working Class: The Politics of Legitimacy* (Austin: University of Texas Press, 1982), p. 64.

4. Raymond Williams, *Marxism and Literature* (Oxford: Oxford University Press, 1977), p. 132.

5. James, *Resistance and Integration*, p. 97.

6. Corradi, *The Fitful Republic*, p. 117.

7. Richard Gillespie, *Soldiers of Perón, Argentina's Montoneros* (Oxford: Clarendon Press, 1982), p. 39.

8. On the military rebellions of the 1990s, see Deborah L. Norden, *Military Rebellion in Argentina: Between Coups and Consolidation* (Lincoln: Uni-

versity of Nebraska Press, 1996). On a comparative study of Argentina's "*carap-intadas*," the Brazilian UDR (Rural Democratic Union), and the Nicaragua's "contras," see Leigh A. Payne, *Uncivil Movements: The Armed Right Wing and Democracy in Latin America* (Baltimore: Johns Hopkins University Press, 2000).

Index

Viola, Navarro, 110
Volpe, Gioacchino, 114–15
La Voz de la Iglesia, 110
La Voz del Plata, 130, 196
La Voz Nacional, 64, 79–80

Waisman, Carlos, 99, 183, 206
Wast, Hugo, 114, 180
Weber, Eugen, 33, 214n.3
Weimar Conservative Revolutionaries, 2,
    211n.3
Whitaker, Arthur P., 213n.6
Wilde, Eduardo, 232n.50
Wilkinson, Fr. Roberto, 179
Wilson, Woodrow, 126
working class, 7, 41, 55, 95, 183,
    234n.80
  and anarchism, 41–46
  and Catholicism, 110–11
  under fascism, 16, 19, 33, 216n.13
  and FORJA, 145
  and integralist nationalism, 17, 34,
    122, 134, 135–41, 168–69, 170, 207,
    208, 237n.51
  and 1943 military revolution, 177
  and Peronism, 13, 34, 60, 186–89,
    190–93, 198, 205–6, 242n.47
  and Radical Party, 56, 59–61,
    224n.69
  and the Semana Trágica, 60–61, 70
  See also Syndicalism
World War I, 9, 59, 61

World War II, 158
  Argentine neutrality in, 12, 123,
    160–68, 173–75, 178, 180, 181, 182,
    184–85, 203–4, 242n.2, 244n.24

Yeats, William Butler, 76
Yrigoyen, Hipólito, 48, 153, 159
  economic policies of, 58, 59, 62, 63,
    65, 145–46
  immigration policies, 61
  labor policies, 59–61, 137, 237n.48
  neutralist policies, 12
  1916 election victory of, 51, 56
  1930 overthrow of, 7, 8, 64–66, 67, 77,
    80, 83, 84–87, 90, 152, 155, 202,
    228n.54
  patronage policies of, 57
  populist nationalism of, 11, 35, 46,
    53, 56–63, 65, 66, 78, 81, 82, 86, 91,
    93, 94, 106, 108, 130, 131, 134,
    136–37, 138, 144, 145, 148, 151,
    155, 156–60, 160, 171, 202–3, 212n,
    225n.80, 226n.85, 237n.48, 240n.13
  relations with the military, 56, 63–66,
    225n.81
  Rosas compared to, 108
  and universal suffrage, 54–55
  See also nationalism, populist

Zeitun, Jackes, 219n.43
Zuleta Alvarez, Enrique: *El nacional-
    ismo argentino*, 212n

ALBERTO SPEKTOROWSKI
is professor of political science at Tel Aviv University
and is co-editor of *Ethnic Challenges to the Modern Nation State.*

www.ingramcontent.com/pod-product-compliance
Lightning Source LLC
Chambersburg PA
CBHW070611270326
41926CB00013B/2498